Blender Cycles: Lighting and Rendering Cookbook

Over 50 recipes to help you master the Lighting and Rendering model using the Blender Cycles engine

Bernardo Iraci

[PACKT] open source ✳
PUBLISHING   community experience distilled

BIRMINGHAM - MUMBAI

Blender Cycles: Lighting and Rendering Cookbook

First published: December 2013

Production Reference: 1191213

Published by Packt Publishing Ltd.
Livery Place
35 Livery Street
Birmingham B3 2PB, UK.

ISBN 978-1-78216-460-9

www.packtpub.com

Cover Image by Bernardo Iraci (bernardo@mccinfo.it)

Credits

Author
Bernardo Iraci

Reviewers
Patrick Boelens

Fernando Castilhos Melo

Acquisition Editors
Akram Hussain

Luke Presland

Lead Technical Editor
Amey Varangaonkar

Technical Editors
Tanvi Bhatt

Kapil Hemani

Akashdeep Kundu

Shiny Poojary

Faisal Siddiqui

Copy Editors
Roshni Banerjee

Brandt D'Mello

Deepa Nambiar

Karuna Narayanan

Shambhavi Pai

Alfida Paiva

Adithi Shetty

Project Coordinator
Navu Dhillon

Proofreaders
Lucy Rowland

Elinor Perry-Smith

Indexer
Priya Subramani

Graphics
Ronak Dhruv

Yuvraj Mannari

Abhinash Sahu

Production Coordinator
Shantanu Zagade

Cover Work
Shantanu Zagade

About the Author

Bernardo Iraci was born in Livorno, Italy in 1985. He followed a standard education career until he graduated in Economics in 2009. He always had a great passion for computers, especially gaming. During the latter part of his studies, he also developed a passion for 3D graphics, and this soon became the main focus of his career. It was at this time that he came to understand that his passion was the most important thing to pursue, more important than even attending university.

Even though Bernardo later participated in various online courses teaching the different aspects of computer graphics, he has been largely self-taught. In 2010, he moved to Warsaw, Poland, where he was finally able to start working full-time in computer graphics as a 3D generalist in the field of movies VFX and advertisments. He also started work as a freelancer.

Bernardo constantly works to improve his skills and knowledge about computer graphics and thinks that this is the only way to keep pace with this field. When he is not busy with graphics, he likes to travel, watch movies, and play the guitar.

I would like to thank my family because they gave me the tools and the spirit to pursue my dreams. It is thanks to them that I am able to do what I do today.

I would also like to thank my girlfriend as she constantly supports, pushes, and inspires me every day of my life.

About the Reviewers

Patrick Boelens is a 3D content creator, programmer, and game designer with a passion for anything in which these fields meet. While studying Communication and Multimedia Design, he started producing video tutorials for the CG Cookie Network, showing people how to make custom scripts and add-ons for the open source software Blender. He was also a part of the team behind the studio's first iOS game, Eat Sheep. He has since worked on a wide variety of projects, including client- and server-side web development, games, and applications.

Fernando Castilhos Melo lives in Caxias do Sul, Brazil, and works in a software house as a software developer and systems analyst. Since 2009, he has been working on 3D modeling in his spare time using the software Blender. He has conducted some lectures on Blender and 3D modeling in several Brazilian free software events such as FLISOL and TcheLinux. Fernando is majoring in Computer Science at the UCS (University of Caxias do Sul). He is developing an integration between Blender and Kinect to generate a 3D animation as his coursework in the university. For more information, access his webpage: http://www.fernando.melo.nom.br/.

I want to thank my fiancée Mauren, my parents Eloir and Miriam, my friends, and my teachers from the university, for the support during the review of |this book.

www.PacktPub.com

Support files, eBooks, discount offers and more

You might want to visit www.PacktPub.com for support files and downloads related to your book.

Did you know that Packt offers eBook versions of every book published, with PDF and ePub files available? You can upgrade to the eBook version at www.PacktPub.com and as a print book customer, you are entitled to a discount on the eBook copy. Get in touch with us at service@packtpub.com for more details.

At www.PacktPub.com, you can also read a collection of free technical articles, sign up for a range of free newsletters and receive exclusive discounts and offers on Packt books and eBooks.

http://PacktLib.PacktPub.com

Do you need instant solutions to your IT questions? PacktLib is Packt's online digital book library. Here, you can access, read and search across Packt's entire library of books.

Why Subscribe?

- ▶ Fully searchable across every book published by Packt
- ▶ Copy and paste, print and bookmark content
- ▶ On demand and accessible via web browser

Free Access for Packt account holders

If you have an account with Packt at www.PacktPub.com, you can use this to access PacktLib today and view nine entirely free books. Simply use your login credentials for immediate access.

Table of Contents

Preface

One of the most advanced 3D packages on the scene, Blender now has a powerful new tool to allow its users to achieve even more astonishing results: the Cycles rendering engine. Cycles is based on an accurate lighting model and realistic shaders. It is also blazing fast, thanks to the fact that it can take advantage of the modern GPU-rendering capabilities. Cycles is definitely a modern and effective tool that every Blender user wants to know in order to get the best results. *Blender Cycles: Lighting and Rendering Cookbook* will take you on a journey through the new great Blender rendering engine Cycles. We will start with understanding the fundamental concepts of this rendering engine, and use them to learn the creation of any kind of lighting, material, texture, and setup. At the end of the book, both beginners and more advanced users will not only be able to create virtually any kind of shader and lighting, but will also be able to find and experiment with new techniques on their own. Thanks to the logical way in which the topics are presented in the book; the readers will be able to create their work without additional tutorials by just using the knowledge they will master by reading this book.

What this book covers

Chapter 1, Key Holder and Wallet Studio Shot, will highlight the fundamentals of lighting, along with the creation of materials in Cycles. Finally, this chapter will teach you how to set up the render parameters in Cycles.

Chapter 2, Creating Different Glass Materials in Cycles, will help us create from the most basic to really advanced glass materials. To achieve this, we will go deeper into the Cycles material creation, learning interesting node trees and techniques.

Chapter 3, Creating an Interior Scene, will help us with the creation of an interior scene, a situation that can be quite challenging without proper knowledge. You will learn how to light a scene in an efficient way, along with new materials and advanced techniques.

Chapter 4, Creating an Exterior Scene, will help you learn the secrets of exterior lighting. Here we will learn how to create a flawless natural exterior lighting using different advanced techniques together with the creation of new materials.

Chapter 5, Creating a Cartoonish Scene, will teach you how to create stylized yet appealing lighting materials, for example, a fake subsurface scattering and hair material, ideal for a cartoon scene.

Chapter 6, Creating a Toy Movie Scene, will show you how to create a lighting setup that will resemble a movie set, together with highly realistic materials. Moreover, you will learn different techniques to give our image an even closer look to that of a cinema movie.

Chapter 7, Car Rendering in Cycles, will help you set up great studio lighting to make the car look great, and of course, will show you how to create complex and captivating car paint material.

Chapter 8, Creating a Car Animation, will help you deal with your first animation and explain to you how to set up Cycles at its best for this purpose. You will optimize the scene to lower the render times while maintaining a high quality and detail level, and learn how to deal with a huge project.

Chapter 9, Creating an Iceberg Scene, will highlight some really advanced material creation in Cycles, and some greatly advanced techniques about seamlessly mixing two materials inside the same mesh. Moreover, you will learn to use information from scene objects to use for even more advanced materials.

Chapter 10, Creating Food Materials in Cycles, the final chapter, will talk about the creation of food, one of the most challenging topics to deal with in Computer Graphics. This chapter will teach you the creation of highly realistic and complex Cycles materials.

What you need for this book

The only program needed to follow the recipes of this book is Blender, which can be freely downloaded from the official Blender foundation website www.blender.org.

Who this book is for

This book is aimed at both beginners and more advanced Cycles users, as it will take you from the very first steps up to quite advanced techniques. Even more advanced users could pickup several new things by reading this book.

Although every topic is described in detail, some basic knowledge of Blender as a package is advisable.

Conventions

In this book, you will find a number of styles of text that distinguish between different kinds of information. Here are some examples of these styles, and an explanation of their meaning.

Code words in text are shown as follows: "Again we will have to duplicate the material and name it `Rim_Light`."

New terms and **important words** are shown in bold. Words that you see on the screen, in menus or dialog boxes, for example, appear in the text like this: "Let's start by going to the **System** tab, and in the lower-left corner, you will see the **Compute Device** setting area."

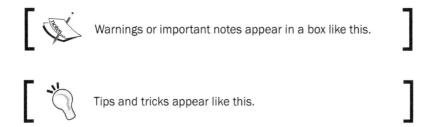

Warnings or important notes appear in a box like this.

Tips and tricks appear like this.

Reader feedback

Feedback from our readers is always welcome. Let us know what you think about this book—what you liked or may have disliked. Reader feedback is important for us to develop titles that you really get the most out of.

To send us general feedback, simply send an e-mail to `feedback@packtpub.com`, and mention the book title via the subject of your message.

If there is a topic that you have expertise in and you are interested in either writing or contributing to a book, see our author guide on `www.packtpub.com/authors`.

Customer support

Now that you are the proud owner of a Packt book, we have a number of things to help you to get the most from your purchase.

Downloading the example code and colored graphics

You can download the example code files for all Packt books you have purchased from your account at `http://www.packtpub.com`. If you purchased this book elsewhere, you can visit `http://www.packtpub.com/support` and register to have the files e-mailed directly to you.

We also provide you a PDF file that has color images of the screenshots/diagrams used in this book. The color images will help you better understand the changes in the output. You can download this file from: `https://www.packtpub.com/sites/default/files/downloads/4609OS_ColoredImages.pdf`.

Errata

Although we have taken every care to ensure the accuracy of our content, mistakes do happen. If you find a mistake in one of our books—maybe a mistake in the text or the code—we would be grateful if you would report this to us. By doing so, you can save other readers from frustration and help us improve subsequent versions of this book. If you find any errata, please report them by visiting `http://www.packtpub.com/submit-errata`, selecting your book, clicking on the **errata submission form** link, and entering the details of your errata. Once your errata are verified, your submission will be accepted and the errata will be uploaded on our website, or added to any list of existing errata, under the Errata section of that title. Any existing errata can be viewed by selecting your title from `http://www.packtpub.com/support`.

Piracy

Piracy of copyright material on the Internet is an ongoing problem across all media. At Packt, we take the protection of our copyright and licenses very seriously. If you come across any illegal copies of our works, in any form, on the Internet, please provide us with the location address or website name immediately so that we can pursue a remedy.

Please contact us at `copyright@packtpub.com` with a link to the suspected pirated material.

We appreciate your help in protecting our authors, and our ability to bring you valuable content.

Questions

You can contact us at `questions@packtpub.com` if you are having a problem with any aspect of the book, and we will do our best to address it.

Introduction

Welcome to the *Blender Cycles: Lighting and Rendering Cookbook*. Before we start, I would like to talk about the new Blender rendering engine.

Cycles is a brand new unbiased rendering engine based on the **path tracing** algorithm that Blender has provided to users. It is still under heavy development but is growing really fast and is already capable of creating astonishing images.

Path tracing is an algorithm that computes how light travels in an environment in a very accurate way. For this reason, it is also a pretty heavy rendering algorithm. The good news is that Cycles can rely on modern video card power to make rendering times shorter.

Cycles also has a **Global Illumination** (**GI**) system. GI is a system that is used to simulate the bouncing of light different different surfaces. Earlier, to achieve similar effects with **Blender internal renderer**, it was necessary to manually fake it. Now, Cycles will do this for us. GI changes a lot in the way we can set up lighting for our scenes, as now each object's color influences and is influenced by other objects around it and in general everything will behave in a way closer to reality.

Another new key feature is the accompanying node-based shader system. It is a really powerful tool that will allow us to create a great variety of shaders, from the simplest to really advanced ones.

One could already be used to working with nodes, since the Blender Internal engine can also use nodes to set up shaders, not to mention the Blender compositing system, which is also based on nodes.

Anyway, the first approach with this system can be a bit hard sometimes. This is why I believe that a brief introduction, where we can see the concepts behind the usage of nodes, will be very useful to fully master the recipes that we are going to see in this book.

Just as a cook must know the ingredients at his/her disposal in order to cook tasty food, we too have to know which tools we can use to achieve the renders we want. When we cook our recipes later in the book, we will cover everything with the attention it deserves. If some passage is not perfectly clear, you can always come back to this introduction in order to understand how the tools that we will use will work.

So, let's see these concepts together!

Knowing your ingredients

Using nodes mainly means one thing: mixing different elements such as shaders, images, colors, and values. What makes nodes so powerful is that we can balance the mix of these elements as we like. We can use a simple value, images, colors, or even complex mathematical operations to decide how much of either value we want to see in our final material. The good thing is that we can repeat this process as many times as we want. However, we cannot mix things randomly. Nodes are powerful, but we need to follow a certain logic in order to make them work properly. To better understand the philosophy behind nodes, I have given an example that I hope will help.

Let's think of a node this way: nodes are like food processors. I am talking about blenders, mixers, and machines to make tomato sauce; ovens and stoves to make pasta, and so on. To use a food processor, you put in some ingredients and it does its work. Then, you take what the food processor has produced and use it in a different food processor until you get the final meal ready. Of course, you cannot put tomatoes directly in the oven to make a pizza. You have to first put them in the tomato sauce machine and only when you have the sauce, can you put it on the pizza.

Well, nodes work exactly the same way. Each node is like a different food processor specialized for doing different things. We will put in some information to the left as inputs and the node will give us an output to the right. When we think that our meal is ready, we will put the result of the nodes' work inside the output node and get our final material.

As I am sure you are eager to start, let's jump straight into Blender! Blender Internal is still the default engine in Blender, so we will first need to select Cycles from the render menu. Now open up a node editor in a separate window and with the default cube selected, select the **Use Nodes** checkbox by clicking on it in the materials menu.

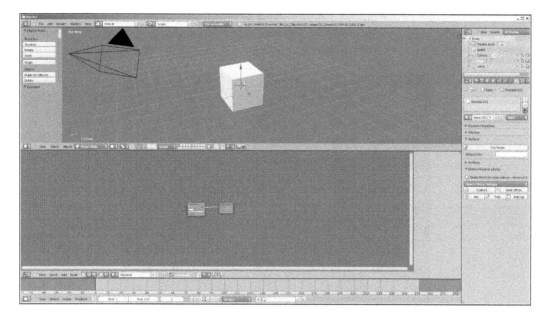

Here you have them... nodes! What you see there is a diffuse node and an output node. The output node is quite important as it will always be the last node of a material but is also quite self-explanatory. So, now let's focus on the **Diffuse BSDF** node for a moment. As you can see, we have some small colorful circles on the left-hand side (inputs) and some on the right-hand side (outputs). You may also notice that these inputs and outputs have different colors. Just as with the food example, we can't just plug any node anywhere. We need to adhere to certain rules. Colors will help us distinguish between the various ingredients in order to mix them in the correct way. Here we have the following types of inputs:

- ▸ **Color** (the yellow circle)
- ▸ **Roughness** (the grey circle)
- ▸ **Normal** (the blue circle)

On the right-hand side, we have the output values. In this case, there's only one: a shader (the green circle). We are using the **Diffuse BSDF** node as an example, but each node has a different combination of inputs and outputs. In Cycles, you will find only these four aforementioned kinds of nodes.

As a general rule, we should always connect nodes by following their colors. Green with green, yellow with yellow, and so on. We will see, however, that it is possible to convert some of these values from where it comes from in order to use them inside an input of a different kind.

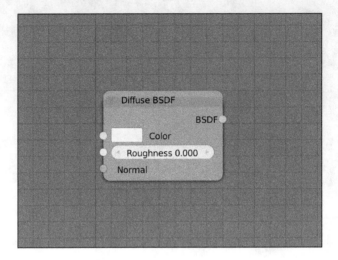

Now let's see what kind of ingredients we can find inside each color group:

- ▸ **The yellow circle**: Here, we have the color information. This means RGB inputs (plain color) or images from files (textures). Cycles' procedural textures can also generate color information.

- ▸ **The gray circle**: These are numeric values. However, black and white images can also be used as numeric values, black being 0 and white being 1. The same thing is true for alpha values. Keep in mind that in many situations 1 will be the maximum and 0 the minimum value. This means that, for example, if we want to mix two shaders, the mixing factor will lie in the range of 0 to 1. At these extremes, only one of the two shaders will actually be visible. Of course, numbers inbetween are endless.

- ▸ **The blue circle**: Under this group, we can find vector information. Vectors mainly are information about the position and orientation of points and surfaces in space. So, for instance, we can use this vector info for normal maps or bump maps in order to tell Cycles what the surface of a certain object must look like.

- ▸ **The green circle**: This is the shader group and contains the information about how surfaces react to light.

As we will see in our recipes, these groups are not completely separate from each other, but there are many ways to convert the information in order to use them for our needs.

Now, let's have a look at the concept of the sequence that a material node tree should usually follow. In the rest of this chapter, we have to picture a node setup. Let's analyze it to better understand what's going on.

We always start from the left-hand side. The first node you see in the following screenshot is a **Texture Coordinate** node, and it is needed to tell Cycles what kind of texture coordinates we want to use for the textures of the material we are creating. This node belongs to the input nodes group. These kinds of nodes (inputs), as the name says, are used to generate some kind of input (values, colors, and so on); so, they only have output sockets. They are used to provide information about the object on which we want to apply the material we are creating.

Proceeding to the right, we can see that there is a **Wave Texture** node. This is a procedural texture built in into Cycles. It receives the information about the vector from the **Texture Coordinate** node. Looking at the node, we can see that there are several empty sockets on the left-hand side. We can change the values manually, but each of these sockets can also receive information from other nodes just as we are doing for the **Vector** socket.

From the right-hand side of the node, you can see that we are plugging the **Wave Texture** node's **Color** output into the **Color** input of a diffuse shader and a **Bump** node. The **Bump** node will convert the color information of the **Color** output of the **Wave Texture** node into vector information, which is used to give a bump effect to the surface of our object.

Moving further to the right, we find two shaders. As we saw earlier, the **Diffuse BSDF** node takes the **Color** input from **Wave Texture**, while the glossy shader has a plain white color. Note that more input sockets are left empty so that we can manually change the values instead of using other nodes as input information.

These two shaders are then mixed using a **Mix Shader** node with a factor of 0.2. This means that the output of this mix node will take 80 percent of the information from the upper input socket (in this case, the diffuse) and 20 percent from the lower one (the glossy).

Lastly, the result is plugged into a **Material Output** node. As said before, this is always the last node of a material.

Looking at the node setup, we can see that each output has the same color as the input into which it is plugged, with the exception of the **Bump** node. This node takes the values from the color information (the node automatically converts any color information into a black and white format) and converts it into vector information.

This simple material setup is helpful in understanding a correct sequence of nodes:

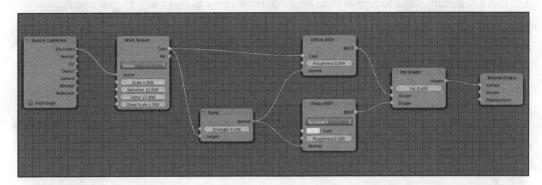

A look at the hardware

As said before, Cycles is a pretty heavy render engine and needs the appropriate hardware to work correctly. Moreover, it gives us the possibility to use the power of modern graphic cards to speed up render time. Not every card will work with Cycles, so I thought it'd be worth it to say a couple of words about this topic.

Cycles can render on both CPU and GPU, even if at the moment it cannot use them at the same time. That being said, GPU render is faster than CPU (at least for the same amount of money spent on these two items), but the first one presents some limitations.

First of all, GPU rendering with Cycles works only with CUDA at the moment. CUDA is a proprietary technology of **NVIDIA**. This means that at the current state of its development, GPU rendering with Cycles only works with cards equipped with an NVIDIA chip, such as **GeForce**, **Quadro**, or **Tesla** cards. A similar technology that will allow Cycles to take advantage of video cards is **OpenCL**. This is an open source technology, which is supported also by **AMD** (and others, but AMD is the main NVIDIA competitor) cards, but unfortunately at the time of writing, developers have still not managed to implement these libraries in a usable way mainly due to the fact that OpenCL is still under heavy development.

So, to summarize, it is good to repeat it once again. At the time of writing these lines if you want to use a GPU to render in Cycles you need an NVIDIA card, and it looks like things are not going to change any time soon.

Now, what video card should we buy to get the best out of Cycles? I guess you are not new to computer graphics, so you may already have guessed the answer. The more you are willing to pay, the better the performance you will get. There are, however, some important points to keep in mind.

First of all, Cycles will load up all the information needed to render the scenes onto the video card memory. When the **VRAM** (**video RAM**) is full, your render will fail. This should make you understand the first important point—Performance is really important, but if you cannot render a scene at all, it is quite useless.

The second important point is that developing features for the GPU is much more difficult than developing them for the CPU. As I am writing these lines for example, new Cycles features such as **strand rendering** and **SSS** are available only for the CPU.

The third important point is that new Cycles releases often brought two things, among others, until now—Faster CPU rendering and slower GPU rendering. At the moment, GPU rendering still has the best performance/price ratio, but it's important to keep in mind the preceding three points while choosing the right hardware.

Choosing the CPU for Cycles is pretty straightforward. Any CPU will work fine, and the faster the CPU, the faster the render time will be. Keep in mind that there are fairly big differences between operating systems here as well. Both Linux and OS X are much faster than Windows while rendering on the CPU. The only way to get similar performances in Windows is by using a **MinGW** (**Minimalist GNU for Windows**) or the Visual Basic 2012 build of Blender. These are Blender versions built using a different compiler from the default one used, and they provide similar render times to Linux and OS X while using the CPU. The problem is that the stability of this version is not guaranteed.

Speaking of video cards, performances among operating systems is quite similar. Here is a brief list of some of the best video cards to use with Cycles in the order of performance. I will not list professional video cards such as Quadro or Tesla as they would require a more in-depth analysis. In my humble opinion, most Cycles users will not benefit from their usage:

- GTX TITAN 6 GB
- GTX 590 3GB
- GTX 690 4GB
- GTX 580 1.5/3 GB
- GTX 680 2/4 GB
- GTX 670 2/4 GB
- GTX 570 1.2/2.5 GB
- GTX 660 Ti 1.5/3 GB
- GTX 560 Ti 1/2 GB

As you can see, apart from TITAN, the fastest single chip video card is still a 580 GTX. Despite the fact that the 6*xx* is newer, the rendering performance remains the same, or in some cases even got worse than the older 5*xx*. However, the 6*xx* comes with a higher amount of memory on board, which is an advantage on its side.

It is important to notice that the GTX x90 models are double chip versions of the x80 cards. They are faster, but the real amount of memory is half of how much is written. This is because the total amount has to be divided between the two chips, so Cycles will only be able to use half of the memory.

Some less powerful video cards than the ones listed here will usually still be faster than many CPUs, so in case you don't want to change the whole computer, it can still be a good deal to buy a cheap video card if you have an old CPU. Anyway, I advise you to always check benchmarks for the specific CPU or video card you are looking for. Keep in mind however, that a new high-end CPU (such as the Intel i7-4770K) under Linux will perform almost as fast as any lower-level card, other than the ones listed before.

Before moving on to the first chapter of this book, I would like to provide you with a useful link where Blender users upload their performance results with Cycles:

```
http://blenderartists.org/forum/showthread.php?239480-2.61-Cycles-
render-benchmark
```

In the first post you will find a link to the benchmark used, another one where you can upload your results, and a last link that will open up a page with a result summary.

1
Key Holder and Wallet Studio Shot

In this first chapter we will learn how to set up **Cycles**. Then, we will create our first materials and lights in Cycles. We will cover the following topics:

- ▶ Setting up Cycles for the first run
- ▶ Creating a three-point light setup in Cycles using mesh emitters
- ▶ Learning environment lighting
- ▶ Using the Glossy shader to create a clean metal material
- ▶ Adding realism to the keys with a bump texture
- ▶ Creating a rubber shader for the key holder
- ▶ Adding color to the key holder
- ▶ Creating a leather material for the wallet
- ▶ Using the Cycles camera's depth of field
- ▶ Setting the Cycles render parameters

Introduction

Here we are at the beginning of our journey. In a short time we are going to set up our first Cycles scene. We will start with some basic lighting and materials, but at the end of this chapter we will have already learned a good amount of knowledge, which we will use to proceed with the other chapters and the creation of more and more complex things in Cycles.

Setting up Cycles for the first run

In this recipe we will see how to set up Cycles for the first run.

Getting ready

Let's open Blender and set Cycles as the rendering engine. If you are using the CPU to render, you are pretty much ready to go. If you want to use your video card, we need to change a couple of settings.

How to do it...

1. Let's go to **File | User Preferences...**. As an alternative you can use the hotkey *Ctrl + Alt + U*.

2. Let's start by going to the **System** tab and in the lower-left corner you will see the **Compute Device** setting area.

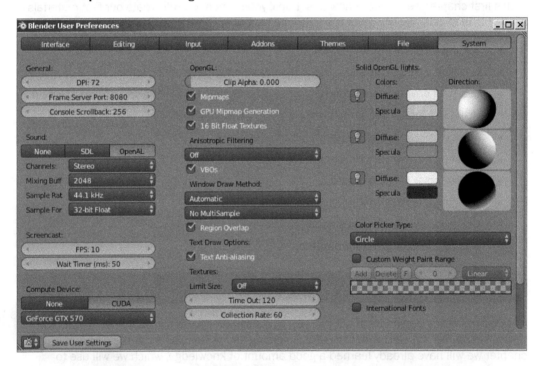

3. As default it is set to **None**, but to use your **Compute Unified Device Architecture** (**CUDA**) device, you need to click on the **CUDA** button. From the drop-down menu, select your device (or devices if you have more than one card installed in your computer).

4. At this point you may want to save the settings. To do this, click on the **Save User Settings** button in the lower-left corner so that Blender remembers these settings at the next startup.

 If you are working with Blender 2.66 or newer, the user settings and the startup scene are kept separate. If on the other hand you are using an older version, clicking the **Save User Settings** button will also save the scene that you have in the viewport at the moment, and it will become the startup scene of Blender. To save the startup scene in version 2.66 or newer, go to **File | Save Startup File**.

5. Now let's close the **Blender User Preferences** window and go to the **Render** menu bar item. From there go to the render menu and change the **Device** from **CPU** to **GPU** Compute.

6. Let's open up the `keys_Empty.blend` file. If we did everything correctly from the previous section, the video card settings should have remained as we set them a while ago.

 Downloading the example code

You can download the example code files for all Packt books you have purchased from your account at `http://www.packtpub.com`. If you purchased this book elsewhere, you can visit `http://www.packtpub.com/support` and register to have the files e-mailed directly to you.

7. As you can see the interface is a bit different from the default one. This is because to set up Cycles materials, we will need a node editor always open. Moreover, Cycles has a new great feature that will help us while setting up our scenes—the interactive viewport.

8. When the interactive viewport is on, we will see our render running in real time in the viewport; in the meantime, we can set up our lights and material.

9. This is why I like to have a small viewport always set on camera view to check out the scene in real time. As the rendering is quite a heavy process, if we don't have a really powerful hardware (such as a dual-video card machine), it is good to keep this window comparatively small, in order not to over charge the system.

10. We will use the main viewport to select and move objects around in the scene, as this operation is not so easy from the real-time viewport.

11. Of course the interface setup really depends on personal tastes, so feel free to change it as you like. For the sake of simplicity in this book, when explaining some passage I will refer to the interface setup you will find in the various chapter's scenes.

12. Well, I think that now we are really ready to set up our first Cycles scene!

Creating a three-point light setup in Cycles using mesh emitters

For our first lighting setup we will look at one of the most important and common ways of lighting: the three-point light setup. As the name suggests, this consists of three lights—the key light, the rim light, and the fill light. With different positions, colors, and intensities we can create a huge variety of moods for our image and this is why every artist should know how to set up this kind of lighting. Let's get started!

Getting ready

From the smaller viewport header, select the **Display** mode and from the drop-down menu, click on the **Rendered** mode.

Here you have it! The awesome real-time viewport. Now the scene is quite empty, so it is not so heavy and Blender should still be quite responsive. Anyway, it is up to the artist to decide when to turn the real-time viewport off if it becomes too heavy.

 When we activate the real-time viewport, in the upper part of it we can see some technical info. The last one on the right is **Path Tracing Samples** x/x. The more samples you have, the more precise and less noisy the viewport will be. If you want to increase the samples for the viewport, go to the render settings section and under the **Sampling** panel, change the **Preview** value. Just keep in mind that higher samples also mean higher render time!

How to do it...

These are steps that we need to follow to create a three-point lighting setup:

1. Right now, the scene is quite dark and boring. So, let's add some light to start. Add a plane, add a material to it from the material menu, and name it `Key_Light`. While the node editor will be needed for the biggest part of materials, for the really basic ones it is still possible to use the old materials menu. So from the **Surface** panel, click on the **Surface** drop-down menu and select **Emission**. Note that a new shader node has been added in the node editor.

2. If you still have the real-time viewport active, you will see that the plane is emitting light. Place the light a bit above our scene and let's take some time to familiarize with it. As we said in the introduction, Cycles is able to calculate lights in a quite accurate way. Indeed, mesh lights will behave like it does in reality.

3. This means that increasing the surface of the emitter will increase the amount of light in the scene. At the same time, the shadows will become more blurred. On the other hand, a smaller surface will be weaker but will cast much sharper shadows.

4. For the mesh emitters the only possible setting is in the materials menu (or in the node editor) and is Strength. Let's give this light an emitting power of `10` and then place it a bit on the right and a bit higher than the camera, and make it face towards the center of the scene. Now set the scale to `3`.

5. Let's copy the plane, place it on the left side of the scene, and scale it up to a value of `16`. Our target is to make the shadows of this light much smoother, this being a fill light. The problem is that now its light is way too strong. By clicking on the button with the number 2 on it, which is right next to the material name, duplicate the material and name it `Fill_Light` and set the intensity of this material to `1`. To make the scene a bit more interesting, we can add a touch of blue to the color of the light. Something like R: 0.600, G: 0.800, B: 0.800 should be fine.

6. Now let's duplicate the emitting plane again and move it behind the objects facing towards the camera and leave the scale as it is. Again we will have to duplicate the material and name it `Rim_Light`. Change the color to a really subtle yellow. Set the RGB value to 0.800, 0.770, 0.600. This small color temperature contrast will help make the scene more interesting.

7. There is just a small problem now. We can see our rim light in the camera, and this is not exactly what we want in a studio shot. Luckily, even if Cycles is a realistic engine, there is still a lot of room for tricks! With the rim light selected, go to the object menu and down to the Ray Visibility panel. Here uncheck the Camera checkbox and our rim light will be gone from the real-time viewport!

8. That's it for our three-point light setup! In the end, our scene should look more or less like this:

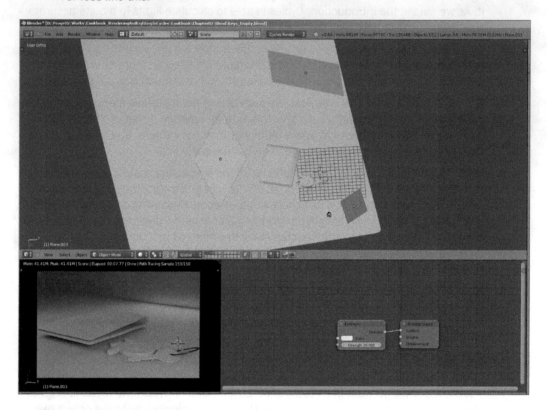

How it works...

As we said at the beginning of this recipe, the three-point light setup is one of the most important setups to master and one of the most commonly used. We are now going to see the concepts behind it in depth.

Key Light

This is the dominant light in the scene. This light plays the main role in determining the mood of an image and in shaping the form of subjects. It is also responsible for most of the shadows. With that said, the key light is not always the brightest one in the scene. More often than not the rim light is the brightest. On the other hand, the key light must always be brighter than the fill light. This light is usually positioned about 30 to 60 degrees to the front and to the right-hand side of the object. This is not a rule, however.

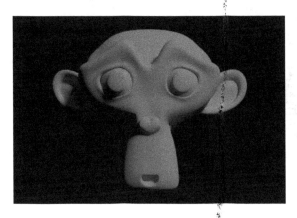

Fill Light

As the name suggests, this light fills in the shadow areas. As we said before, it is always of lesser visual intensity than the key light. The fill light is also really soft. This is because it is used to control the contrast of the image. A stronger fill light will result in a less-contrasted (and so with less visual tension) image, while a weaker fill light will leave the image with a higher contrast (and thus a more dramatic and visually tense image). In the real world, the fill light is always generated by the reflected or scattered light from where it takes its soft look. The fill light is usually positioned across from the key light, in order to better fill the shadows left by the latter. Still it should cast its light from the camera side.

Rim Light

This light is also called Backlight and its primary function is to make the subject stand out from the background. It creates a thin line of light around the shape of the subject that helps to enhance the illusion of depth and emphasize the subject. This light is positioned behind the subject, more or less opposite to the camera point of view.

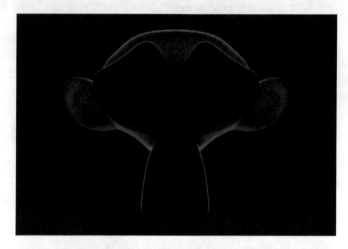

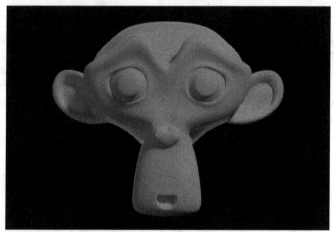

The three-point light setup became so popular thanks to its versatility. Playing with the intensities, colors, and position of the lights will greatly change the mood of the image, from a happy fairy look to a dark and sinister one. A good technique is to find references from images, for example, movies, and try to recreate the look of that image. You can be sure that in almost any of the movies out there, the lighting of the subjects was done with a three-point setup.

In this link *Ben Simonds* will explains a lot of tips and tricks with the three-point light setup, including how to give different moods:

`http://bensimonds.com/2010/06/03/lighting-tips-from-the-masters/`

Learning environment lighting

Even if we already set up a proper three-point light system, a real studio shot usually has some more elements around the scene that will contribute to the reflections on the object.

Getting ready

To recreate the environment that will contribute to the lighting and the reflections, it won't be necessary to model a whole scene. Instead, we can use an image to fake the environment around the scene and give our objects something to reflect.

How to do it...

To create the environment lighting, we will be following these steps:

1. Let's go to the World node editor and add the following three nodes:
   - **Texture Coordinate**
   - **Environment Texture (Add | Texture)**
   - **Mapping (Add | Vector)**

2. The environment texture is the kind of texture that we always have to use for a World **BSDF (Bidirectional Scattering Distribution Function)**. The Mapping node is really useful. It allows us to move, rotate, and scale an image on a surface or, as for this situation, on the environment. Let's plug the **Generated** output socket of the **Texture Coordinate** node in the **Vector** input of the **Mapping** node and the output of the latter in the **Vector** input of the **Environment Texture** node. Finally, as we would do for a normal shader, let's plug the texture in the **Color** input of the **Background** node.

3. Now the sky will have a purple color. That's because we still haven't loaded any image in the **Texture** node. Let's do it now, and from the browser, load the `studio019.hdr` file. Here we go! Now the environment will resemble the look of a real photographic studio. You can move around in the scene in the perspective mode, or look through the camera and the picture will move accordingly.

4. All we have to do now is to set the **Z** rotation in the **Mapping** node to `-90` degrees in order to place the image accordingly to our scene. Finally, let's set the intensity of the **Background** node to `0.6`.

To see the final effect, remember to activate the layer with the lights and deactivate the **Clay material overwrite** option from the **Render** menu.

Here is how the World node setup should looks like:

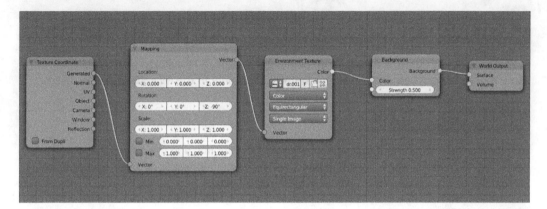

How it works...

Let's have a brief look at the environment lighting system built in Cycles in a more general way. As for the materials, we have two ways of setting it up. We can use the menu as it works for **Blender Internal** (**BI**) or we can use the node editor.

Of course, the node editor will give us more versatility for the creation of the environment. Anyway, before we can use it, there is one thing to do. Let's go to the World menu and on the **Surface** panel click on the **Use Nodes** button. Now we are ready to move to the node editor and start playing with the environment.

In the lower header of the node editor, click on the World icon (it is the same icon of the World menu). What you should see is a **Background** node plugged inside a **World Output** node. The concept behind the environment is exactly the same as for the Shader node system. Here, things are a bit more straightforward as the only shader node which we have to worry about is the **Background** one. For the rest, it works exactly in the same way.

To familiarize with the environment lighting, let's switch off the layer with the mesh lights for a moment. Also, to speed up the scene rendering, we will use a clay material for the whole scene. Don't worry, we won't be changing materials one after another. It is enough to go to the **Render** menu, and from the **Layers** panel, select the material **Clay** inside the material space. This is just a gray diffuse material that I included in the file. All the materials we created are still where we left them, but for now every object of the scene will render with the Clay material. To come back to the original situation, it will be enough to erase the material from where we just placed it.

Now, let's activate the real-time viewport. Remember that Cycles have **Global Illumination** (**GI**). This means that the environment will always influence the scene. Of course we also have the possibility to deactivate it, but this is an important concept to keep in mind. If we set the color to pure black, as there are no lights, the scene will look pitch black. As we make the color lighter, we will start to see things in our scene. As it is now, which is a plain color, the environment works as a constant source of light which is uniformly distributed around our scene. It will not cast shadows, but we will be able to see the occlusion of the objects. In a moment, we will see that it is possible to make the environment non-uniform, in order to resemble the different kind of places or lighting or whatever we want, without physically having them in the scene.

In the World menu, right below the **Surface** panel, there is the **Ambient Occlusion** panel. In Cycles, the ambient occlusion works only in the **Add** mode. By activating it, you will see that the occluded areas of the scene look much brighter. We can adjust the intensity and the distance at which the AO affects the objects of the scene. For this particular scene, we will not be using the AO, so switch it off for now.

Even below the **Settings** panel there is the **Multiple Importance Sample** checkbox. I quote from the Cycles manual:

> *"By default, lighting from the world is computed solely with indirect light sampling. However for more complex environment maps this can be too noisy, as sampling the BSDF may not easily find the highlights in the environment map image. By enabling this option, the world background will be sampled as a lamp, with lighter parts automatically given more samples."*

So, this option will help us reduce the noise when dealing with complex images used as environments. The map resolution will increase the accuracy of the MIS, but also increase the render times and memory used.

There's more...

At the beginning of this chapter, we talked about Bidirectional Scattering Distribution Function (BSDF from now on). We will have a lot to do with this from the next recipe, so it is time to have a better understanding of what it is. Said in a really simple way, it represents a big part of the shaders present in Cycles. As the name suggests, it is the function used by Cycles to distribute the light when a surface is lit. So, when we apply a BSDF to an object, the light will be distributed following the function of the BSDF we used, depending on the one we use. As we will see, there are several BSDFs, such as Diffuse, Glossy, Glass, and others. Each one of these is a different light distribution function, which imitates real-life materials. With each chapter of the book, we will see in depth each BSDF present in Cycles and learn to use it at its best.

It is important to say that there is also a second kind of scattering function called **Bidirectional Surface Scattering Reflectance Distribution Function** (**BSSRDF**). This is another kind of function which is used for some particular shader, for example, the subsurface scattering which we will see for the first time in *Chapter 3, Creating an Interior Scene*.

See also

▸ The following link directs you to Blender Wiki for Cycles shader. It is really useful to have a general overview of each one of the BSDFs and BSSRDFs present in Cycles at the moment:

```
http://wiki.blender.org/index.php/Doc:2.6/Manual/Render/Cycles/
Nodes/Shaders
```

Using the Glossy shader to create a clean metal material

Now that the lighting is ready, we need to add some material to the objects of our scene. Let's start with the key.

Getting ready

Select the key from the scene, add a new material and name it Key. Even if the key material alone will be quite simple, this time we are going to use the node editor in order to set it up.

By default when we add a new material, Cycles will add a Diffuse shader node and of course, the material output. For the key metal we will also need this node, so let's leave it where it is. Moreover, we are going to need a glossy shader in order to add reflections to the key surface.

How to do it...

These are the steps to create the materials of this recipe:

1. To add a new node, we need to keep the cursor on the node editor and press *Shift + A* to make the **Add** menu appear. Now let's go to **Shader | Glossy BSDF**. A new Shader node will appear where your cursor stands.

2. Now we need to mix the **Diffuse BSDF** and the **Glossy BSDF** nodes. To do this, we can use the **Mix Shader** node. You will find it again in the **Add** menu, **Shader** section. Now let's take the output from the **Diffuse BSDF** node and plug it into the first **Shader** input of the **Mix Shader** node, and the output of the **Glossy BSDF** node into the second **Shader** input of the **Mix Shader** node. As a last thing, take the output of the **Mix Shader** node and plug it into the **Surface** input of the **Material Output** node.

3. In the real-time viewport you should already see that the key is looking much better than with the plain white material it had before. Anyway, we need to make a couple of tweaks to make it look as it really should.

4. First of all we need to change the mix factor in the **Mix Shader** node. Let's change the face value to `0.800`. In this way 80 percent of the output will come from the lower shader input, where we connected the **Glossy BSDF** node. Now the key should have stronger reflections on the surface.

5. Anyway if we observe a real key, we will notice that reflections are quite sharp when objects are close to the surface, while they get a bit blurred as the distance increases. Our key right now has definitely too blurred reflections, and to make them sharper, we need to change the **Roughness** value of the **Glossy BSDF** node. Set it to `0.060` and now we can see that the reflection of the close objects are much sharper.

6. The last thing to do is to change the diffuse color to a gray one (set RGB values as `0.200, 0.200, 0.200`).

The final node setup should look like the following screenshot:

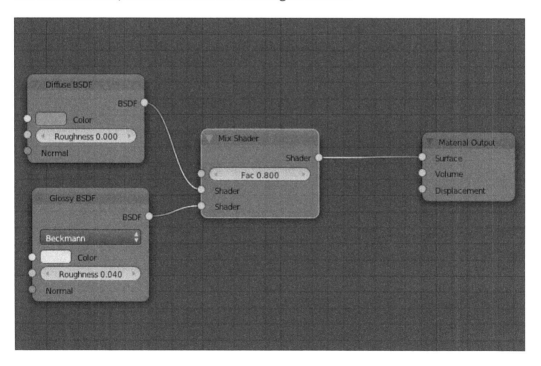

And that's it! We just created our first Cycles material!

How it works...

In this first material we are mixing two different BSDFs to obtain the desired result. While the Glossy BSDF is important to get reflections on the surface of the key, it is also true that the metal of which the key is made of does not behave as a mirror. This means that even if it is strongly influenced by the colors and lights around it, in most cases it will maintain its grayish color. This is why we mixed the Glossy BSDF with a bit of Diffuse BSDF. The Diffuse BSDF is useful to give a plain color to a surface. It will still be influenced by surrounding objects and lights, but it will help the surface to maintain its gray color in most environment situations.

There's more...

You will see the BSDF acronym next to every shader node in Cycles. Applying a shader to a material will change the way in which the lights interact with the surface of that material. Each different shader node contains a different BSDF.

Adding realism to the keys with a bump texture

In this recipe we will learn how to use **bump maps** to distort the surface of an object or at least create the illusion of it.

Getting ready

Now the surface of our key is reacting in a realistic way to light, but it is still missing something. Every real key has got some word or pattern on it. To obtain this effect, we are going to add a bump texture at the key material in order to add these details on the surface.

How to do it...

These are the steps we are going to follow to create the bump for our material:

1. Let's go to our node editor and add a new node. To do this press *Shift + A* and go to **Inputs | Texture Coordinate**. This node will allow us to tell Cycles what kind of coordinate we want to use for the textures of our material. Now we need to add an **Image Texture** node. We will find it in the **Textures** section of the **Add** menu. Before we start to link the nodes, we need the last one. From the **Vector** section of the **Add** menu, add a **Bump** node.

2. Now let's link the **UV** output from the **Texture Coordinate** node to the **Vector** input of the **Image Texture** node and the **Color** output of the latter to the **Height** input of the **Bump** node. As a last linking we need to put the **Normal** output of the **Bump** node into the **Normal** input of both the **Diffuse BSDF** and **Glossy BSDF** nodes. We are almost ready, as we just need to add the image that we want to use as a bump map. To do this we need to click on the open image icon in the **Image Texture** node. From the file browser go to the `Chapter01/Blend/Textures` folder and open the `Key_Bump.png` image.

3. That's it! Looking at the real-time viewport we can see the bump map doing its work on the key surface. Without changing anything of the mesh geometry we can see really fine details, affecting the way the light reacts on the surface of the key.

4. There is one last thing to change. The strength of the bump node is definitely too much. To adjust this, let's change the **Strength** value of the **Bump** node to `0.030`.

The final node setup of the key material will look like the following screenshot:

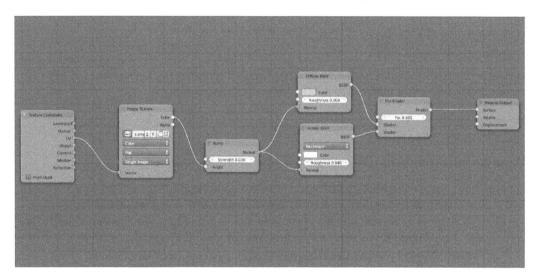

How it works...

We used the **Texture Coordinate** node to tell the **Image Texture** node where to place the image on the surface of our key. Then with the **Bump** node we converted the black and white image information into vector information which is readable by the BDSFs.

When we use a bump map, Cycles will treat the surface as it would be lower in correspondence to the black areas of the image and higher in correspondence to the white ones. Of course all the grayscale in the middle will give information about the position of the surface. Taking this information in account, the BDSFs will calculate the behavior of the light bouncing on the surface of the object.

There's more...

A bump map is a black and white image which contains information about the shape of the surface of an object. It is used to add details to a mesh without actually changing the geometry of it. This means that during the rendering process, Cycles will take to account the information taken from the bump map and make the light react accordingly even if the surface is actually flat. A bump map will not change the silhouette of the object, it will just fake the details on the surface. To actually change the geometry we need to use displacement, but we will cover this technique later on in the book, in *Chapter 8, Creating a Car Animation*, in the *Creating the materials for the exterior environment* recipe.

Creating a rubber shader for the key holder

Now we will create a material for the **key holder**. It will be a soft rubber material and something completely different from the metal of the key.

Getting ready

Before we start to create the material we need to add it to the mesh. Let's select the key holder mesh, add a new material to it, and name it KeyHolder.

How to do it...

These are the steps we are going to take to create the rubber material:

1. Now, erase the **Diffuse BSDF** node from the node editor as we will not use it. Instead, we will be using the combination of **Translucent BSDF** and **Glass BDSF** nodes. Add them from the **Shader** section of the **Add** menu. Also add a **Mix Shader** node and link the **Translucent BSDF** node to the first **Shader** input and the **Glossy BSDF** one to the second **Shader** input of the **Mix Shader** node. Also set the **Fac** value to 0.100.

2. As you can see in the viewport, the key holder now has a white milky material, with the light scattering inside itself. Anyway, to give it a rubber-like look we need to tweak the **Glass BSDF** node a bit.

3. Let's change the **Roughness** value of **Glass BSDF** to 0.500. Doing so, we will make both the refractions and the reflections generated by this BSDF quite blurry, to resemble the look of a piece of rubber. Also set the **Glass BSDF** color to pure white.

4. The last thing we need to do is to set the correct **IOR** value for the rubber. On the Internet you can easily find information about the IOR (Index of Refraction) of different materials. Rubber for instance has an IOR of 1.5191. Let's set the IOR value in **Glass BSDF** to 1.5191.

Here is how the final node setup will look like in the following screenshot:

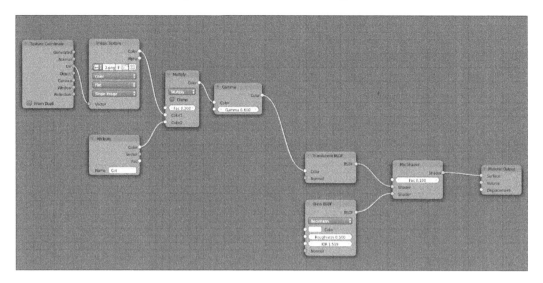

How it works...

A rubber material needs the light to be scattered inside itself. Moreover, it will have a slight amount of reflection on its surface and refractions within its volume.

With the **Translucent BSDF** node we make the light scatter through the key holder. As we need a touch of reflections and refractions, we will use a small amount of the **Glass BSDF** node. As both reflections and refractions are quite blurry for a piece of rubber, we increased the roughness value of the **Glass BSDF** node.

The color of the **Glass BSDF** node is really important. As we will see, especially in the next chapter, really small changes make a big difference. In order to not make a glass look dark and almost dirty the color needs to be pure white. Even a slightly darker color will not make the glass look good.

There's more...

The Translucent BSDF allows the light to pass through the object and get scattered within. The surface, as in the Diffuse BSDF, is without reflections. On the other hand, a Glass BSDF, as the name tells us, is a shader used to recreate glass materials. While for the Translucent BSDF we can just choose the color, and for the glass we can change the glossiness of the refractions and the IOR. This last value represents the ratio between the speed at which the light travels in vacuum compared to the speed in the object. This is the reason why when we look through a piece of glass we see things distorted. Moreover, the Glass shader generates not only refractions, but also reflections on the surface of the object.

Adding color to the key holder

In this recipe we will learn how to use a color texture inside a material. We will also learn a really interesting technique to make the material more realistic and "live".

Getting ready

As you will have probably noticed our key holder has the shape of the Blender logo. Of course we cannot have just the shape, we need to add proper colorization!

How to do it...

To effectively use a color texture, we need to follow these steps:

1. First of all let's add the colors of the Blender logo to it. In the node editor add a new **Image Texture** node and a **Texture Coordinate** node. Also, for these textures we will use the UV coordinates.

2. Now link the **Color** output of the **Image Texture** node to the **Color** input of the **Translucent BSDF** node. It is already much better! Now we have a nice Blender logo! Some could say that we could even stop here, but let's tweak this material even further.

3. It would be nice to have a bit of dirt in the occluded parts of the the key holder. To obtain this kind of effect, we will be using vertex paint.

4. First of all let's paint the vertices of our key holder. From the lower header of the viewport, select from the **Mode** menu, **Vertex Paint**. Now our key holder will have a shadeless white color in the viewport. From the lower viewport header, in the **Paint** menu select **Dirty Vertex Color**. Looking at the viewport we can now see that the color of the key holder has changed. This function will give a black and white color to the surface of the object following things such as occlusion and topology. We could say that our key holder is a bit dirty, and this is what we wanted.

5. Let's see how we can use this color in our material. Go back to object mode. If we go to the **Object Data** menu, we will see that in the **Vertex Color** panel a new entry has been added. This is the color information we created a while ago. Change the name to KeyHolderDirt, and copy it (you can use *Ctrl + C* as in the desktop environment). Now let's go to the node editor and add an **Attribute** node. We can find this inside the **Input** section of the **Add** menu. Now paste within the **Attribute** node field the name of the vertex color with *Ctrl + V* and we are ready to go. The **Color** output of this node will now work as a texture with the information of the vertex **Color**.

6. Now let's add a **Mix Color** node, which can be found in the **Color** section of the **Add** menu. Take the output of the **Image Texture** node which was plugged in to the **Translucent BSDF** color input and plug it into the first **Color** socket of the **Color Mix** node. In the second socket we will plug the **Color** output of the **Attribute** node. Finally, let's change the mixing mode of the **Mix** node to **Multiply**, change the factor to 0.300, and plug the **Color** output to the **Translucent** node's **Color** input.

7. As a last touch, let's add a **Gamma** node (go to **Add | Color**) and place it between the **Mix** node's **Color** output and the **Translucent BSDF** node's **Color** input. We will use this node to lighten the overall color a bit as now it is too dark. Change the **Gamma** value to 0.600.

8. Our rubber key holder is ready!

This is how the final node setup should look like, in the following screenshot:

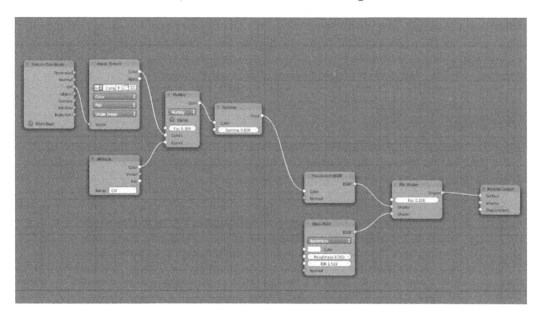

Before we move on to the next recipe, let's add a fast material to both the chain and the keyring. It can be the same material for both. Add a new material and name it KeyHolderChain. Now let's move for a while to the key material. In the node editor select just the two BSDFs and the relative **Mix** node and press *Ctrl + C*. Now go again to the KeyHolderChain material and in the node editor erase the default **Diffuse BSDF** node. Press *Ctrl + V* and the node that we copied before will be pasted into the node editor. We will just have to link the **Mix** output to the **Material** output and we are ready to go.

How it works...

The first part of the creation of this material follows a workflow that we already saw in the previous recipes. However, we mixed two new BSDFs. While we will have a whole chapter to talk about the Glass BSDF, let's have a look at how the Translucent BSDF works.

As we saw, a BSDF is useful to scatter light within an object. The amount of light scattered by the object depends on the color we set in the node. A totally white color will give the highest amount of light scattered through the object, while a black color means no light scattered at all.

When we used the texture and the vertex color as the input for the **Translucent BSDF** node's color, we not only changed the amount of light scattered, but we also changed the color of the light that scattered through the key holder.

Another important thing we learned in this material is that BSDFs have to be mixed in a different way than colors. While for BSDF we need a Mix Shader node, for the colors we have to use a normal Mix node, exactly like the one that we use in the compositing node editor. You can easily see the difference of the two nodes by the colors of the inputs and outputs. Moreover, the Color Mix node has several ways of mixing the colors.

There's more...

Vertex painting is a technique used in computer graphics to assign color information directly on the vertices of a mesh. It can be used simply to give color over a surface or as a map to achieve different effects when setting up, for instance, a material.

When you are creating a complex material, it is a good idea to check some passages with a much simpler setup. For example, if we need to check the color of some texture or the effect given by some node, we can use a temporary diffuse node. Plugging, for instance, a texture inside the color input of a Diffuse BSDF and the diffuse output directly in the Material Output node will give us a good idea of what is going on.

See also

▸   In the following link there is a really nice add-on which will allow us to create worn edges using the vertex paint within Blender:

    http://oscurart.blogspot.com.ar/2013/05/blender-addon-worn-edges-bordes.html

Creating a leather material for the wallet

Now let's see how we can create a material for a wallet. We want to recreate a smooth, worn eco leather.

Getting ready

First of all we need to add a new material to the wallet. Let's select the wallet mesh, add a new material to it, and name it `Wallet`.

How to do it...

To create the leather material, we will be following these steps:

1. Now in the node editor add a **Glossy BSDF** node and mix it with the default **Diffuse BSDF** node using a **Mix Shader** node. Set the mix factor to 0.300 and the **Glossy BSDF** node's **Roughness** value *to* `0.100`. Still not so great looking... is it? Let's make this material look a bit better! To do so we are going to use a combination of image textures and procedural textures.

2. First of all let's add our **Texture Coordinate** node (**Add | Input**). Then we need to add a procedural texture. From the **Texture** section of the **Add** menu, click on **Noise Texture**. Link the **Vector** input to the **Generated** output of the **Texture Coordinate** node.

3. For this material we just need to set the **Distortion** to `1.000`, while for the other values the default settings of the **Noise Texture** node will be good for our needs, so we can leave them as they are. If you want to see how this texture looks, remember that you can use a Diffuse BSDF node.

4. We will now be using a second procedural texture to recreate the smaller imperfections of the leather. It will again be a noise texture type. So let's duplicate the one we just created using *Shift + D*. In this one we need to set the scale to `100.000`, while we will set **Details** *and* **Distortion** to `5.000`.

5. Now we need to mix the two procedural textures with a Mix node in mix mode, with a **Fac** of `0.050`. We will be needing the black and white info of the textures, so we need to use the **Fac** output of the procedural textures, not the **Color** one. The **Noise Texture** node with the lower scale value (**Scale** `5.000`) have to be plugged in the first socket, while the **Noise Texture** node with the higher scale vale (Scale `100.000`) in the second socket.

6. As we will see, this node setup will soon start to be a little bit crowded. It is a good thing to keep things organized, so let's name some nodes. Press the N key to bring out the properties panel. When you have a node selected in this panel, you will get some info and some settings about the node. With the last-created **Mix** node selected, write PROCEDURAL in the label space. Looking at the node, we can see that now it will not have **Mix** written on it anymore, but the name we just gave it. Note that you can also change other settings such as the name and the color of the node.

7. Now let's add an **Image Texture** node and from the browser, select the scratches. jpeg image. This time as the texture coordinate we will use **UV**.

8. To recreate the leather, we will be using another **Image Texture** node as well. Let's duplicate the previous **Image Texture** node and press the **X** button on the node to erase the path and load instead the image called stains.jpeg. Also for this texture we want to use UV coordinates.

9. As we did for the procedural textures, let's mix these two **Image Texture** nodes. Plug them into a **Mix** node, scratches.jpeg in the second socket and stains.jpeg in the first one, **Mix** mode, **Fac** 0.20. As we also want to use the black and white information from the image textures, we need to convert them. To do this from the **Convertor** section of the **Add** menu, click on **RGB to BW** and link the **Color** output of the **Image Texture** nodes to the input of the node we just added. Let's label this Mix node **Images**.

10. Now we want to mix the procedural texture and the image texture. To do this we will again use a Mix node. Plug the Mix node labeled **Proc** in the first socket and the one labeled **Images** in the second. For this particular situation we want to change the Mix mode to **Add** and set the **Fac** value to 1.000. Let's label the node **GlossyCOLOR**. Now let's plug the output of this Mix node to the **Color** input of the **Glossy BSDF** node. If we change the **Diffuse BSDF** node's color to a brownish color (RGB 0.150, 0.075, 0.030), we will see that now the wallet material starts to resemble leather, but the reflections are way too strong. To fix this, we need to darken the color of the **Glossy BSDF** node. Let's add a **Gamma** node between the **GlossyCOLOR** Mix node and the **Glossy BSDF** node and set the value to 1.750. The reflections now will be much weaker. Anyway, the material is still looking really flat and boring.

11. To give some interesting variation to the surface, we will use the same color we are using for the **Glossy BSDF** node's color as a bump. Let's add a **Bump** node (**Add | Vector**), plug the **GlossyCOLOR** Mix node into the **Height** input, and the **Vector** input of both the **Diffuse BSDF** and the **Glossy BSDF** nodes into the **Normal** output of the **Bump** node. Now the surface is starting to be more interesting. All we need to do is set the strength to -0.030.

12. Let's give a final touch to this leather. We want to have more glossiness variation between the worn and the lesser worn parts of the wallet. Add another Diffuse BSDF node and set the color to RGB `0.500, 0.400, 0.250`. This will be the color of the scratches and worn areas. Now let's add a **Mix Shader** node and plug in the second **Shader** socket **BSDF** output of the **Diffuse BSDF** node and in the first **Shader** socket plug in the mix between the other **Diffuse BSDF** and **Glossy BSDF** nodes **BSDF** outputs. This time we will not set manually the **Fac** value. Instead let's plug in it the output of the **GlossyCOLOR** Mix node. Finally plug the output of the **Mix Shader** node into the **Material Output** node and we are ready to go!

Here is how the final node setup will look like, in the following screenshot:

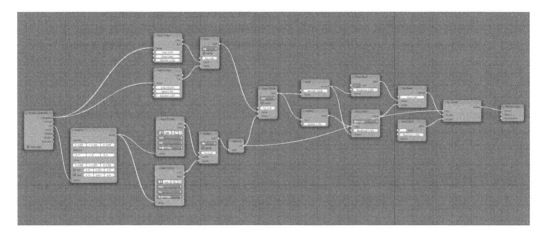

For the stitches it is enough to use a diffuse material with an RGB value of 0.650, 0.400, 0.250. We will name the material `Stitches`.

How it works...

In this leather material we can really start to see the power of nodes. First we created the map of the color by mixing different procedural and image textures. Then we used the very same node group, or part of them for the bump input and to mix two different BSDFs.

When we converted the two image textures to black and white color information, we were able to use it as a factor input for the last Mix node, telling Cycles how much we wanted of each one of the BSDF inputs. Precisely, black areas received influence from the first socket (the leather) and white areas from the second one (the material inside the scratches).

In this situation the scratches material was made using just a **Diffuse BSDF** node, but we could have created another big and really complex node setup if needed. As anticipated in the introduction, this kind of operation can be done in reality any number of times we want, making the possibilities virtually endless.

There's more...

A procedural texture is a computer-generated image that tries to resemble different natural patterns using functions, for instance, fractal noise and turbulence. These functions try in a different way to represent the "randomness" of nature. Procedural textures are set with different numerical values and can be seamlessly mapped over surfaces, even without the usage of UV maps.

Using the Cycles camera's depth of field

Creating images using a 3D program is often all about imitating reality. When we take a picture, something that often occurs is that some of the objects are out of focus. Such an effect is called **depth of field** (**DOF**) and is what we are going to recreate in this recipe.

Getting ready

Our first scene in Cycles is almost ready. However, we can still do a couple of things to make it look even more realistic. We will now see how to add a nice DOF effect.

How to do it...

To recreate the DOF effect in Cycles, let's follow these steps:

1. Let's jump in now to our scene in Blender and select the camera. First of all we need to set the point in the scene where we want to keep the focus. To do this we need to select the camera and go to the **Object Data** menu (the one with the little camera icon).

2. From here we need to activate the **Limits** option in the **Display** panel. In the viewport we will see that the camera now has a line going towards where it is looking and a yellow cross at the beginning. This cross represents the focus point.

3. To set the focus point where we want it, we need to change the **Distance** value in the **Depth of Field** panel. We want the keyholder to be the focus point of the scene, so let's set the **Distance** value to 16. The yellow cross will now be placed over the key holder.

4. For the DOF intensity, let's use **Radius** with a value of 0.0500. We do not want an effect that is too strong. For this particular scene we will simulate a round iris so that the default values are ok. Now we have a nice DOF effect in our scene that helps add realism to it. This is how the camera settings should look like if we did everything correctly in the following screenshot:

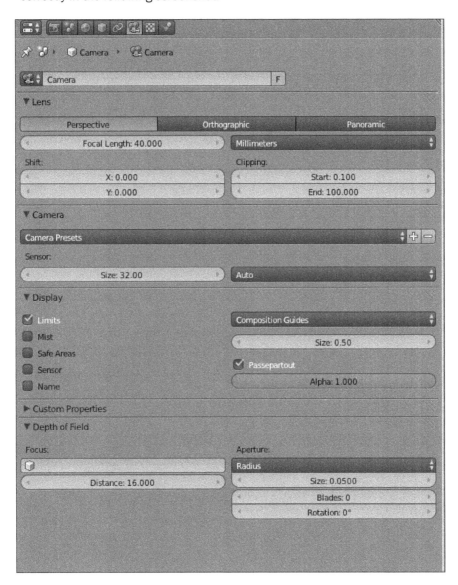

How it works...

With Blender Internal, the only way of adding this kind of effect is in compositing. Even if this method is still possible—also in Cycles—we now have another way of achieving the DOF effect.

Cycles has a DOF system built inside the camera. This means that now we dispose of a real ray-traced DOF effect which is much more accurate than the previous one. It is necessary to remind you that this new method also has some drawbacks. For instance, we will be dealing with render passes, and we will see that DOF generates a big amount of noise around edges, which can make it difficult sometimes to composite the scene. Another drawback is that once we render the image, we will not be able to change the DOF until we render the image again. This can be a problem especially for animations.

Anyway, apart from these two aspects the method of achieving DOF is fast and the final quality is really high.

There's more...

Another method of setting the focus point is to use an object. Right above the **Distance** value there is a field where you can put the name of the object on which you want to set the focus. The yellow cross will now automatically follow this object. It is important to remember that this doesn't mean that the camera will follow this object, just the distance of the focus.

On the left of where we set the distance value for the focus of the camera, there are the settings for the DOF. We can use two methods to set the intensity of the DOF: Radius and F/stop (focus stop). Bigger values for the radius will mean stronger DOF. On the contrary, with the focus stop method we need to lower the value to have a stronger DOF.

Right under the intensity value there are the iris settings, which will determine the shape and rotation of the **bokeh effect**. We can decide what shape and rotation the latter will have. If we want to have a circle iris it is enough to leave the Blade value to 0.

Setting the Cycles render parameters

In this recipe we are going to learn how to set the parameters for the final render. We will learn how to make our image noise-free and how to set the parameters in order to optimize our render times as best as we can, without losing quality.

Getting ready

We are getting closer to the conclusion of our first scene in Cycles. It may sound strange but even if we have already set up materials, lighting, and DOF, we still didn't actually render anything yet by pressing the render button. We only looked at the scene through the real-time viewport! So we can see how powerful the Cycles real-time viewport is. But the time for the final render has come, so it's time to talk about render settings.

How to do it...

I thought that a description of each render setting would be better than a mere list of the values I used in this scene. In this way, we can understand better how and why we are doing something like this. Anyway, the following is a screenshot of the render settings used for this render:

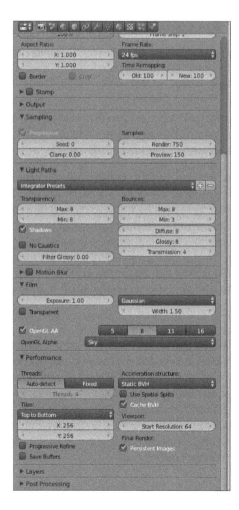

How it works...

Let's jump to the **Render** panel. Many of the settings are the same as they were in BI, so we will skip the **Dimensions**, **Stamp**, and **Output** panels. We already saw in the first part of the chapter how to set up the settings concerning the device to use, CPU or GPU.

Let's have a look instead at the **Sampling** panel. Here lies some really important settings for our render. On the right we can read **Samples**. Every time a light path in the scene hits a surface, Cycles will compute a new sample for that pixel. The higher the number of samples, the less noise the render will have. The setting of this value will depend on the scene. In general, we will need to keep increasing it till the noise disappears, or at least will be at an acceptable level.

We can see that there is a **Render** and a **Preview** value. The first is the number of samples that Cycles will compute for the final render, while the second represents how many samples will be computed in the real-time viewport. Let's set the **Render** value to 750 for this scene.

> The **seed** value is really important for animation as it will avoid the noise to be static. We will talk again about this in *Chapter 7, Car Rendering in Cycles*.

The **clamp** value is a setting that will help us reduce fireflies in our scene. A firefly, also known as **burned pixels**, is a mistake made by the engine while calculating areas with strong light. They will appear as white pixels with totally crazy RGB values.

There are many ways to avoid fireflies, but the fireflies will still occur from time to time. Clamp will help us reduce them at the cost of the accuracy of the scene. This setting will indeed clamp out the highlights over a certain value to avoid getting burned pixels. Anyway, if set a value too high, clamp can also cut out some highlights that we would like to have in the scene. Leaving this value as 0 will disable clamping, while low values will mean stronger clamping of light and higher value will mean less clamping. Usually it is not good to go below values like 3, as by doing so it may compromise the lighting of the scene. For this particular scene we won't be needing clamp anyway, so we can leave the value to 0.

We will learn in the next part of this chapter about the non-progressive integrator.

Now let's move to the **Light Paths** panel. Here we will find the settings about the precision of the rendering. As for the samples, it is good that the settings will change depending on the scene. Each setting that you see represent the number of light path bounces that we want to have in the scene. In general, the higher the number of bounces the more precise the render will be, but it will also increase both render time and noise. It is important to find the right balance. The number of bounces needed depends on the level of complexity of the materials in the scene. For instance, a complex glass material could require a high-transparency bounces number in order to render correctly.

We also have the possibility of switching off shadows and/or caustics computation. While it is really hard to find a scene where shadows are not needed, if not in particular situations, we will see especially in *Chapter 2, Creating Different Glass Materials in Cycles*, that sometimes caustics can generate a lot of noise, and it is a good idea to turn them off, especially because it is possible to fake them.

Finally, the **Filter Glossy** value can help us reduce noise on glossy surfaces in some situations. Of course nothing comes for free and as for the clamp, filter glossy will decrease the accuracy of the image. For this reason it is better to use it only if strictly necessary.

You will also see at the top of this panel a cascade menu with a couple of presets. You can also add your own presets, but as I said every scene is a story on its own.

In general, it is quite hard to find scenes that will require bounce numbers higher than 16 (and 8 for the min values). This is a quite safe area that will be capable of rendering the majority of scenes without any lack in quality and precision. On the other hand, it could also be too much for other scenes. However, a method that I like to use is to set the **Full Global Illumination** preset and make a render. Then I will start to lower down each value until I see that there is a little change in the image. It is important to check areas with transparencies, reflections, and caustics, as they are the first to change depending on the settings.

Moving down we have the settings regarding **Motion Blur**, which we will see in depth in *Chapter 7, Car Rendering in Cycles*.

In the **Film** panel, we can find settings regarding the exposure, the **Anti-Aliasing** algorithm, and the option to make the background transparent. Making the background transparent will preserve any lighting or reflections coming from it. It will just be rendered as an alpha channel.

Another important panel is **Performance**. Here we can find some settings which, if correctly set up, can speed up our render times. First of all let's talk about **tiles**. To save up memory and take advantage of multithreading, Cycles will divide the render into smaller tiles. Here it is very important what we use to render. In case of GPU the tile size should be bigger, around 256 x 256. On the other hand, when using a CPU we should make tiles smaller. Depending on the number of cores we have, good values are 32 x 32 or 64 x 64. Anyway, you will have to test it and see which is the best setting for your computer. Keep in mind that this setting can really change render times. We can also decide in what order we want the tiles to be rendered.

The **Progressive Refine** option will render the image in a single big tile. The render will be slower, but it can be stopped when we believe the noise level is acceptable and we can see the overall look of the image from the beginning.

The **Save Buffer** option will allow Cycles to write some information on the hard drive instead of the RAM. This will allow us to save some memory and could come in very handy in some big scene especially when using the GPU for the rendering.

On the right side of the panel, we will find options concerning the **Acceleration Structure**. When Cycles starts the render, a **bounding volume hierarchy** (**BVH**) of the scene will be built. Without going too deeply into technical details, BVH can be defined as the geometrical structure of the scene. Even when we will be using GPU to render, this operation will be computed by CPU and there are some different ways BVH can be built.

First of all, we can decide between a **static** or **dynamic BVH** build. The first one will require a complete reconstruction of the BVH for each rendering, but the sampling phase of the render will be faster. On the other hand, the dynamic one will allow faster BVH updates at the cost of sampling speed.

The **Spatial Split** option works in a similar way. When this option is activated, the BVH building will be slower, but the sampling will be faster.

Another interesting option is **Cache BVH**. This option will allow Cycles to cache the BVH on the RAM so that it will not need to compute it again for the next render. It is important to keep in mind anyway that this will work only if no mesh in the scene is deformed. A good kind of scene to use this option is when the only thing which is animated is the camera.

 A good thing to keep in mind is that Blender has a really good tips pop-up system to help understand the settings. Just hover the cursor over an option or a button and after a while, a pop up with a brief description will pop up.

This is the conclusion of the first chapter. If you encountered any difficulty in following some part of the recipes, you will find a ready version of the scene in the blend folder named `keys.blend` which is available in the code bundle of this book.

2
Creating Different Glass Materials in Cycles

This chapter contains the following recipes:

- ▸ Creating a simple glass shader
- ▸ Creating a glass full of water
- ▸ Using default Cycles caustics
- ▸ Creating custom fake caustics
- ▸ Creating a custom and more versatile glass shader
- ▸ Creating more complex glass materials
- ▸ Obtaining a dispersion effect
- ▸ Creating an absorption glass shader

Introduction

In this chapter, we will focus totally on glass materials. Cycles has a great Glass BSDF, which allows us to easily create really good looking glass. Anyway, we do not want to create just a simple glass, but to really master the art of creating any kind of glassy material. We will see how to create custom glass shaders to have more control over different settings, like reflections and refractions, but also caustics, dispersion, and absorption.

Creating a simple glass shader

To start getting acquainted with the glass shader, we will use a simpler scene than the one we will be creating later. To get all the objects we will use now, we need to select just layers 1, 3, and 5. Layer selection area is in the lower viewport header. Now let's add a new material to the `Empty_Glass` object (the first glass on the right when we are in camera view) and name it `Clean_Glass`.

Getting ready

First of all let's open Blender and open the `Glass_Empty.blend` file, which you will find in the `blend` folder of this chapter. As we saved the user settings before, everything should be ready.

How to do it...

To create the first recipe of this chapter, we will be performing the following steps:

1. Let's now go to the **Material** node editor and start creating our shader. First of all we need to delete default **Diffuse BSDF** and instead add **Glass BSDF** (**Add | Shader**).

2. Let's now link it to **Material Output** and activate the real-time viewport. Everything is black because there are no lights and the environment is black. So let's select the **Emitter01** mesh in the scene, add a material, and name it `Emit01`. Change default **Diffuse BSDF** with **Emission** and set the strength to `6`.

3. Now we can see our glass in the viewport. It is already looking quite good. As we said, the default Cycles glass shader does a very good job for simple glass materials. Of course we have to make a couple of changes even in this simple glass shader.

4. We can see that the glass is quite dark. This is because of the color of **Glass BSDF**, which is not pure white. Let's fix this, changing the color in the **Material** node editor to a pure white (RGB 1, 1, 1). Now it is much better. The glass does not look so dark anymore.

5. Let's leave the roughness to `0`, as we want a clear glass. On the other hand we want to change the IOR.

6. Our simple glass is quite a thin material, so we can set the IOR to `1.52`. This is an IOR which will fit for a lot of objects of this kind.

7. Finally, from the drop-down menu on the **Glass BSDF** node, let's change the algorithm used to calculate refractions and reflections from **Beckmann** to **Sharp**.

How it works...

The important points to learn in this first recipe are the IOR and the algorithm. Glass materials can have different IOR values, depending on the kind and thickness of the object. Most of the time, the IOR for a glass is a value between 1.44 and 1.9. The rule of thumb states: *the higher the IOR, the thicker the material*. When we are dealing with really thick glass objects we will see that even higher IOR values will be useful to fake the fact that in the real world the object is full, while in our 3D scene we can only have the outside shell.

Beckmann and GGX can both use the roughness values to get blurry. The first one fits better for inorganic materials, such as plastic or metal, while the GGX has a more organic look, even if the differences are pretty subtle. Finally, the Sharp algorithm will not take into account the roughness values and will always return sharp reflections and refractions. It is definitely fit for our glass, so that's the one we will be using.

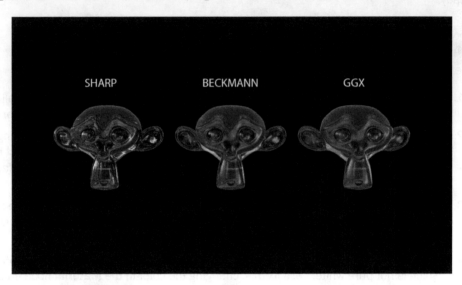

There's more...

In this recipe we have seen the IOR value for the first time. **IOR** stands for **Index of Refraction**. The IOR is the relation between the speed of light in the air and inside a different vacuum, which for example, in our case is the glass. When the light hits the glass surface, a part of it is reflected, while a part of it travels inside the glass, but at a lower speed than in the air, which was the previous vacuum. The difference between the speeds changes the way we see the light, and this is why we see things distorted through glasses and lenses or even water.

To give a more practical example, the IOR of water is 1.33. This means that the light travels 1.33 times slower in the water, than it does in the air. It is really important to set the IOR correctly in order to give the correct look to our materials.

See also

▶ This link is a really big list with the IOR of different materials: http://forums.cgsociety.org/archive/index.php/t-513458.html

Creating a glass full of water

Now that we have created a nice glass, let's pour some water in it. In this recipe we will learn a really efficient way to create a glass full of water.

Getting ready

Select the **Water_Glass** object on the left of the scene and assign the **Clean_Glass** material previously created to it. To do this, we need to click on the small sphere on the left of the **New** button in the **Material** panel.

Now select the water object, which is the plane inside the glass. Add a new material to it and name it `Water`. We are almost ready to start. Select the **Water_Glass** object again and go inside the **Object Data** menu. In the **Vertex Groups** panel there is an entry named **MixingSurface**. Let's go into the edit mode by pressing the *Tab* button. Make sure that none of the parts of the mesh are selected (press *A* to select/deselect everything) and click on the **Select** button from the **Vertex Groups** panel.

A part inside the glass will be selected. Now go to the material menu, add a new material slot with the **+** button on the right, add a new material, and name it `MixingSurfaceWater`. Finally, click on the assign button to apply the material we just created to the part of the mesh which is selected right now. Now let's go back to the object mode. We are ready to start!

How to do it...

The following steps will explain us how to create a glass of water:

1. In the real-time viewport, our water inside the glass looks more like plaster. Definitely not what we are looking for.

2. Let's select the `Water` object and start creating our water material. In the **Material** node editor we need to erase **Diffuse BSDF** and add a **Glass** node. Let's change the algorithm again to **Sharp** and set **IOR** to `1.333`. Also set the color to pure white.

3. The shader is ready, but the glass still looks wrong. We need to set the material inside the glass. Select the **Water_Glass** object and then **MixingSurfaceWater** in the **Material** menu. In the **Material** node editor let's again cancel **Diffuse BSDF** and add a **Glass** node. Here, let's set the **Sharp** algorithm and **IOR** to `1.14`.

4. Now things are much better!

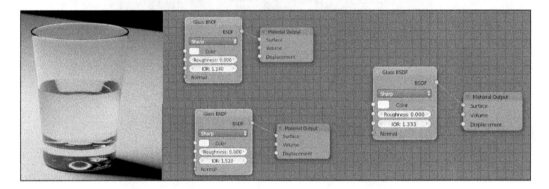

How it works...

The concept behind this recipe is quite similar to the previous one. The interesting thing here is what to do when two refracting surfaces interact. When a liquid is poured into a glass, the water and the portion of the glass touching each other interact with light as a single surface.

Sometimes in **CG** (**Computer Graphics**), it is not possible to use the technique we are using now. For example, if we need to animate water falling inside the glass, we should find another way to deal with the scene. On the other hand, for a still picture like this it is perfect.

While water and glass have their own IOR, when they come together they become like one single surface and the new IOR is equal to GlassIOR/WaterIOR. In this case we have *1.52(glass) / 1.333(water) = 1.14(mixed surface)*.

There's more...

Another advantage of this technique is that we have less interpenetrating polygon problems. This is in general a thing to avoid in CG, even more when dealing with glass materials. As we will see in the next recipe, shadows of glass shaders can be quite a tricky issue. The strategy of avoiding interpenetration of surfaces will also help a lot with this.

See also

At the `http://www.yafaray.org/documentation/userguide/material` link, you will find more information about the technique we used to recreate the water in the glass. This is the Yafaray documentation (another rendering engine supported by Blender), but the concept works really well for any rendering engine.

Using default Cycles caustics

Caustics are quite an important aspect in a computer graphic image. They represent the light scattered through a transparent material on its own shadow. In order to obtain a really realistic image, we cannot have a totally dark shadow for such materials as the glass or water and for this we need caustics. We will learn in this and the next recipe how to obtain this effect using different techniques.

Getting ready

If we look at the glass, it looks right. What does not look right is its shadow. Right now it is fully dark, and a piece of glass does not cast a dark uniform shadow.

How to do it...

To enable Cycles caustics, we need to follow these quick steps:

1. To obtain this effect we need to activate an effect called caustics. Let's go to the **Render** menu and in the **Light Path** panel, uncheck the **No Caustics** option.

2. In the real-time viewport we can see that now the shadows of the glasses are different. They do not look so dark anymore.

How it works...

When the light hits the surface of the glass, part of it is reflected and part of it is refracted. Depending on the shape of the glass surface, the rays get distorted and when they hit another surface we can see their projection, which is called caustic. Cycles is able to reproduce this effect in an accurate way. To obtain realistic caustic, it is really important to have good geometry of the object, as for the biggest part, their look depends on the shape of the glass object.

There's more...

There is a big drawback in using caustics. The noise generated by activating this option is really big and getting a clean render can be really hard. Another big drawback of caustics is that they work only with mesh emitters. When using lights such as point, sun, and so on, obtaining caustics this way will not be possible.

Finally we do not have much control on the look of caustics. Once the shape of the object and the lighting is set, we cannot change how caustics look. This is realistic, because in the real world caustics work exactly this way. Anyway in CG, it is always nice to have more control over things, even with little fakes. In the next recipe, we will see that we have another way to get caustics.

See also

▶ Here you will find a nice tutorial from *Sebastian Koenig* that will show you a trick to reduce the noise generated by Cycles caustics: `http://cgcookie.com/blender/2013/01/14/reducing-caustic-noise-blender-cycles/`

Creating custom fake caustics

The caustics we created in the previous recipe are the default ones generated directly by Cycles. They are the most accurate you can get, but there are ways to obtain fake caustics, which render much faster and with less noise. This is what we will learn in this recipe.

Getting ready

Let's now see how to create caustics using another method. Inside Blender, we will need to tweak each glass shader in our scene. We will start with our **Clean_Glass** shader. So let's select it and go to the material node editor. Just one last thing before we start. We need to activate the **No Caustics** option again in the menu rendered, as we do not need them with this method.

How to do it...

1. Inside the material node editor we need to add three nodes: **Transparent BSDF** (**Add** | **Shader**), a **Mix** node (**Add** | **Shader**) and a **Light Path** node (**Add** | **Input**).

2. Let's use the **Mix** node to mix the glass and **Transparent BSDF**. We will connect the glass in the first socket and **Transparent BSDF** in the second. As a mixing factor, we will use the **Is Shadow** output of the **Light Path** node. Looking at the real-time viewport, we can see that now our glass has no shadow at all, and this is not what we want.

3. Let's now add these nodes: a **Geometry** node (**Add** | **Input**), a **Vector Math** node (**Add** | **Convertor**), a **ColorRamp** node (**Add** | **Convertor**), and a **Math** node (**Add** | **Convertor**).

4. From the **Geometry** node, plug the **Normal** and **Tangent** sockets in the two vector input sockets of the **Vector Math** node. Here, select the option **Dot Product**. Then we need to plug the value output of this node to the **Fac** input of the **ColorRamp** node and the **Color** output of the latter to the first **Value** socket of the **Math** node.

5. Finally in this node, let's change the mode to **Multiply** from the **Cascade** menu and let's plug the **Value** output to the **Color** input of **Transparent BSDF**. Something is already going on in the real-time viewport. We can see that the shadow is changed. We can now tweak it further, changing **ColorRamp** to something like this:

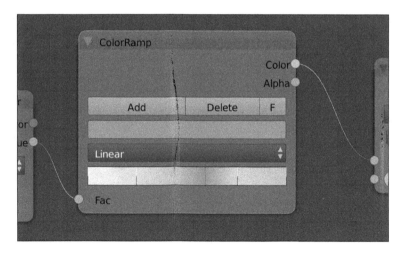

As a last touch we need to put a value of 1.7 in the **Multiply** node.

We will need to do the same thing for the **Water** and **MixingSurfaceWater** materials as well. The structure will be exactly the same. Each material will need little tweaks in the **ColorRamp** node and multiply value in order to get the right look to its caustics.

Remember that we can copy nodes from one material to another just using *Ctrl + C* and *Ctrl + V*.

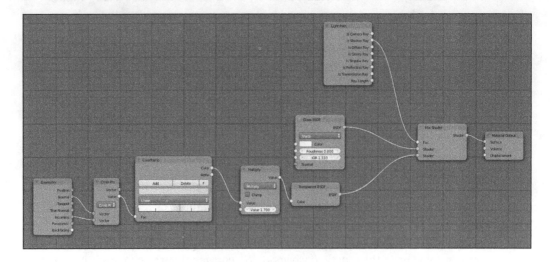

This is how the final node setup should look:

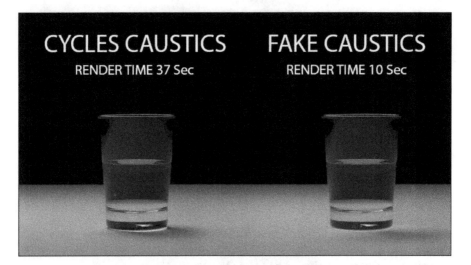

How it works...

Here we have a couple of really interesting techniques to look at. The first is the ability to control how every single part of the material (**Diffuse**, **Glossy**, and **Shadows**) interacts with other materials.

In this particular situation we separated the shadow of the glass material, and set a shader group on its own, which controls how shadows look. In other words, with the **Light Path** node we asked Cycles to render a glass object, but to take the shadows cast by it from **Transparent BSDF**. This is something extremely powerful, which give us a big amount of control when creating materials. Another thing we learned here is that we are able to tweak materials taking into account the geometry and shape of an object.

From the **Geometry** node we took information about the normals and the tangent of the object. Then we were able to combine them using the **Vector Math** node, obtaining rough information about the shape of the object and use the result to distribute the color among the shadow accordingly. Finally the **Math** node allowed us to increase the power of the ramp color in order to obtain the slightly burned effect of the caustics. It is exactly a multiplication. The node takes the value from **ColorRamp**, which is black and white so that it can be easily translated to a single numeric value and multiplies it for the value we inserted in the node.

With this method we get two big advantages over the normal caustics. First of all they generate much less noise. Getting a clean image with the Cycles default caustics can be a bit challenging, while these methods do not generate additional noise. The second big advantage is that while the default caustics work only with mesh emitters, now we are free to use whatever light source we want. The caustics will be there.

Of course there is also a drawback as nothing comes for free. As the name suggests, these caustics are fake. Therefore they are not as accurate as the default one. Moreover, with this method, we are able to generate only the caustics coming from the refractions of the glass, while the caustics generated by the reflection will not be taken into account. Anyway, if you are not looking for absolute realism, the effect will work perfectly for most of the scenes.

There's more...

With the **ColorRamp** node, we can also control the color of the caustics. So we are able to recreate believable caustics for colored glass materials. There is one thing we have to care about though; the **Math** node after the color ramp will convert the color info from the latter node into a black and white one. So any color information different from a grey scale will disappear. To avoid this issue, we need to use another node instead of **Math** to boost the effect of the caustics, for instance, an **RGB Curves** node.

Creating a custom and more versatile glass shader

Cycles gives us a great versatility and even if creating transparent materials using the Glass BSDF is fast and effective, this is not the only way. In this recipe we will learn how to create a shader setup that will give us a greater control over the look of the material.

Getting ready

Now we need to change our scene a bit to get its final look. We will just need to change the layers we use. Deselect layers 3 and 5 and select layers 2 and 4. So right now we will be working with layers 1, 2 and 4 as shown in the following figure:

This means that our source light will not be a mesh emitter anymore but a sun lamp, as now we are using our custom caustics. We also added some more objects to our scene in order to learn different glass materials.

Right now we want to create a material, which is quite similar to the previous one, but will allow us more control over its look compared to the default glass shader. Now in the scene there is a new glass with a liquid inside. They are respectively called Glass_Thea and TheaLiquid. Let's start by selecting the TheaLiquid object and adding a new material to it. We will name it TheaLiquid.

How to do it...

To create this material, we will be following these steps:

1. In the **Material** node viewport, let's delete default **Diffuse BSDF**. Instead, we will add two different BSDFs. So from the **Add** menu, in the **Shader** section, select **Refraction BSDF** and **Glossy BSDF**. We also need to add an **Add Shader** node.

2. Let's link the two BSDFs' output to the **Add** node and the **Add** node to the **Material** output. As this is an **Add** node, the order is not important.

3. For **Glossy BSDF**, let's change the **Roughness** value to 0. Also set the color to RGB 0.5, 0.45, 0.175.

4. In the refractions BSDF, change the roughness value to 0.02 and the color to RGB 0.8, 0.29, 0. Also set the IOR to 1.333.

5. Copy the fake caustic node setup part from the **Water** material (*Ctrl + C*) and copy them into the **Thea** material (*Ctrl + V*).

6. Change the colors in the **ColorRamp** node so that all of them are yellowish. Check the following figure for a reference.

7. Erase the **Math** node and add the **RGB Curves** node. Set the curve and then connect the various nodes as shown in the following figure:

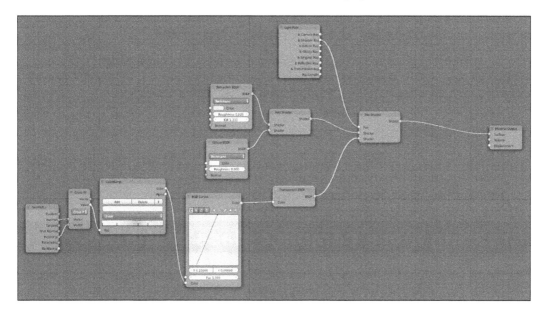

8. Now select the `Thea_Glass` object and add the **ClearGlass** material to it.

9. We need to add the material to the glass for the area which is touched by the liquid. As for the `Water_Glass` object there is a vertex group that includes the one to which we need to add this material. In the *Getting ready* section of the *Creating a glass full of water* recipe there is a detailed explanation on how to do this. We will name the new material **MixingSurfaceThea**.

10. Erase the default **Diffuse** node and then copy the nodes from the **Thea** material and paste them into the **MixingSurfaceThea** material.

11. Change the IOR value of **Refraction BSDF** to `1.14`.

How it works...

The material we created here is quite simple in terms of nodes, but it allows us a greater control over the glass. With the standard glass material, the reflection and refraction controls, such as color or roughness, are linked together. Now we are able to change them independently. Here, for example, we created a material, which has sharp reflections (glossy roughness to 0) and slightly blurred refractions (refraction roughness to 0.02).

In this recipe, we also changed the color of the fake caustics with the **ColorRamp** node. In order not to lose the color information, as mentioned before, we had to replace the **Math** node with an **RGB Curve** node in order to boost their effect.

There's more...

This is just one of the possible materials that we can create with this combination of BSDF. Especially interesting can be the way we mix them. After the **Add** node, use a **Mix** node and plug into it the result of the **Add** node and the output of **Glossy BSDF**.

Now try different solutions to mix them. For example, we can use a **Layer Weight** node (**Add | Input**), or play with the **Geometry** node as we did for the fake caustics. The possibilities are many and experimenting is the best way to master a lot of different techniques.

See also

In this chapter's files you will find a blend named `GlassMaterials`. Inside this file there is some interesting glass material that you can use as an inspiration. Do not stop there though; use them as a base to create your own shaders!

Creating more complex glass materials

Now we will be creating the material for the table. The effect we are aiming for is some kind of frosty glass. The refractions have to be really blurred, while we need sharp reflections.

Getting ready

Before we concentrate on the material we need to add a nice HDR in order to make the scene more interesting. In the **World** node editor, add **Environment Texture**, a **Mapping** node, and a **Texture Coordinate Input** node.

Load `Newport_Loft_8k.jpg` into the **Environment Texture** node and then set up the nodes as shown in the following figure:

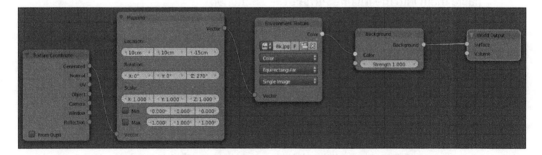

Make sure to set the position to 10cm, 10cm, -15cm and the **Z** rotation to 270. Now let's select the GlassTable object and add a new material. Name it FrostedGlass.

How to do it...

To create the material for the table, follow these steps:

1. Let's go into the **Material** node editor and erase the default **Diffuse BSDF**.

2. Add **Glossy BSDF** and **Refraction BSDF**.

3. Now we need to mix the two BSDFs we just added using an **Add Shader** node.

4. Set **Glossy BSDF** color to RGB 0.2, 0.35, 0.41 and the roughness value to 0.005.

5. Set the Refraction BSDF color to RGB 0.45, 0.85, 1 and the roughness to 0.075.

6. Add **Diffuse BSDF** and mix it to the output of the **Add Shader** node with a **Mix Shader** node. Make sure the diffuse BSDF is inside the second socket.

7. Set **Diffuse BSDF** color to RGB 0.7, 0.915, 1.

8. Now we need to change the **Mix Shader** face value to 0.275

9. As a final touch we need to add the same fake caustic we used before to this glass. Copy the setup from the **Thea** material and paste it here.

10. Let's change the color to a subtle blue and then link the nodes as shown in the following figure:

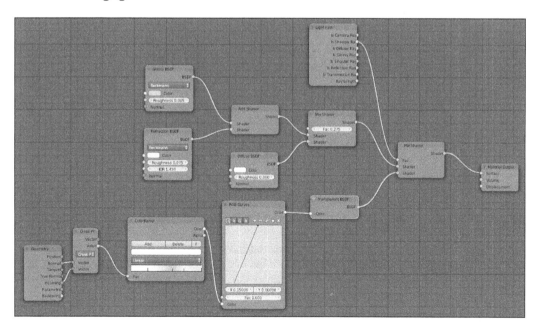

11. The `TableLegs` object has two material slots on it. The first one is for the metal of the legs. Add a new material to it and name it `Metal`. Create a Diffuse and Glossy mix for this material.

12. Add a material in the second slot and name it `Rubber`. Also here a Diffuse and Glossy mix will be fine. Check the following figure as a reference for these two shaders:

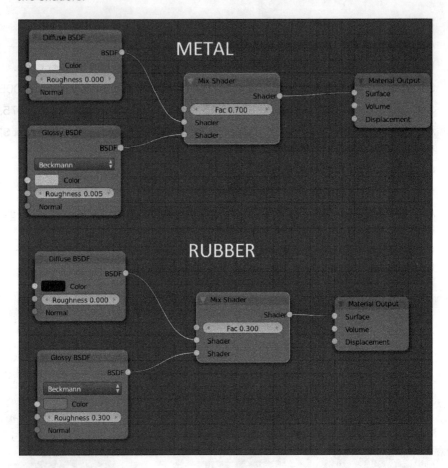

How it works...

In this recipe we went a bit deeper with the technique we learnt in the previous recipe. This time we increased the roughness of the refractions in order to obtain a frost glass effect. On the other hand, the low glossy roughness allowed us to keep reflections on the surface sharp.

Another thing to notice is that we used the color to trim the amount of reflections that we wanted. Making the blue of **Glossy BSDF** a bit darker makes the reflection weaker. In this shader setup there is a further passage. We mixed **Diffuse BSDF** in the end. In this way we were able to obtain a more solid material, which receives shadows on its surface, like frosty glass does in reality.

Finally we used the fake caustic technique that we learned earlier in the chapter, to adjust the color according to the material.

There's more...

We can make a slight change to this material. Instead of **Refraction BSDF** we could use **Translucent BSDF**. This could be useful if we wanted to obtain a really frosted glass material.

Translucent BSDF will allow the light to get scattered inside the object as **Refraction BSDF** does, but unlike the latter we will not be able to control the roughness. This will be always really blurred and, in general, the amount of light that will pass is less than with **Refraction BSDF**.

Moreover we can create interesting color variations of the glass using a **Layer Weight** node to distribute different colors along the surface of our object. The following image is a good reference to start experimenting:

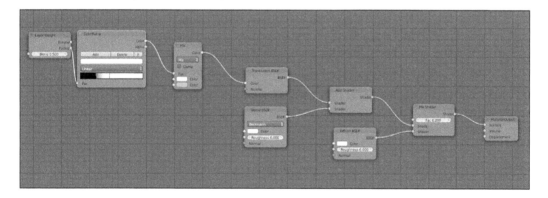

Obtaining a dispersion effect

In this recipe we will start to dig a bit more in the endless world of possibilities that Cycles' node **Shaders** offers us. What we will be creating now is a dispersion effect of the glass. This is a phenomenon which happens when the light travels through certain kinds of vacuums and gets spatially separated due to the different frequency of the colors it is composed of. Probably the most famous dispersion effect in nature is the rainbow.

Getting ready

Despite this brief physical introduction, what we will be doing in Cycles is fake, but it is really believable to the eye.

To start, let's select the `Glass_IcoSphere` object and add a new material to it. We will name this material `DispersionGlass`.

How to do it

These are the steps we will follow to create the dispersion glass:

1. In the **Material** node editor, add a **Separate RGB** node (**Add | Convertor**), a color **Mix** node (**Add | Color**), and **Glass BSDF**.

2. Set the mode of color **Mix** node to **Color** and the fac to `0.95`. Then duplicate both, the color **Mix** node and **Glass BSDF**.

3. Connect the three output sockets to the **Separate RGB** node to the first color input of the three color **Mix** nodes. Now set the colors of the second input of the three color **Mix** nodes respectively to pure red, green, and blue.

4. Connect the output of each color **Mix** node to the color input socket of each one of **Glass BSDF**. Now we need to mix the three glass BSDFs using the **Add Shader** nodes.

5. Let's now set the roughness values of **Glass BSDF**. We will set the one coming from the red color **Mix** node to `1.64`, the one coming from the green node to `1.65`, and finally the one coming from the blue node to `1.66`.

6. We also need to set the color input of the **Separate RGB** node to pure white.

7. Finally, let's add the usual fake caustics setup in the node editor. The white color in **ColorRamp** in this case will be fine. The following figure shows how the final node setup should look:

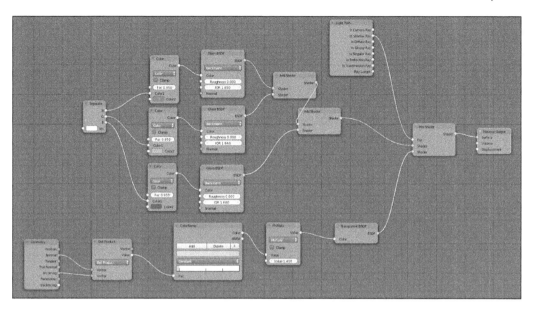

How it works...

This kind of setup is fake, because the dispersions created with this do not follow the laws of physics, but what we are doing here is actually separating the colors of the rays that get through the glass.

The **Separate RGB** node is made exactly for this. Anyway, the information it returns is not RGB information, so we need to convert them for our purpose. After this node we used the color **Mix** nodes in order to translate the output of the **Separate RGB** node to the colors we needed and then plugged them into glass BSDFs.

And here is where the magic happens. The IOR value actually changes the way we see the environment through the glass. Giving a different IOR to the three glass BSDFs makes sure that the three different colors we divided the main one in, are shifted inside the glass object, giving us a dispersion effect.

We finally reunited the colors into one using the add nodes.

There's more...

We can change the color of the glass by changing the input color of the **Separate RGB** node.

Moreover, also in this more complex setup we can use the techniques we learned in the previous recipes. We just need to create the setup we want for each one of the colors. It is important to remember that the setup for the dispersion is quite heavy, because each BSDF has to be computed three times. So we need to be careful not to make it too heavy.

The following figure shows an example of a different glass material, which also has the dispersion property. Notice that increasing the roughness value of **Refraction BSDF** makes the dispersion effect harder to see.

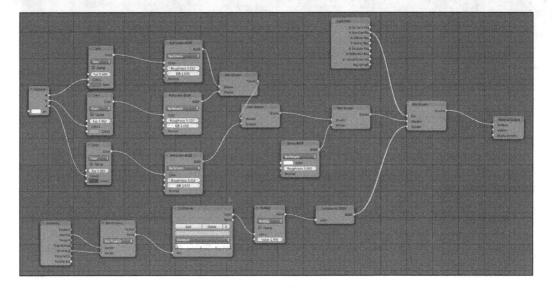

Finally it is important to notice that we didn't use the value 1 for the color **Mix** node factor because doing so actually generates more noise and some strange dark areas in the material.

Creating an absorption glass shader

We have arrived at the last recipe of this chapter. Now we are going to create a material, which involves some mathematical operation in Cycles. The absorption is a phenomenon that makes the look of a material change depending on its thickness. The idea is that when the light travels through a piece of glass, it gets weaker little by little, because of the absorption of the material. So, the longer the length of the path made by the light through the material, the weaker the ray will be when it exits on the other side. A weaker ray means less transparency.

Getting ready

The object to which we will be applying the absorption material is `Glass_Artifact`. So let's select it and add a new material to it, by the name of `GlassAbsorption`.

How to do it...

To create the dispersion glass, we will be following these steps:

1. In the **Material** node editor, let's delete **Diffuse BSDF** and add **Glass BSDF** and **Glossy BSDF**.

2. Mix the just added BSDFs with a **Mix** node, mixing 10 percent of **Glossy BSDF** and 90 percent of **Glass BSDF**.

3. Set the Glossy roughness to 0 and the color to RGB 0.6, 1, 0.6. Then set the Glass IOR to 1.52.

4. Now we need to add a **Light Path** node and a **Geometry** node. Also add 6 **Math** nodes.

5. This setup of nodes is quite complex to describe with the text. Let's use the following figure to setup our nodes properly. We will then discuss the details in the *How it works* section.

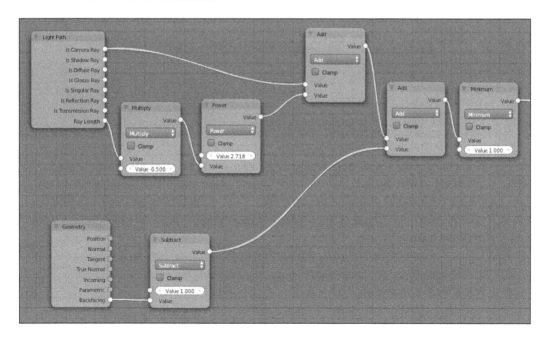

6. Let's now add three **ColorRamp** nodes. Connect the output of the last **Math** node to two of the **ColorRamp** nodes. Connect the remaining **ColorRamp** to the output of one of the other two.

7. Set the three **ColorRamp** nodes as shown in the following figure:

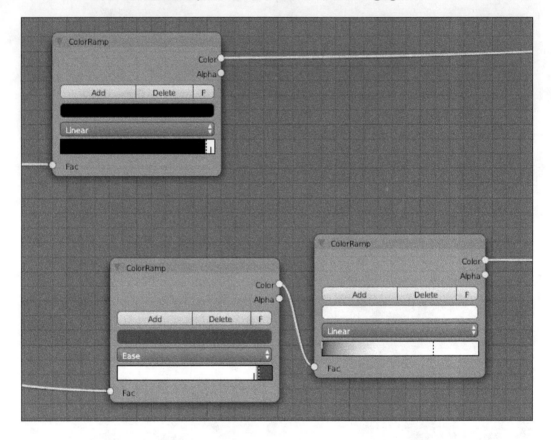

8. Now connect the single **ColorRamp** to the **Fac** input of a color **Mix** node. Leave the mode to **Mix** and set the first color to pure green and the second to pure white. Finally connect the output of the color **Mix** node to the **Color** input of **Glass BSDF**.

9. Let's connect the output of the couple of **ColorRamp** nodes to the **Roughness** input of **Glass BSDF**.

10. The last thing to do is to create the fake caustic setup. We will need to use a greenish color for our caustics this time. The following figure shows the final setup for this material:

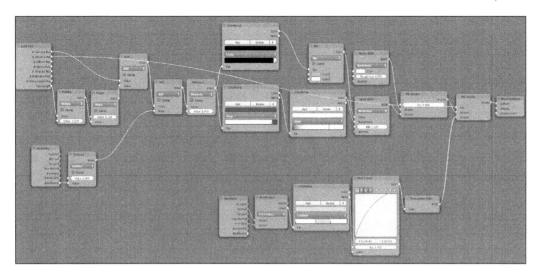

How it works...

The really interesting part of this recipe is the way we obtained the absorption—through a mathematical operation. We can even write down this operation as we would do on a piece of paper. In this book we will not go too deep with the mathematical explanation. In simpler words, what we are doing with this equation is converting the distance traveled by the rays through the material into something readable by Cycles.

All the information starts from the **Light Path** node and the **Geometry** node. From the first node we used **Ray Length**, which gives us information about how long a ray travels through the object. Of course this information is directly used to calculate the absorption. The **Backfacing** output from the **Geometry** node is used to exclude the transmission rays, which are outside the object, making calculations much easier for Cycles.

We then used the **ColorRamp** nodes to fine tune the result from the equation to adjust it to the dimensions of our object. Finally we used what we obtained to set the color and the roughness of **Glass BSDF**. Pure white equals to 1, while black is 0. With this mix we were able to tell Cycles to give a white color and sharp refractions to the glass where the object is thinner.

There's more...

The **Light Path** node is a crucial node in Cycles, which gives us a number of possibilities when creating materials. Basically it allows us to control the influence of the material we are creating on the other objects of the scene.

At first sight the node looks quite difficult to master, but after a while it will become quite self-intuitive. With the **Light Path** node and the rays, we are able to subdivide the rays bouncing off our object depending on what they are hitting next in the scene.

Let's take a really simple example. Let's say we have a green diffuse material. Now, for some reason, we would like that the image of this object reflected on the other object of the scene is not green, but blue. We can use **Is Glossy Rays** to mix our green **Diffuse BSDF** with a blue one, as shown in the following figure:

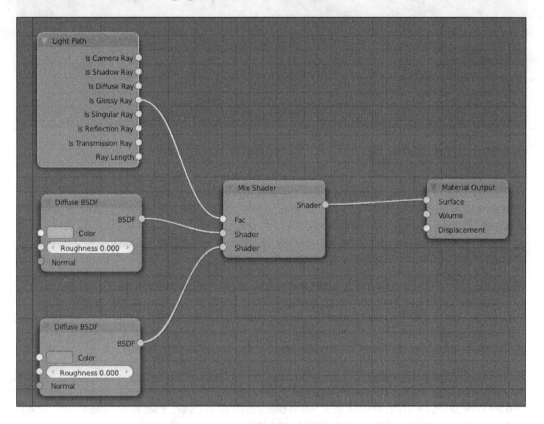

Now the reflected image of the object will not be green, but blue. We can apply the same principle for every output of the node; we already did when we faked our caustics, for example, changing what the shadows of our object look like.

See also

At these two links, there are really useful resources about absorption in Cycles. The first one is a video tutorial by *Gottfried Hoffman*. The second is an entry blog of Agus 3D. In this page there is also a link with a detailed explanation of the math behind this node setup. Moreover there are some really interesting variations of the material we created in this recipe.

- `http://www.blenderdiplom.com/index.php/en/tutorials/item/104-tutorial-absorption-in-cycles`
- `http://agus3d.blogspot.com/2012/05/blender-cycles-ray-length-node-output.html`

The following link is a great tutorial from *Bartek Skorupa* about the **Light Path** node:

- `http://cgcookie.com/blender/2013/02/26/blender-cycles-light-path-node/`

3

Creating an
Interior Scene

In this chapter, we will cover the following recipes in detail:

- ▶ Creating fake portals to decrease the noise in the scene
- ▶ Creating a parquet material
- ▶ Creating materials for the plant in the scene
- ▶ Creating a different kind of leather
- ▶ Creating the materials for the lamp
- ▶ Creating a carpet using hair particles
- ▶ Setting up night lighting
- ▶ Using IES files in Cycles

Introduction

In this chapter, we are going to face a pretty common situation in computer graphics: interior architectural visualization. We will see how we can get the best out of Cycles in this difficult lighting situation and learn how to create some new beautiful materials.

Creating fake portals to decrease the noise in the scene

Before we start, it is important to state one thing about the scene we are going to prepare in this chapter. Cycles is a path tracer, and for path tracers, closed spaces are hard to render. This is a chronic problem of this kind of renderer. There are several methods to help reduce noise, but as Cycles is still under development, they haven't been implemented yet.

Getting ready

In this first recipe, we will observe a couple of tricks to make the situation a bit better, but in general, it is good to know that to have this scene noise-free, we will need a lot of samples and a lot of time to render.

Now that we know this, let's open up the `Chapter03_Empty.blend` file and start setting up our scene!

How to do it...

To create fake portals, follow these steps:

1. In the **World** settings, set the surface color to RGB 0.85, 1, 1 and **Strength** to `0.600`.

2. Turn on **Ambient Occlusion**. Set **Intensity** to `0.700` and the **Distance** to `12`.

3. Add a sun light and orient it so that we have a nice light coming in from the window, which goes over the pouffe and the plant.

4. Set the sun's size to `0.010` and the **Intensity** to `3.000`. Let's also set the color to a really subtle yellow (RGB: 1, 0.95, 0.85).

5. Add an **Area Light** and name it `DayPortal`. Place it right outside the window so that one of the faces will look perpendicularly inside the room. Change the size to `4.600` and uncheck the **Cast Shadows** option.

6. Set the area light **Intensity** to `8.000` and change the color to RGB: 0.85, 1, 1.

7. In the **Render** menu, set the **Exposure** to `1.400`. We can find this setting in the film panel.

The following screenshot shows how the lights are positioned in the scene:

How it works...

In this first recipe, we already used some new interesting things. A new function that we used here is **Ambient Occlusion**. We already talked about its effects in the first chapter, in the recipe on render settings. In this kind of situation, it is of big help.

As we said in the beginning of this recipe, closed spaces are difficult for path tracers. This is because the light has to bounce around a lot to light the scene properly. **Ambient Occlusion** (**AO**) is a good way to fake Global Illumination where there is only indirect lighting; indirect lighting is one of the biggest problems faced in Cycles.

In the BI, we had the possibility to use the AO in the **Add** or **Multiply** mode. Right now in Cycles, we can use it only in the **Add** mode, but it is good for this situation.

Increasing the distance setting makes the effect of the AO visible on more distantly occluded objects.

Another technique we used here is the fake portal. A portal is one of those tricks that render engines use to make things easier for interior rendering. What a portal does is help the engine understand from where the light will come into the room and optimize the rendering accordingly.

Cycles does not support this function yet, but we can fake it. The method we used of course does not do the things that a real portal would. Regardless, like the AO, it helps Cycles to brighten the most difficult areas, helping a lot with the noise. It is important to uncheck the **Cast Shadows** option because we want only the real-light source to be the sun, and as you don't have any other artificial lights in the scene, other shadows would look wrong.

There's more...

The room in our scene has only got 3 walls, while one side is open. This is another way to help Cycles light up difficult areas. In this situation, the wall on the side of the camera is not needed and not visible. Taking it out from the scene will further help us with the rendering.

There is another really quick and easy method to improve the lighting in dark areas. We can add a sun light perpendicular to the ground and deactivate the **Cast Shadows** option. The intensity doesn't need to be high, around 0.500 is usually fine. This method is really effective in lightening up dark corners of interior scenes.

However, it is not completely correct to say that all the methods we saw help us reduce noise. Or say, they do not do this directly. We have two ways of increasing light in dark areas, where the only source is indirect light. We can increase light bounce, which will lead to more noise and more rendering time, or we can use some trick as we did to fake the indirect light without pushing the light bounce up. By using these methods, we can remove the dark areas without having to push the render settings. This will greatly reduce the noise.

This is how these methods helped us reduce the noise. Thanks to them, we can set the light paths of our scene as shown in the following screenshot and still have proper lighting. Notice that 250 samples will not be enough to get a clean scene at the end, but they are a good compromise for test renders.

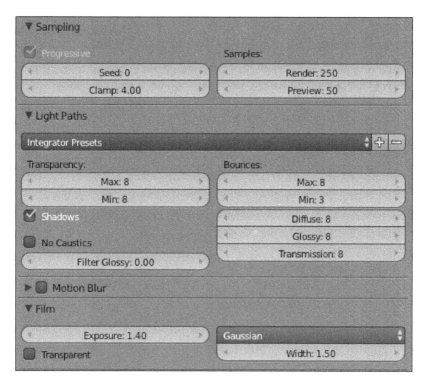

 A last note about the fact that all the methods we used here will lead to a slightly increased render time. This is true looking only at the amount of samples. To get similar images in terms of noise and light, not using these techniques would lead to a much bigger render time.

In this scene, it is also good to set the acceleration structure to **Static BVH** and activate both **Spatial Splits** and **Cache BVH** (to learn more about these options, refer to the *Setting the Cycles renders parameters* recipe in *Chapter 1, Key Holder and Wallet Studio Shot*). Also notice that the final render will require at least 1,000 samples to get a decent image.

Creating a parquet material

Now that our scene lighting is ready, we can start adding the materials to the scene. A really important material is the floor, followed by the material of the wall, which in this scene will be very simple.

Getting ready

Let's start by selecting the object named **Floor** and add a material to it. Let's name the material **Parquet**.

How to do it...

To create the parquet material, follow these steps:

1. Let's go to the material node editor and add a **Glossy BSDF** and a **Mix Shader** node. Change the Glossy BSDF **Roughness** to 0.040 and the Diffuse BSDF roughness to 1.000.

2. Mix the Glossy and the Diffuse BSDFs with the **Mix Shader** node (diffuse on the top) with a **Fac** of 0.300.

3. Now add an **Image Texture**, a **Texture Coordinate**, and a **Mapping** node. Link the output to the diffuse BSDF **Color** input.

4. In the image texture, let's load the texture_seamless_parquet.jpg file located in the Textures folder.

5. For this texture, we want to use UV coordinates. Also place the mapping node between the texture coordinates and the image texture, and set the scale for X, Y, and Z to 2.000.

6. Now let's add a **ColorRamp** (**Add | Convertors**) and plug the image texture into its **Color** input, the image texture. Press the **F** button to flip the colors and then set the node as shown in the reference screenshot at the end of this section.

7. Now add a **Color Mix** node and set the mode to Color. Plug the output of the **ColorRamp** into the first socket and the output of the **Image Texture** into the second. Set the **Fac** to 0.400.

8. Duplicate the **Image Texture** node and click on the button with the number **2** right next to the image path to make this a unique texture. Then click on the open texture button and select the texture_seamless_parquet_DISP.jpg file.

9. We want to use the exact same coordinates for this texture, so for the vector input, plug in the output of the mapping node.

10. Add a **Bump** node (**Add | Vector**) and plug the output into its height socket, the latterly added image texture. Then plug the normal output into the normal socket of both the Diffuse and Glossy BSDFs.

11. Set the bump node **Strength** to 0.030.

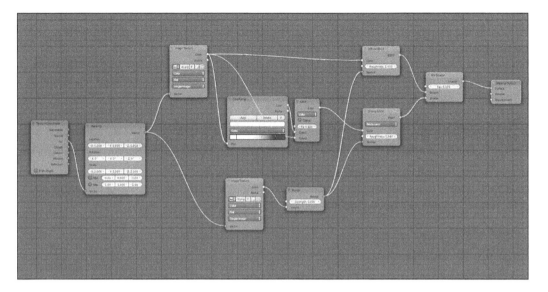

How it works...

Although we already saw the idea behind this pretty simple setup previously in the book, we introduced some new techniques here, which are interesting to explore further.

If we look at a parquet material in real life, we can see that the places where the reflections are more visible are the darker areas. So what we did here to obtain a reflection map for the **Glossy BSDF** is we inverted and then tweaked the original Color map. To do this, we used a **ColorRamp** node. We flipped its colors and then adjusted them accordingly to obtain smoother transitions between dark and bright areas.

Also, we didn't want the reflections to be completely white, but instead, slightly follow the colorization of the floor. We were able to do this with a **Color Mix** node using the color mode. This particular mode of the **Color Mix** node will allow us to paint a color over an image without changing its lighting. The higher the factor, the higher the saturation the output will have.

There's more...

Another interesting thing to talk about is the Diffuse BSDF roughness. By default, it is set to 0, and this means that the node follows the **Lambertian** reflectance model. Setting it to 1 will change this model to an **Oren-Nayar** one.

Without going into too much technical detail, the **Oren-Nayar** reflectance model will take into account the roughness of a surface. A parquet, even if it is a flat surface, has a lot of small differences in the surface orientation, which we recreated using the bump. The **Lambertian** model is not adequate for this kind of surface, and even if the difference in the final image is very subtle, it will help to get the right look for our parquet.

Creating materials for the plant in the scene

In this recipe, we will have our first brief contact with organic materials, which is a really challenging topic in computer graphics. We will go more in depth on this in the last chapters of the book, but this will be a good introduction.

Getting ready

It is time to create the material for the plant in our scene. To start, let's select the object named **Plant** and add a material to it. Name the material Leaf01 and go to the materials' node editor.

How to do it...

To create the plant materials, follow these steps:

1. Add a **Glossy BSDF** and **Mix Shader** node. Set the Glossy roughness to 0.080 and change the algorithm from **Beckmann** to **GGX**.

2. Mix the default **Diffuse BSDF** and the **Glossy BSDF** with the **Mix Shader** node. Put the Diffuse on top and the Glossy at the bottom, and use a **Fac** value of 0.200. Also set the **Diffuse** roughness to 1.000.

3. Now, let's add a **Translucent BSDF** and an **Add** shader node. Add the output of the previously added shaders and the **Translucent** node with the **Add** shader.

4. Now add a **Mix Shader** node and plug in the first socket, the output of the mix of the **Diffuse** and **Glossy BSDFs**, and in the second socket, the output of the addition of the **Translucent** and the **Mix** node. Set the **Fac** value to 0.800.

5. Now add a **Texture coordinate** node and an **Image Texture** node. We will use UV coordinates. In the **Image Texture** node, load the image named LeafCOLOR.png and plug the output into the **Diffuse BSDF Color** input.

6. Add a **Color Mix** node and plug the output of the LeafCOLOR image texture into it. Leave the mode as **Mix** and set the **Fac** value to 0.500. Finally, plug the output of the **Color Mix** node into the **Color** input of the **Glossy BSDF**.

7. Leave the second input of the **Color Mix** node empty and adjust the color until we get the desired glossy intensity. To set the color, click on the **HSV** button right under the color wheel and set the **Value** to 0.600.

8. Add a **Hue Saturation** node and plug the LeafCOLOR image texture output into its **Color** input. Set the **Saturation** to 0.700 and the **Value** to 1.200. Finally, plug the output into the **Color** input of the **Translucent BSDF**.

9. Duplicate the **Image Texture** node and click on the user data number next to the path to make the texture unique. Then load the LeafNORM.png file. The following screenshot shows the node tree for the leaves material:

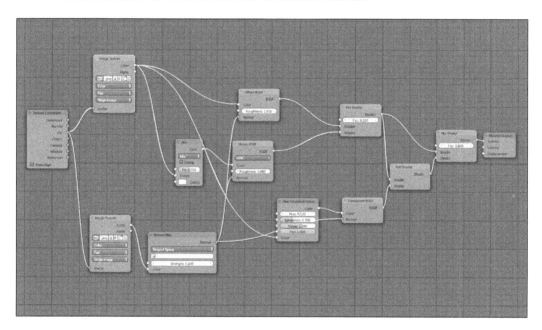

10. Add a **Normal Map** node (**Add | Vector**) and plug the LeafNORM Image Texture **Color** output into its **Color** input. Set the **Strength** to 0.100 and plug the output into the **Normal** input of each BSDF in the editor.

11. Now we need to add two new materials to our plant. In the material menu, click twice on the **+** button next to the shader list. For each new material slot, select the original leaf material from the drop-down menu that we can see, by clicking on the little ball button on the left side of the **New** button.

12. For both of the new materials, click on the **User Number** button to make the material unique. Name the first material Leaf02 and the second material Leaf03, as shown in the following screenshot:

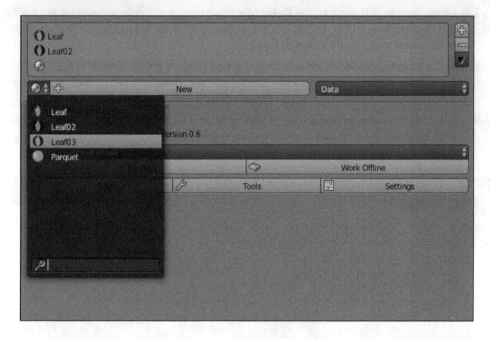

13. Go into the edit mode and then into the face selection mode by pressing *Ctrl + Tab*. Make sure no face is selected by toggling the *A* key. Now, from the lower viewport header, navigate to **Select | Random**. Press the *F6* button to show the operator menu and set the percent to 0.120. Finally, press *Ctrl + L* to select linked faces and press the **Assign** button in the material menu while the Leaf02 material slot is selected.

14. Repeat the same operation for the Leaf03 material.

15. In the node material editor, we will now perform some changes in terms of color, glossiness, and so on, to give the plant some variation. We can use different methods for this. For reference, you can have a look at the finished blend file.

16. For the Vase object, the material can be a simple mix of a grey **Diffuse BSDF** (20 percent) and an Anisotropic BSDF with a roughness of 0.015 (80 percent).

How it works...

To create the material for the leaves, we first created a mix of different BSDFs to get the right shader. Later, we applied the textures. To give the illusion of the imperfections on the surface of the leaf, this time we used a normal map. This kind of map works like a bump map but is more precise. While a bump map uses greyscale values to assess the height of the surface, the normal map is also able to provide information about the orientation of the surface.

As a **Color** input for the different BSDFs, we used the same color map, which is tweaked each time to get the result we want for a specific situation. While for the Diffuse BSDF it is alright to use the clean color map, for the Glossy and Translucent BSDF, it is nice to get a slightly brighter colorization. Also, remember that in this case the color also affects the intensity of the BSDF, and a brighter texture will give a stronger glossiness and translucency.

There's more...

There are different kinds of normal maps. In this situation, we used the tangent space type normal map. This kind of normal map is probably the most commonly used. It can be baked out of high-res geometry or even be created from a color map using several standalone programs or plugins for image editors such as Photoshop or GIMP.

The other kinds of normal maps are the World space and the Object space ones. If we want to use one of these kinds of normal maps, it will be necessary to specify it in the drop-down menu of the **Normal Map** node. It is also possible to specify the UV layer that we intend to use. In case there is only one UV layer, Cycles will automatically use that one.

See also

The following are some interesting free and commercial programs to create every kind of map that is needed:

- `http://www.mapzoneeditor.com/?PAGE=HOME`: This is a free node-based map generator
- `http://www.xnormal.net/1.aspx`: This is a free map creator
- `https://code.google.com/p/gimp-normalmap/`: This is a free GIMP plugin for creating maps
- `http://www.crazybump.com/`: This is one of the best known and intuitive commercial map generators
- `http://quixel.se/ndo/`: This is a powerful suite of commercial plugins for Photoshop

Creating a different kind of leather

In the real world, the same type of materials can have a lot of different variants. For example, there are different kinds of leather. In this recipe, we will learn how to create leather of a different kind from the one that we used to create a wallet in *Chapter 1, Key Holder and Wallet Studio Shot*.

Getting ready

We will now create the leather material for the pouffe. The kind of leather will not be the same as the one we created for the wallet, which was smooth. Here we will apply a lot of wrinkles, which will give us a really nice leather effect.

Select the pouffe object, add a material, and name it `puff`.

How to do it...

1. Add a **Glossy BSDF** and a **Mix Shader** node. Set the Glossy node to GGX mode and set the roughness to `0.350`.

2. Mix the Diffuse and the Glossy BSDF giving 80 percent for the Glossy and 20 percent for the Diffuse BSDF.

3. Add an **Image Texture** node and a **Texture Coordinate** node. Use the UV coordinates. Also add a **Mapping** node and set the scale to `13.000` for every axis.

4. In the **Image Texture** node, load the file called `Leather.jpg` and plug the **Color** output into the diffuse BSDF **Color** input.

5. Duplicate the texture node and make it accessible to a single user using the button next to the path. Load the image named `Leather_SPEC.png`.

6. Add a **Color Mix** node and plug the last added texture into the first color socket and leave the second slot empty with a color of RGB: 0.5, 0.5, 0.5. Set the **Fac** to `0.200` and leave the mode to **Mix**. Finally, plug the **Color Mix** output into the Glossy BSDF **Color** input.

7. Let's duplicate the **Image Texture** node and make it accessible to a single user again. Now load the `Leather_NRM.png` image.

8. Add a **Normal Map** node (**Add | Vector**) and plug the `Leather_NRM` texture into its **Color** input. Set the **Strength** to `0.300` and plug the output into the **Normal** input of the two BSDFs of the material.

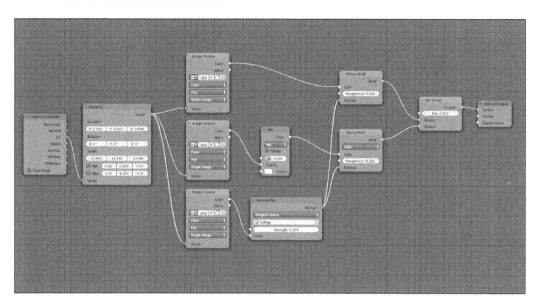

How it works...

This node setup is a pretty simple one. Once again we used a normal map to simulate the bumpiness of the surface.

We also used a specular map for our **Glossy BSDF**. Since the original map was a bit too contrasted, we used a **Color Mix** node to mix it with a neutral grey and to lower the contrast between the dark and the bright parts.

To obtain a more interesting effect, we can use a **Layer Weight** and a **Color Ramp** node to differentiate between the glossiness over the surface of the pouffe. The **Layer Weight** node gives us the possibility to tell Cycles which part of the surface is looking towards the camera, and which is tangential to its point of view. The **ColorRamp** node will be useful to make fine adjustments and obtain the desired effect. There is a reference to this kind of setup shown in the following screenshot:

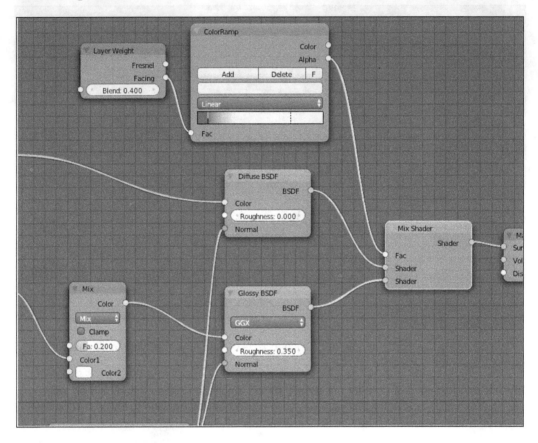

There's more...

It is also possible to recreate a leather material with procedural textures. This method requires a bit more work while creating the shader, but it does not require the model to be unwrapped in order to correctly map the textures over it.

See also

Check out the file for the additional materials provided (named `AdditionalMaterial.blend`) for a procedural leather shader.

Creating the materials for the lamp

Now we will create the shaders for the lamp. Among others, a really interesting material will be the marble for the base. For this particular shader, we will be using a new node, subsurface scattering, which is often written as SSS.

Getting ready

To start, select the object called **Lamp**, add a new material to it, and name it `LampMarble`.

How to do it...

To create the materials for the lamp, follow these steps:

Assigning the different materials

To assign different materials, follow these steps:

1. With the lamp object selected, let's go into the edit mode by pressing the *Tab* key and make sure no vertex is selected. With the mouse cursor over the piece of geometry that we want to select, press the *L* key on the keyboard to select the entire part of the mesh. Using this method, let's select the two spheres at the top of the lamp.

2. Add a new material slot by pressing the **+** button in the material menu. Create a new material and name it `Lamp`, and then click on the **Assign** button.

3. Repeat the operation described in step 1, but this time, select the cylinder pipe and the two support spheres. Add a new material slot and a new material. Name this material `LampMetal` and click on the **Assign** button.

Creating the marble

To create the marble, follow these steps:

1. Let's select the marble material and add a **Glossy BSDF** and an **Add Shader** node. Add the default **Diffuse BSDF** to the Glossy one and set the Glossy BSDF's roughness to `0.100`.

2. Add a **Subsurface Scattering BSDF** (**Add | shaders**) and a **Mix Shader** node. Mix the output of the sum of the Diffuse and Glossy BSDFs with the SSS node. Put the SSS in the lower input socket and set the **Fac** value to `0.400`.

3. Add an **Image Texture** and a **Texture Coordinate** node. Connect them using the generated coordinates. In the **Image Texture** node from the second drop-down menu, set the projection method to **Box**. A **Blend** slider will appear. Set it to `1.000`.

4. Load the image called `Marble.jpg`. Add a **Mix** node and connect the **Image Texture** node to its **Color1** input. Set the **Color2** to RGB 0.15, 0.15, 0.15, the **Fac** to `0.800`, and leave the mode to **Mix**. Finally connect the output to the Diffuse BSDF **Color** input.

5. Now let's add an **RGB Curves** node and connect the Marble texture to its Color input. Set the curve as shown in the following reference screenshot and connect the output to the Glossy and Subsurface Scattering BSDF's **Color** input.

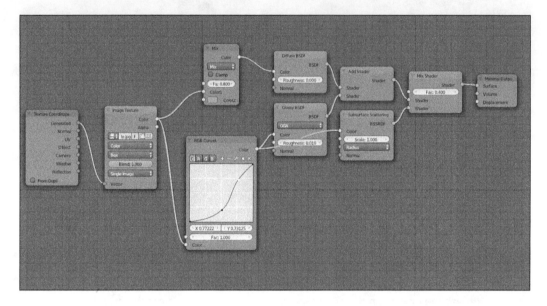

The material setup for the **Lamp** and the `LampMetal` are really easy mixes of BSDFs. We can see how they are made in the following two reference screenshots:

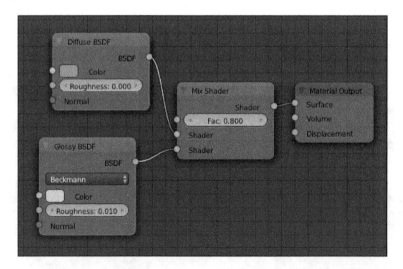

Finally, the node setup for the lamp itself is done as follows:

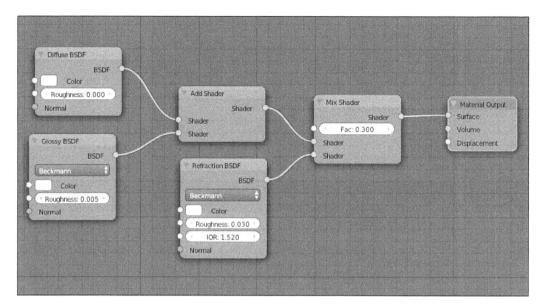

How it works...

In the marble shader, we assigned the color of the surface using mainly the Glossy and the SSS BSDFs. The **Diffuse BSDF** only gets a really weak input from the texture. This is because we want to obtain a sort of layered effect, typical of a really smooth marble with a highly reflective surface.

With a darker and less defined diffuse color, the **Glossy BSDF** has a much stronger effect on the surface of the object. To make the effect even stronger, we used an RGB curves node to increase the contrast of the image.

Finally, the SSS gives the marble the final touch, allowing the light to get scattered inside the object. As for other BSDFs, the intensity (the amount of scattered light) of the SSS is driven by its color. Using the color map, we were able to give some variation to the SSS effect.

There's more...

At the moment of this recipe's writing, the SSS BSDF has just been added into Cycles (2.68). This means that it is still under development and is missing a couple of features.

First of all, it is not possible to use the GPU to render SSS materials. Rendering with GPU will result in SSS being ignored and treated as a normal **Diffuse BSDF**. The second missing feature is that it is not possible to add any bump to the SSS node at the moment, even though the normal input is already in place.

However, it could be that by the time you read this recipe, these features will already be working.

In the following link, you will find a thread about a skin shader for Cycles. It is a node group created by a user on Blender Artist who tried to recreate the Arnold skin shader in Cycles. It definitely is a good reference to learn from!

```
http://blenderartists.org/forum/showthread.php?287516-Arnold-skin-
shader-ported-to-Cycles
```

Creating a carpet using hair particles

Now we will create the hair for the carpet under the coffee table in our scene. For the creation of the hair, we will cover just the part regarding the rendering in Cycles. Then we will see how to create the material for it.

Getting ready

First of all, we have to check a couple of render settings. At the moment of this recipe's writing, hair rendering is a new feature, and the support for GPU rendering is being added right now. By the time you read this, everything will already be supported, but right now, to activate hair rendering on the GPU, we need to go to the **Render** menu, and in the render panel, set the **Features** drop-down menu to **Experimental**.

Now we are ready to start. The first step is to select the object called **Carpet** and add two materials to it. We will call the first one `Carpet` and the second `CarpetHair`.

How to do it...

1. Let's go to the particles menu with the carpet object selected. In the render panel, we will check that the **Material** slot is set to `2.000`.

2. Let's go down to the **Cycles Hair Rendering** settings. From the **Mode** drop-down menu, select **Accurate**. Below that the **Cycles Hair** settings is present. Here we need to set the **Shape** to `-0.970`, and in the thickness panel, set the **Root** to `0.200` and **Tip** to `0.150`, and make sure the **Close tip** option is off.

3. Now let's go to the material node editor with the `CarpetHair` material selected. Add a **Glossy BSDF** and a **Translucent BSDF** and two **Mix Shader** nodes.

4. Mix the **Diffuse BSDF** and the **Glossy BSDF** with the Glossy influence to 5 percent. Also, set the Glossy roughness to `0.400`.

5. Now mix the output of these two BSDFs with the **Translucent BSDF** and set the translucent influence to 10 percent.

6. Now let's add a **Hair Info** node (**Add | Input**) and a **ColorRamp** node. Plug the **Intercept** output from the **Hair Info** node into the **ColorRamp** node and set the color ramp as shown in the following screenshot.

7. Let's add a **Wave Texture** node. We want to use UV coordinates and also a **Mapping** node to set the Z rotation to 30. Inside the **Wave Texture** node, set the scale to 3.000 and the distortion to 15.000.

8. Add an RGB Mix node and plug the **Wave Texture Color** output into the **Fac** input and the **ColorRamp Color** output into the **Color1** input of the **RGB Mix** node. Set the mode to **Multiply** and the **Color2** to RGB 0.14, 0.11, 0.07. Finally, plug the RGB Mix node output into the Diffuse **Color** input.

9. Select the **Carpet** material and change the diffuse BSDF color to a medium dark brown (RGB 0.25, 0.2, 0.15).

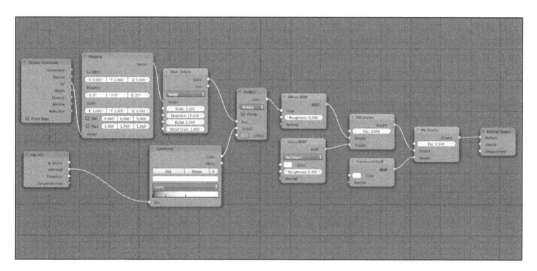

How it works...

First of all, let's talk about Cycles rendering settings for the hair. As we saw, they can be found in the particles panel. There are several modes we can select to render the hair. Basically, the lowest option (**Fast Planes**) is the least accurate but the fastest to render, while the highest (**Smooth Curves**) is the best looking one, but also the slowest in terms of render time. There is also an option to create a custom setup, but in general, the presets are quite good.

Usually, the **Accurate** mode is suitable for the majority of situations, providing a good balance between quality and render time. The smooth curves provide additional quality at the cost of a much higher render time. It can help if we have to render a close up that shows hair in detail. It is also possible to give a minimum pixel width for the strands. This is useful if we have really thin hair, which can give us some aliasing problems. This option can help to fix these kinds of issues.

In the **Cycles Hair Settings**, we can choose the thickness of the hair at the root and at the tip. The way the thickness changes from the **root** to the **tip** depends on the shape option. Negative values will make the influence of the root value stronger even when we get close to the tip, while positive values will make the tip thickness visible much lower along the hair. The **Close tip** option will set the tip of the strands to zero, no matter what value we set in the tip thickness. We also have a multiplier for the thickness, which is the scaling option. Changing this, we can change the whole thickness of the strands without changing the ratio between the root and tip thickness.

In the material we created for the hair, a really important node is the **Hair Info** node. This node gives us a lot of useful input to use for strand rendering. In this situation, we used the **Intercept** value. This value gives us information about the position along the strand. Using the **ColorRamp** node, we were able to set the color from the root to the tip of the strands (left to right). This was useful to give some variation to the color, making it a bit darker at the root. We also used a **Wave Texture** node to give some interesting pattern to the color of the carpet. Using this method, we can apply any kind of texture and recreate, for example, beautiful animal fur patterns. We used the texture as the **Fac** input for the **Color Mix** node in order to decide where we want the original color of the strands to be multiplied by the color we set in the **Color Mix** node.

There's more...

There is another way to assign a material to strands while rendering with Cycles. In this recipe, we used the old method, which also worked in the Blender Internal render engine, which is selecting the number of the material slot from the rendering panel of the particles settings.

With Cycles, we can use the **Is Strand** output of the **Hair Info** node as a **Fac** input to mix two different node setups inside the same material. Everything going into the second socket of the **Mix Shader** node will be the material used for the strands. Remember to set the number of the material slot inside the particles settings to the material that is assigned to the mesh (in our scene, this is the **Carpet** material, therefore slot `number1`).

For any other material in Cycles, the fact that we can use nodes to create the materials for strands gives us a lot of flexibility. The number of effects that can be obtained using this setup are practically endless. For example in the following screenshot, we can see a node setup to map a texture on each strand, which was created by a user on Blender Artists:

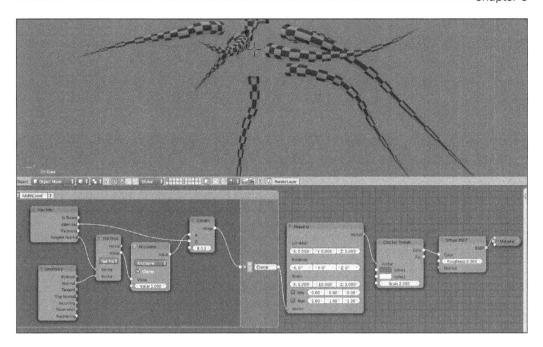

Shown in the following screenshot is another node setup, also created by a BA user, which shows how to apply color to strands horizontally:

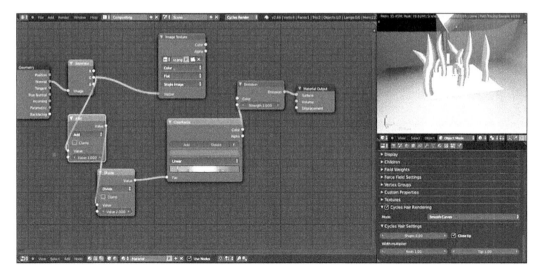

See also

In the following link, you can find a really good tutorial about hair. The most interesting thing, however, is an in-depth overview of the settings available for strand rendering in Cycles.

`http://www.blenderguru.com/videos/how-to-render-hair-with-cycles/`

Setting up night lighting

Now that our scene is ready, let's play a bit with the lighting. Let's see how we can set up a nice night lighting system. We will try to create two separated setups so that it will be easy to switch from day to night.

Getting started

The first thing that we want to change is the environment. Let's go to the World Settings and rename the **World** to Day. Also click on the **F** button, as doing so will assign a fake user to the world to prevent Blender from erasing it, if it isn't in use when closing the file. Then click on the plus button on the right side and rename the new world as Night. Press the *F* key for the Night world as well.

How to do it...

1. Let's change the color of the Night world to a dark blue. Something like RGB 0, 0, 0.01 will be fine. Also set the **Strength** to 0.100.

2. Set the **AO Factor** to 0.050.

3. In the viewport, select the area light for the window and the sun, and move it to layer 2. To do this with the two lights selected, press the *M* key and click on the layer we want to move them in.

4. Activate layer 2 to see the lights again. Select the Area Light and copy it with *Ctrl + D*. Move the new light to layer 3. Deactivate layer 2 and activate layer 3.

5. Name the new Area Light NightPortal. Set its color to a blue lighter than that of the world, for example, RGB 0.3, 0.3, 0.7. Also let's activate the **Cast Shadows** option.

6. Create a plane (press *Shift + A* and then navigate to **Mesh | Plane**) and go into the edit mode by pressing the *Tab* key. Press the *W* key and select **Subdivide** from the drop-down menu. Remember to always keep the mouse cursor in the viewport while performing these operations.

7. Select the central vertex and move it down slightly. Also, scale the whole plane down to a quarter of its original size.

8. Exit the edit mode and name the new plane `Emit01` from the object menu. Add a new material and name it `Emit01`.

9. From the surface panel in the material menu, select **Emission** and set the **Strength** to 20 and the color HSV to 0.15, 0.4, 0.8.

10. Now let's move to the material node editor and add a **Geometry** node, a **Mix Shader** node, and a **Diffuse** BSDF.

11. Plug the **Backfacing** info from the **Geometry** node into the **Mix Shader** node's **Fac** input. Then plug the **Diffuse BSDF** into the upper socket and the **Emission** node into the second one.

12. In the 3D viewport, duplicate the Emit plane (*Alt + D*) and place it as shown in the following screenshot:

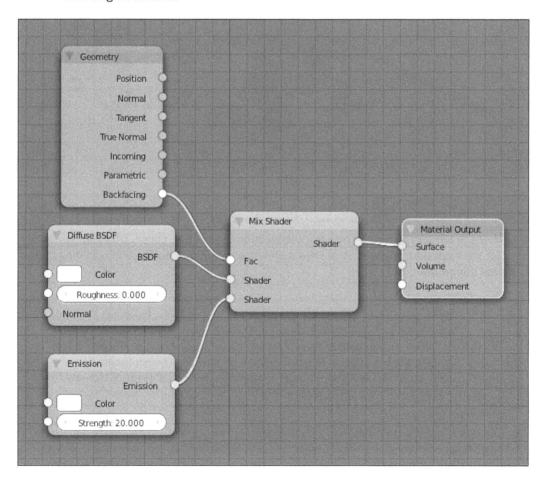

The following screenshot shows the **NightLighting** setup seen from the 3D viewport:

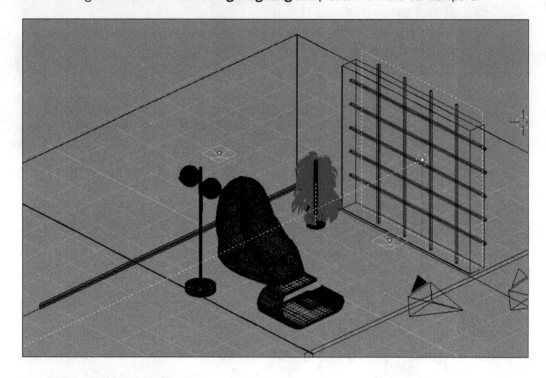

How it works...

A night scene still has some light in it. It must be dark, but not pitch black. The settings we used for the night world allowed us to have a dark scene, but maintained some lighting thanks to **Global Illumination** (**GI**).

 While we are setting up lighting in our scene, it is always a good idea to check every source of light individually to see the effect it has on the scene. Thanks to GI, the environment is also a light source in Cycles. For this reason, it is good to see the effect of the environment on the scene without any other light, in order to see how the room would look with the lights off. In this way, we can see if we created believable environment lighting for our scene.

We used a blue color, both for the environment and for the portal because this is the most prominent color of the environment at night. We also activated the shadows for the portal because the light entering from the window at night is mainly indirect light, which bounces around outside the window. This means that unlike the sun, which casts sharp and well-defined shadows, the shadows coming from the window at night will be subtle and blurry. The size of the area light is enough to give us this kind of effect.

After the environment, we added some artificial lighting inside the room. The particular setup that we used allows us to apply the emission shader only on one side of the plane. As the light sources are outside our view, we didn't need the light to bounce on the ceiling as this would just have added a lot of noise to our scene.

The color of the artificial light is yellow, as these kinds of lights are usually warmer when compared to natural lighting coming from the outside, especially by night. The third layer contains a plane that closes the open side of the room. In this night scene, without this plane, the opening in the wall would have been visible in the reflections. Moreover, the night scene has the strongest sources of light inside, so the opening in the wall would not have been of great help here compared to the day setup.

There's more...

In the end, using **Duplicate Linked** on the plane instead of copying it gives us different advantages. Duplicates share several settings with the original. This means that we can still modify the size, position, and rotation in the object mode, but if we change something in the edit mode, every single duplicate will be modified as well. Moreover, duplicates also share the same memory during the rendering process. This can be of great help in cases of complex scenes where the memory usage is really high. Duplicates can be obtained by pressing *Alt + D* as we have seen in the recipe, or by using particle instances or arrays.

Since in the night lighting, the fact that the portal light casts shadows is acceptable, we can also use an emitting plane instead of the area light. This could allow us to map a texture onto it, to reflect on the floor whatever kind of background we would like to use as the exterior of our room. Note that this technique can also be used in the case of day lighting if the sun light does not come directly inside the window. In this case, the light would be coming from indirect bounces just like the night scene, and using the **Cast Shadows** option would be acceptable.

If we would like to use mesh emitters as portals, we will have to remember to deactivate the camera and shadow ray visibility for the plane in the object menu. The following screenshot shows how to set up the **Ray Visibility** panel for the emitter.

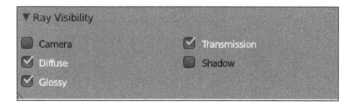

Using IES files in Cycles

The final step for this recipe will be to add the light for the big lamp next to the pouffe.
To do this, we will use Illuminated Engineering Society (IES), which is a file format used
to store photometric data. Thanks to IES files, we will be able to recreate the distribution
of lights based on specific lamps inside programs that support this format.

Getting ready

Cycles, by default, does not support IES files, but we can use a script for it. You can find the
script at the following page on the Blender Artists' website: `http://blenderartists.`
`org/forum/showthread.php?276063-IES-Lamps-to-Cycles`.

 The script is also included with the recipe files of this cookbook.

To install the script, we need to navigate to the **User Preferences | Addons** section of Blender.
In the lower-left part of the window, we need to click on the **Install from File...** button, shown in
the following screenshot, after which a browser will open. Let's go to the location of the python
file (`//chapter03/blend/script`) and double-click on the `IES.py` file. Finally, let's activate
the script that will appear in the list by checking the square checkbox on the right side.

How to do it...

1. After installing the add-on, navigate to **File | Import | IES lamp data (.ies)**. If there is no such option in the **Import** menu, we need to activate the add-on as shown in the *Getting ready* section.

2. In the browser, load the L6441.IES file from the following path:

   `\\IES\ALG\IESFiles\Lithonia_Lighting\Fluorescent\Parabolic_Louvers\9PMO\L6441.IES`.

3. A point light and a mesh will be created. By moving the mesh around, we will also move the point light. We need to place the IES rig inside the two lamps of the stand next to the puff as shown in the following screenshot:

4. Once the rig is placed inside the lamp, let's go to the properties shelf by pressing the *N* key while the cursor is over the 3D viewport. When the mesh of the IES rig is selected, at the bottom of the properties shelf, there is a lamp properties panel. In this panel, we want to set **Strength Multiplier** to 400 and **Color** to RGB 1, 0.9, 0.7.

5. Now we need to copy the rig (*Ctrl + D*) and place it inside the second lamp sphere. When we copy the rig, we need to make sure that both the mesh and the point light are selected.

How it works...

The usage of IES allows us to easily achieve effects, which would otherwise require the creation of additional geometry. As we have seen several times already, when Cycles has to deal with a lot of bounces, a lot of noise is generated, and this is exactly the case when achieving this effect with geometry. Using an IES will not require the creation of any additional memory.

It is important to choose the right IES file for each light in order to achieve a believable result. IES files can be found for free on a lot of lamp producers' websites where they often show from which real lamp a certain IES comes from. This is a good way to learn if a certain IES is suited for our lamp.

There's more...

Observing the effect of an IES file can be quite tricky from the viewport, but we have a much better and faster method to see how an IES file will look in our final render.

We can use a program called IES viewer. It is a really useful freeware program, which allows us to quickly inspect IES files without having to render them in Cycles. Using this program is quite simple. We just need to go to the location of our IES files from the browser on the top-left part of the screen. Then choose one of the files from the big window in the middle. As we select one file, we will be able to see the graph in the lower left part of the screen. Pressing *Ctrl + R* or clicking on the render button under the file browser will show us the IES rendered. What we see is how our light would look on a surface. Notice that this program is for Windows only.

The program can be freely downloaded from `http://www.photometricviewer.com/`.

See also

There are a lot of websites where you can download IES files. The following websites are some of them where you can find good IES files:

- `http://www.cooperindustries.com/content/public/en/lighting/resources/design_center_tools/photometric_tool_box.html`
- `http://www.lithonia.com/photometrics.aspx`

In the following link, on the other hand, there is a small program that will allow us to create our own IES files from scratch:

`http://www.tom-schuelke.com/ies-gen3.exe`

4
Creating an Exterior Scene

In this chapter, we will cover the following recipes in depth:

- ▸ Setting up the lighting with an external plugin
- ▸ Creating the road material
- ▸ Creating the grass material
- ▸ Texturing the tree trunk and creating realistic leaves
- ▸ Adding flowers to the scene
- ▸ Creating the wood material for the table and the fence
- ▸ Giving final touches to the image using render passes

Introduction

After learning how to create an interior scene, we will now see how to set up an exterior scene. Here, we will use different techniques to achieve incredibly natural lighting and see new and beautiful shaders.

Setting up the lighting with an external plugin

In this recipe, we will deal with exterior lighting. This is a much easier situation for cycles to render, and getting rid of the noise will be much easier than the interior scene.

Getting ready

We will be using a combination of **IBL (image-based lighting)** and sunlight in this scene. To combine them properly, there is a really useful plugin that we can use, called Sun Position. It can be found among the chapter files and it is named `SunPosition.zip`. The procedure to follow to install the add-on is the same as we saw for the IES add-on (you can install the ZIP file directly without extracting it). Once the add-on is installed, let's open the `Chapter04_Empty.blend` file.

How to do it...

1. Activate layer 2 and add **Sun Lamp** to the scene. In the **Lamp** menu, set the **Size** to `0.010`.

2. Let's go to the **World** node editor and add a sky texture (**Add | Textures | Sky Texture**) and connect it to the **Background** node's **Color** socket.

3. Go to the **World** menu. If we correctly activated the add-on, we should see a new panel called **Sun Position** in the lower part of the menu. Click on **Enable** and check the **Cycles sky** and **Use object** functions. From the drop-down menu, select the **Sky Texture** and **Sun Lamp** object.

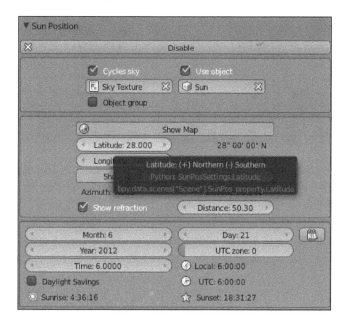

4. Set **Latitude** and **Longitude** to 28.000 and 7.000. Also, set the **North** offset to -15 and the **Time** to 6 as shown in the preceding figure.

5. Now disable the add-on and click on the **Preferences** button that will appear on the right.

6. Under **Usage Mode**, select **Sun + HDR texture** and click on **Done**. Enable the add-on again.

7. In the **World** node editor, add **Environment Texture** and from the browser, select the sky.jpg file. Copy the **Background** BSDF using *Ctrl + D* and connect **Environment Texture** to the newly copied node. Finally, connect it to the **Surface** socket of the **World Output** node.

8. In the **Sun Position** panel of the **World** menu, select **Environment Texture** in the **Use environment texture** drop-down menu and **Sun** from the **Use sun object** menu.

9. Click on **Release binding** and then on **Sync Sun to Texture**. The texture will appear in the viewport. Click on the area of the texture where the Sun is and then click on **Sync Sun to Texture** again.

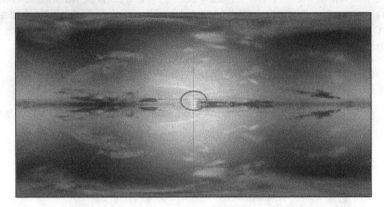

10. Activate the real-time viewport and set the rotation until the Sun appears to be rising from the right side of the screen, in a position similar to the one we set before with **Sky Texture**.

11. Finally, go to the **World** node editor and add an **Add Shader** node. Connect the two **Background** BSDFs to **Add Shader** and the output to **World Output**.

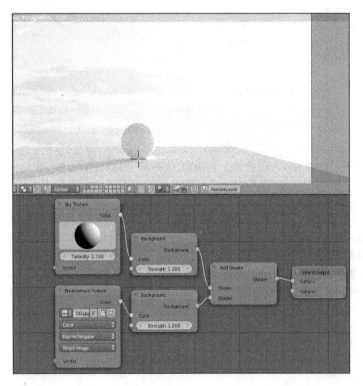

How it works...

In this recipe, we saw for the first time a more complex environment setup. We used the combination of two different textures to obtain the final effect and we could do this exactly as if the world would be a normal shader. Given the power of the **Shader** node system, the creation of the environment gives us great flexibility. Moreover, here we used an external plugin that helped us to set up all the different parts in a realistic way. The first thing we did was to set up the built-in Cycles' **Sky Texture**. In general, it is possible to set up **Sky Texture** by just rotating the sphere in the node by clicking and dragging the mouse cursor over it. Doing so makes it is possible to set the sky lighting for every moment of the day; but this method is not very precise, as it is difficult to set it in the position we want. Thanks to the add-on, we were able to get exactly the kind of sky we wanted.

Once the sky looked right, we added an environment texture to make the sky look interesting. Again it would be possible to manually set the rotation of the Sun and of the texture, but the add-on made this operation much easier. The real-time viewport also comes in handy in this situation to see what is going on with great precision. As a final step, we combined the two **Background** BSDFs with an **Add Shader** node, exactly as we would do for any other shader. This gave us the combined effect of the Cycles' physical **Sky Texture** and **Environment Texture**.

There's more...

The **Sun** add-on is really useful to correctly set the general position of the Sun, **Environment Texture**, and **Sky Texture**. This does not mean that we have to be totally bound to it. If, for example, the Sun should have a very steep angle, we can always manually change it by a small degree after the operations we did in this recipe. In this way, we can set the length of the shadows without losing the correct position of all the elements. It is good to remember that the Sun is only affected by its rotation, while changing the position does not have any effect on the lighting.

Regarding the **World** material, we said that it works exactly as other materials. This means that we can use a lot of the techniques we learned until now. We could, for example, want to slightly change the color of a texture. To do so, it would be enough to insert any of the color correction nodes between the texture and the **Background** BSDF. We can also use any of the procedural textures included in the Cycles to create different kind of effects.

See also

▸ Once you click on the download link of the Sun position add-on, you will see a lot of useful information about the usage of this great plugin: `http://wiki.blender.org/index.php/Extensions:2.6/Py/Scripts/3D_interaction/Sun_Position`

Creating the road material

Now that the lighting is ready, let's start creating the materials for our scene. We will start with the creation of the asphalt and the land that will be covered by the grass.

Getting ready

Before we start, we need to move **Sun Lamp** to the first layer and then activate that layer. So with **Sun Lamp** selected, press *M* and then click on the first layer. In case the scene is too heavy, we can move the the elements that we won't be needing to another layer, for example, the tree. Moreover, in the modifier panel, we can deactivate the viewport visualization of the grass and flower particle system of the ground. To do this, select the **Ground** mesh and from the **Modifier** menu, click on the eye button next of the two last modifiers of the list. In this way, the grass and the flowers will not be shown in the viewport, which will greatly benefit speed. Note that in case of a render they will be rendered regardless, but they will not show up in the real-time viewport. Let's add a material to the **Ground** mesh and let's name it `Land`.

How to do it...

Let's see how to create the shaders for the road.

Creating the asphalt

1. With the **Ground** mesh selected, jump into the **Vertex Paint** mode by selecting it in the drop-down menu in the lower bar of the 3D viewport and paint the road black using the draw brush. Then using the blur brush, make the border of the road less sharp. Finally, in the object data menu, from the **Vertex Color** panel, rename the **Vertex Color** entry as `Road`.

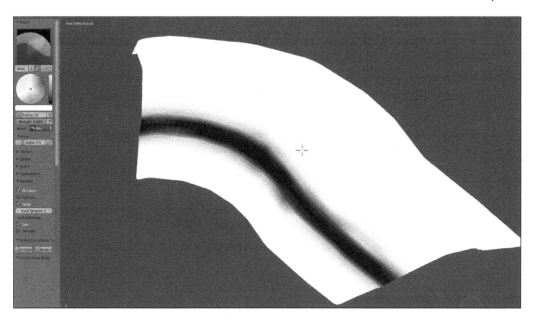

2. Go back to **Object Mode** and go to the **Material** node editor. Add **Glossy BSDF** and mix it with the default Diffuse using a **Mix Shader** node. Set the **Fac** value to `0.400`, with **Diffuse** in the upper socket and **Glossy** in the lower one.

3. Add an **Image Texture** node and load the `Asphalt.jpg` file. We will use the UV coordinates for it by using a **Texture Coordinate** node. Also, add a **Mapping** node and set **Scale** to `2.500` for each axis.

4. Plug **Texture** into the **Diffuse BSDF** color input node. Add a **Gamma** node and put it between **Texture** and **Diffuse BSDF**. Set **Gamma** to `1.400.`.

5. Duplicate the **Image Texture** node and make the texture single user. Load the `Asphalt_SPEC.png` file and plug it into the color input of **Glossy BSDF**. Add a color **Mix** node and place it between the **Texture** and **Glossy BSDF**. Set the mode to **Add** and **Fac** to `0.500`. Also, set the second color to RGB 0.15, 0.15, 0.15.

6. Duplicate **Image Texture** once more. After making it single user, load the `Asphalt_NRM.png` file. Add a **Normal Map** node and plug it into the **Normal** sockets of the **Diffuse** and the **Glossy** BSDFs.

7. For the two last textures, we will use the exact same coordinates as the first one, including the **Mapping** node.

8. Select the **Mix Shader** node and from the **Properties** panel (*N*), label it `Asphalt`.

Creating the mud

1. Within the same material add **Diffuse BSDF** and move it down in the editor. From the **Properties** panel, label it Mud.

2. Add **Image Texture** and a **Mapping** node. For this texture, we will use **Generated** coordinates. We can use the same **Texture Coordinate** node that we used from the asphalt.

3. Place the **Mapping** node between the **Texture Coordinate** and **Image Texture** nodes and set the **Scale** value to 20.000 for each axis.

4. In the **Image** node, load the Mud.jpg file and plug it into the **Diffuse BSDF** color socket.

5. Duplicate the texture and make it single user. Load the Mud_DISP.png file. Add a **Bump** node and plug the texture into the **Height** socket.

6. Set the **Strength** to 0.200 and plug the **Bump** node into the **Diffuse BSDF** normal socket.

Mixing the two node groups

1. Add an **Attribute** node and a **Mix Shader** node. In the **Attribute** node name, write Road and plug the **Color** output into the **Fac** socket of the **Mix** shader node.

2. Link the **Asphalt Shader Mix** node to the upper socket and the **Mud Diffuse** node to the lower one.

3. Plug the output of the last **Shader Mix** node into **Material Output**.

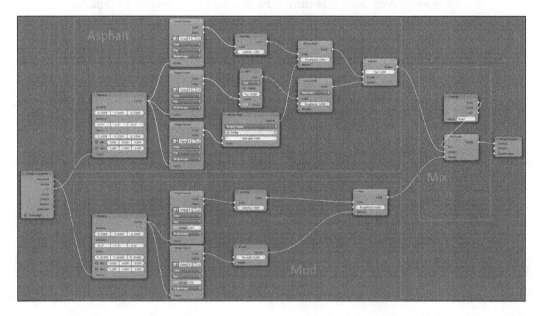

How it works...

In this recipe, we once again used **Vertex Paint** for the creation of our shaders. This time, it allowed us to create two completely different node groups and mix them together in the end. It is like having two different materials in one, but the advantage is that we can mix them in a much smoother way.

There's more...

As an alternative to **Vertex Paint**, we could have created a map in an external program to obtain an even more complex and organic transition between the road and mud. Remember that with these techniques, we can mix not only the colors but also every single element of the shaders.

Creating the grass material

We will now create the grass. In this case, we will use meshes instanced on the **Ground** mesh using a hair particle system.

Getting ready

To start, let's go to layer 5 where all our meshes that will be instanced are. It can be a good idea also to move the Sun to this layer temporarily, so that we are able to set up the materials with the final lighting. Let's select the **Grass01** mesh and add a new material to it. We will call it **GlassBlade01**.

How to do it...

1. In the **Material** node editor, add **Glossy BSDF** and a **Mix Shader** node.

2. Mix **Glossy BSDF** with the default **Diffuse** and set the **Fac** to 25 percent Glossy and 75 percent Diffuse.

3. Set the Glossy color to RGB 0.25, 0.3, 0.17 and the model to GGX.

4. Add **Texture Coordinate** and an **Image Texture** node. Use the UV coordinates and open the `grass_blade.jpg` file. Connect the texture to the **Color** input socket of **Diffuse BSDF**.

5. Add a **Hue Saturation Value** node and place it between the **Image Texture** node and **Diffuse BSDF**. Set **Hue** to `0.450`, **Saturation** to `0.900`, and **Value** to `0.900`.

6. Add a **Gamma** node and place it between the **Hue Saturation Value** node and **Diffuse BSDF**. Set **Gamma** to `1.800`.

7. Add **Translucent BSDF** and a **Mix Shader** node. Mix the last BSDF with the output of the first **Mix Shader** node. Set the **Fac** to 0.200 (**Translucent BSDF** in the lower socket).

8. Select the other three grass meshes by holding the *Shift* button (**Grass02**, **Grass03**, and **Grass04**). Select **Grass01** last so that it is the active selection. Press *Ctrl + L* and select **Materials** from the menu.

9. Select the **Grass02** mesh and from the **Material** menu, make the material single user by clicking on the button with **2** on it. Change the name of the material to GrassBlade02.

10. In the **Material** node editor change **Hue Saturation Value** to 0.470, 1.100, 0.600 and **Gamma** to 1.600.

11. Select the **Grass04** mesh and in the **Material** menu from the drop-down material datablock menu, select the **GrassBlade02** material.

12. Move back to layer 1 (if you moved the Sun, remember to bring it back to the right layer).

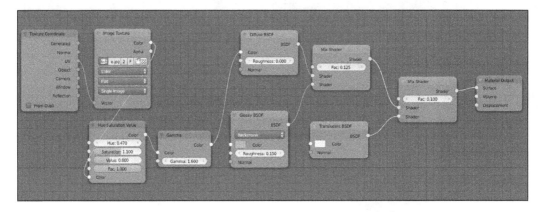

How it works...

The creation of the **Grass** shader is quite fast. We have a mix of **Diffuse BSDF** and **Glossy BSDF** with a color map and then the addition of a translucent effect to obtain the organic feel of the grass. We used two different materials to give some variation to the grass surface. We can even use more than two materials if we want. Moreover, we can even create more different meshes to use as instances to add more variation. Once created, we'll need to add them to the proper group.

To do this, go to the **Object** menu and in the **Group** panel, click on the **Add to Group** button. From the menu, select the **GrassBlade** group. Now, the new mesh will be instanced together with the others over the ground surface.

Thanks to the particle system we were able to take one or more meshes we created and distribute them over another mesh. In this way we created instanced meshes. The big advantage of using this technique is that all the meshes that we see on the scene use the data from the few original meshes. This allows us to save a tremendous amount of memory, still being able to render huge quantities of polygons. Using the particles system settings we can tweak the size and orientation of the instanced meshes, while to change the actual shape of the instanced meshes we should modify the original meshes in edit mode.

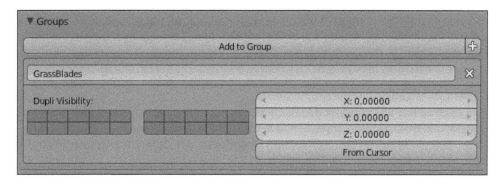

As an alternative to mesh instancing, we could also use pure hair particles to generate the grass, exactly as we did for the carpet. To change the particle visualization from mesh to hair, go to the particles menu with the Ground mesh selected. Select the **GrassBlades** particle settings and go to the **Render** panel. From here, change the option from **Group** to **Path**. Note that it will be necessary to change the **Material** settings to obtain a proper effect with this method. For more information about rendering hair particles, refer to the *Creating a carpet using hair particles* recipe in *Chapter 3, Creating an Interior Scene*.

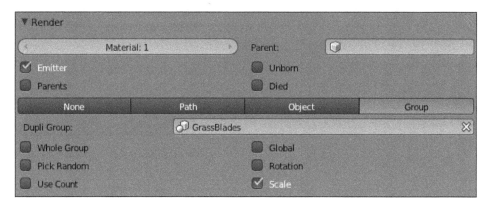

There's more

We can tweak the look of the grass by changing some of the settings of the particle system. Let's go to the **Particles** menu and select the **GrassBlade** particles settings. Now let's go to the **Velocity**, **Rotation**, and **Physics** panels. Here, we can tweak the size and the rotation of the particles. If, for example, we would like to have bigger grass, we can change the **Normal** value from the **Velocity** panel or the **Size** value in the **Physics** panel.

We can also change the rotation of the blades coming out from the ground. Note that being the particle instanced meshes; we will not be able to change the actual shape of the blades, but only the rotation of the mesh as a whole. One of the advantages of using hair particles instead of an instanced mesh would be to have control on the actual shape of the blades from these settings.

There is another way to give some additional variation to the shape of the blades even when using instanced meshes. From layer 5, add to each of the **GrassBlade** meshes a displace modifier using the **Cloud** texture. For **Texture Coordinate**, use **Object** and create an empty object to map the texture on. Set **Strength** to 0.100. You will now see that on moving the empty object, each grass blade is deformed in a different way from each other. This effect will be applied to all instanced meshes. This technique is also useful to add a light wind animation to the grass field, in case we would like to create a video. Then, it is enough to key the position of the empty object through the time of the animation.

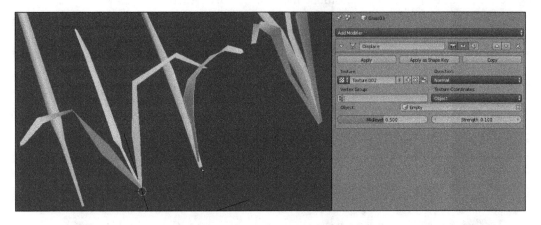

Texturing the tree trunk and creating realistic leaves

Now, we will deal with the tree of our scene. We will create the trunk and the leaves. For the leaves, we will again be working on instances that are located on a different layer than the main scene. The actual leaves on the tree are set to be displayed as **Bounding Box** to make the viewport easier to manage. In case you want to visualize the actual geometry of the leaves, you will have to select the original meshes on layer 5 and from the **Object** menu, select the **Textured** type from the **Display** panel. Note that even if the **Bounding Box** type is selected, the leaves will appear as usual when using the real-time viewport, so it is a good idea to leave the display type to **Bounding Box**.

Getting ready

First, we will create the bark material for the tree. Let's select the tree mesh and hit / on the numeric keypad to go into the local mode and solo the object in the viewport. This will allow us to have a much more responsive real-time viewport. Add a new material to it and call it `TreeBark`.

How to do it...

Let's see how to create the shaders for the tree.

Creating the bark

1. Add **Glossy BSDF** and a **Mix Shader** node. Mix **Glossy BSDF** with the default **Diffuse** node using a 20% contribution of **Glossy BSDF**. Also, set **Roughness** of **Glossy BSDF** to `0.4` and **Roughness** of **Diffuse BSDF** to `1`.

2. Add a **Texture Coordinate** node, a **Mapping** node, and an **Image Texture** node. Let's use **Generated Coordinates** with a **Scale** value of `13` on every axis. In the **Image Texture** node, load the `Bark.jpg` file.

3. In the **Image Texture** node, set the 2D projection method to **Box** and **Blend** to `0.6`. Link the output of **Color** to the **Color** input socket of **Diffuse**.

4. Add a **Gamma** node and place it in between the **Bark** image texture and **Diffuse BSDF**. Set **Gamma** to `1.2`.

5. Duplicate the **Bark** image texture and make the texture single user. Load the `Bark_DISP.png` file and leave the other settings as they are.

6. Add a **Bump** node and plug into its **Height** socket the **Bark_DISP** texture. Then link the **Normal** output to the **Normal** input socket of both **Diffuse BSDF** and **Glossy BSDF**. Set the **Strength** to `0.075`.

7. Duplicate one of the two **Image Texture** nodes again and make the texture single user. Load the `Bark_SPEC.png` image and plug the **Color** output to the **Color** input socket of **Glossy BSDF**.

8. Add **Noise Texture** and set the **Scale** value to `30`, **Detail** to `10`, and **Distortion** to `2`.

9. Add an **RGB Curves** node and plug the **Fac** output of the **Noise** texture into its **Color** input. Create an **S** shape with the curves as shown in the following figure.

10. Add a **Color Mix** node and plug the **Color** output of **RGB Curves** into **Fac**. Set **Color1** to RGB 0.02, 0.015, 0 and **Color2** to RGB 0.1, 0.1, 0.03.

11. Add another **Color Mix** node and place it between the **Gamma** node from the **Bark** texture and **Diffuse BSDF**. Set the **Mode** to `Color` and **Fac** to `1`. Plug the **Color Mix** node from the noise texture into the **Color2** input and the **Gamma** output from the **Bark** texture into the **Color1** input.

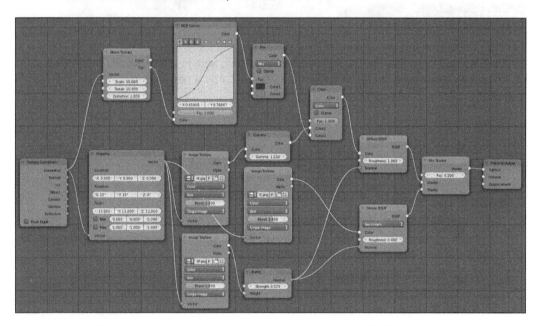

Creating the leaves

1. Go to layer 5 and temporarily bring the sunlight in this layer too.

2. Select the **Leaf01** mesh and add a new material to it, naming it `Leaf01`.

3. In the **Material** node editor, add **Glossy BSDF** and mix it with the default **Diffuse BSDF** using a **Shader Mix** node. Leave the factor to `0.5`.

4. Add a **Texture Coordinate** node and an **Image Texture** node. Use the UV coordinates and load the `Leaf.jpg` file into the **Image Texture** node.

5. Connect the **Image Texture** node to the color input socket of **Diffuse BSDF** and put a **Hue Saturation** node in between. Set HSV to 0.45, 0.8, 1.2.

6. Duplicate the **Image Texture** node and make the texture single user. Load the `Leaf_SPEC.png` image and connect it to the color input socket of **Glossy BSDF**.

7. Add **Translucent BSDF** and mix it with the Diffuse-Glossy mix using another **Mix Shader** node. Plug the **Translucent** node into the second socket and set **Fac** to `0.35`.

8. Duplicate the **Image Texture** node again and after we've made it single user, let's load the `Leaf_TransMAP.jpg` image. Plug the node into the color input socket of **Translucent**.

9. Add a **Color Mix** node and it place between the **Leaf_TransMAP** texture and **Translucent BSDF**. Set the **Mode** to `Color` and **Fac** to `1` and set **Color2** to RGB 0.56, 0.63, 0.175.

10. Duplicate the **Image Texture** node and make the texture single user. Load the `Leaf_DISP.png` file. Add a **Color Mix** node and set **Mode** to `Muliply`. Connect the **Leaf_TransMAP** image to the second socket and the **Leaf_BUMP** to the first.

11. Add a **Bump** node and plug it into its **Height** input socket the **Color Mix** node. Let's then connect the **Normal** output to the **Normal** input socket of the **Diffuse**, **Glossy**, and **Translucent BSDF**. Set **Strength** to `0.080`.

12. Duplicate an **Image Texture** node again and make the texture single user. Load in the `Leaf_ALPHA.jpg` image.

13. Add a **Mix Shader** node and connect **Leaf_ALPHA** to the **Fac** input socket. In the second **Shader** input socket, add the mix between **Diffuse**, **Glossy**, and **Translucent** BSDFs. Finally, add **Transparent BSDF** and connect it to the first **Shader** input socket.

14. Add a **Light Path** node and a **Math** node (**Add** | **Converter**). Connect the **Is Shadow Ray** output from the **Light Path** node to the **Math** node's first socket and the **Leaf_ALPHA** color output to the second one. Set the **Mode** to `Multiply`.

15. Add another **Mix Shader** node and **Transparent BSDF**. Plug into the first **Shader** socket the output of the last **Mix Shader** node and in the second one the last **Transparent BSDF** node added. Set the **Color** to RGB 0.26, 0.45, 0.125. Plug the **Math** node to the **Fac** input.

16. Let's now add a Frame (**Add | Layout**). Select all the nodes we created apart from every **Image Texture** node, the **Color Mix** node that is plugged into the **Bump** node. And the **Material Output** node. Drag them into the frame using the G button, so that when you click the left mouse button, they will be included inside the frame.

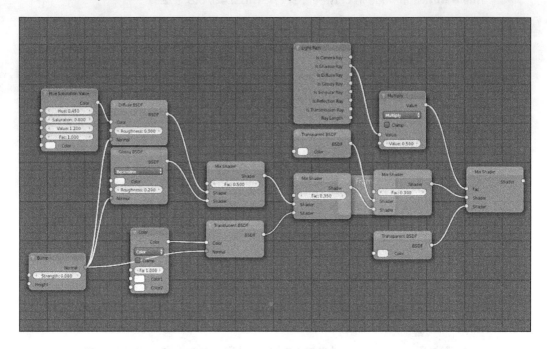

17. Now using Box, select (*B* button), select the frame and all the nodes inside it, and duplicate them using *Ctrl + D*.

18. When the frame is selected, we can rename it in the **Properties** panel (*N*), by changing the label name and changing its color by checking the custom color box. Let's name the first frame UpSide and color it green, and the second frame DownSide and color it yellow.

19. Now, we need to connect all of the textures to the DownSide frame exactly as they are connected in the UpSide frame.

20. In the DownSide frame, let's also change all the colors to a more yellowish green, decrease the intensity of **Glossy BSDF**, and increase the intensity of the **Translucent** one. Also invert the bump strength.

21. Finally, let's add a **Shader Mix** node and a **Geometry** node outside of the frames. Use the **Backfacing** output of the **Geometry** node as a **Fac** input, and connect the UpSide Frame's last **Shader Mix** node output to the first **Shader** socket and the DownSide frame's last **Shader Mix** output to the second **Shader** socket.

22. Apply the material to all four leaves meshes. We can also duplicate it and make some small changes on a couple of the leaves to give more variation to the tree.

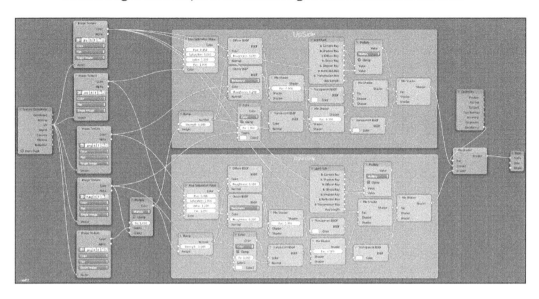

How it works...

With the creation of the bark material, we saw an interesting way of mapping a texture that allowed us to use generated coordinates instead of UVs. This method creates a virtual box around the object that will apply the textures on the six faces of the box. It will then project the image on the surface of the object depending on the normals. We can use this technique when we have to apply irregular textures on organic objects seamlessly. The blend value determines how much the seams of the texture will be blurred. With the creation of the leaves, we saw several new interesting techniques. We saw how to use textures to determine the transparency of a surface. We mixed our material with **Transparent BSDF** using a black and white map to determine where we wanted opaque and transparent areas. As with every other situation in cycles, gray parts of the map will give intermediate values of the **Shader Mix** node, with black being 0 and white 1. We also used the **Lightpath** node to change the color and intensity of the shadows of the leaves. Because we are using an **Alpha** map, we had to multiply **Is Shadow Ray** with the **Alpha** map, since the **Light Path** node takes information from the geometry of the object, also taking into account transparent parts. We also saw how to apply different materials to the two sides of a plane. This was extremely useful here as leaves have a very different appearance on either side.

There's more...

Another interesting thing we learned in this recipe is how to frame node groups in order to keep complex node setups clean and clear. If we want to remove a particular node from a frame, it is enough to press *Alt + P* while it is selected, exactly as we would do to unparent any other object. Moreover in the **Properties** panel we can change the size of the label font by changing the **Label Size** value. By default the frame will resize itself depending on the position of the nodes contained within. However, we can also resize manually, but to do so, we need to uncheck the shrink option in the **Properties** panel. Finally, we can create **Color** node presets by clicking on the **+** button next to the color picker.

See also

▸ A really good tutorial on the usage of node frames can be found at the following URL: `http://cgcookie.com/blender/2012/10/30/using-frame-nodes-blender-clean-organized-node-setups/`

▸ Also, here is an alternative **Leaf** node setup (in this thread of BA, there are also a lot of interesting node setups): `http://blenderartists.org/forum/showthread.php?216866-Cycles-tests-the-new-blender-CPU-GPU-renderer-of-awesomeness&p=2138175&viewfull=1#post2138175`

Adding flowers to the scene

We will now add some flowers to our scene to give some life to the grass field. We will be using instanced meshes Again, those that can be found on layer 5.

Getting ready

It is a good idea to move the sun lamp to this layer while we create the shaders for the flowers. Select the **Flower01** mesh. There are already three material slots, ready and assigned to the right parts of the mesh. Select the first slot and add a new material to it. Name it `Stigma`.

How to do it...

Let's see how to create the shaders for the flowers.

Creating the stigma

1. Add **Image Texture** and a **Texture Coordinate** node. Use the UV coordinates and load the `Margaret.jpg` file.

2. Plug **Image Texture** into **Diffuse BSDF** color input socket. Set the Diffuse **Roughness** to `1`.

3. Add an **RGB to BW** node (**Add | Converter**) and a **Bump** node. Connect **Image Texture** to the **RGB to BW** node and the output of the latter to the **Bump** node **Height** input. Finally, connect **Normal** of **Bump** to the **Normal** of **Diffuse BSDF** input.

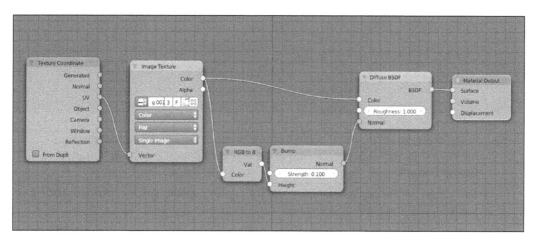

Creating the petal and the stem

1. Now add a new material to the second material slot and let's name it `Petal`.

2. In the **Material** node editor, add **Velvet BSDF** and a **Mix Shader** node. Mix **Velvet BSDF** with the default **Diffuse BSDF** with a velvet influence of 30%.

3. Add **Translucent BSDF** and another **Mix Shader** node. Mix the Diffuse-Velvet mix with **Translucent BSDF** with an influence of 60% for **Translucent BSDF**.

4. Set **Translucent BSDF** color to RGB 0.88, 0.88, 0.72. Also, set the Diffuse **Roughness** to `1`.

5. Add an **Image Texture** node and a **Texture Coordinate** node. Use UV coordinates and load the `Margaret.jpg` image.

6. Connect the Color output of **Image Texture** to the **Color** input socket of the **Diffuse BSDF** and the **Velvet BSDF**.

7. Apply the **Petal** material and the **Stigma** material to the second and first slot materials of each **Flower** mesh, respectively.

8. Select the **Flower 01** mesh and make the **Petal** material single user by clicking on the small number next to the name of the material. Rename the new material `YellowPetal`.

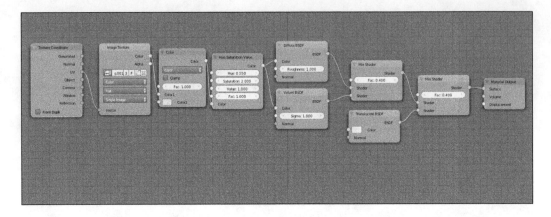

9. In the **Material** node editor, add a **Color Mix** node. Set the **Mode** to **Color** and the color 2 to RGB 0.5, 0.4, 0. Plug into the color 1 socket the **Color** output of **Image Texture**.

10. Add a **Hue Saturation Value** node, place it between **Color Mix** and **Diffuse BSDF** and **Velvet BSDF** and set the **Saturation** value to 2.

11. In the third material slot, create a new material and name it `Stem`. Change **Diffuse BSDF** color to a dark green and put the same material in the third material slot of each flower mesh.

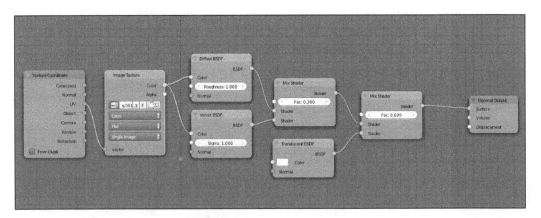

How it works

The materials we created in this recipe are quite simple. We saw how in some situations we can use a color texture as a bump effectively, by just converting it to black and white as we did for the **Stigma** material. We also used **Velvet BSDF** for the first time. As the name says, this BSDF is really well suited to create cloth-like materials. The sigma value changes the amount of shine on the material. In this case, it is really useful to give a delicate, silky look to our petals.

There's more

It is always important to keep in mind the detail that we want to give to a certain object. The mesh that we used for the flowers is quite simple, but in our scene, they will be seen from a very long distance. It would be quite useless to use a super detailed mesh for something that is barely visible, as it would only result in increased render times and memory consumption without any real gain in quality. The same argument goes for the stem material as it is almost impossible to see.

This does not mean that we do not have to pay attention to detail, but when creating a complex scene, it is vital to keep things as optimized and simple as possible without sacrificing quality.

See also

> ▸ In case we need to create a super detailed scene of flowers, this tutorial is really useful: `http://www.blenderguru.com/videos/how-to-make-cherry-blossom-flowers/`

Creating the wood material for the table and the fence

The last material we will be dealing with in our scene is the wood of the table and the fence.

Getting ready

We saw how to create a parquet material in *Chapter 3, Creating an Interior Scene*, but this kind of wood is different. It is worn, and hence much less reflective. Let's see how we can deal with it. Let's move the sunlight back to the first layer and select the table mesh. Add a new material to it and name it `WoodPlanks`.

How to do it...

Let's see how to create the wood for the picnic table:

Creating the wooden planks

1. Add **Glossy BSDF** and a **Shader Mix** node. Mix **Glossy BSDF** with the default **Diffuse BSDF** and set the Glossy influence to 15%.

2. Change **Roughness** of **Diffuse BSDF** to 1 and **Glossy BSDF** distribution model to GGX.

3. Add an **Image Texture** node and a **Texture Coordinate** node. Use UV coordinates and load the WoodPlanks.jpg texture.

4. Connect **Image Texture** to the Color input sockets of **Diffuse BSDF** and **Glossy BSDF**.

5. Add **RGB to BW** and an **RGB Curves** node and put them between the **Image Texture** node and **Glossy BSDF** with **RGB to BW** before **RGB Curves**.

6. Lower the upper-right point of the **RGB Curves** node and add another point in the middle, and lower it down a bit as shown in the figure.

7. Add a **Bump** node. Connect the **RGB to BW** output to **Height** of the **Bump** node input and then connect the output of **Normal** to the **Normal** inputs of **Diffuse BSDF** and **Glossy BSDF**. Set the **Strength** to 0.010.

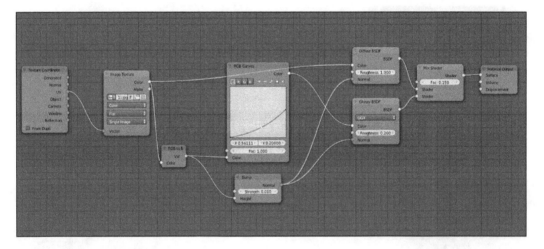

Creating the wooden poles

1. Select the fence mesh and add a new material slot and a new material to it. Name it WoodPole.

2. Add **Glossy BSDF** and mix it with the default **Diffuse BSDF** with an influence of 30% for **Diffuse BSDF**.

3. Set the **Glossy Distribution Model** to GGX and **Roughness** of **Diffuse BSDF** to 1.

4. Add an **Image Texture** node and a **Texture Coordinate** node. Use UV coordinates and load the WoodRough.jpg image. Connect the **Image Texture** node to the **Color** input socket of **Diffuse BSDF**.

5. Duplicate the **Image Texture** node and make the texture single user. Load the WoodRough_BUMP.png file.

6. Add a **Bump** node and plug in its height and input the WoodRough.png image texture. Set **Strength** to 0.080 and connect the output of **Normal** to the **Normal** input sockets of **Diffuse BSDF** and **Glossy BSDF**.

7. Duplicate the **Image Texture** node and make the texture single user again. Load the WoodRough_SPEC.png file and connect the texture to the **Color** input of the **Glossy BSDF** node.

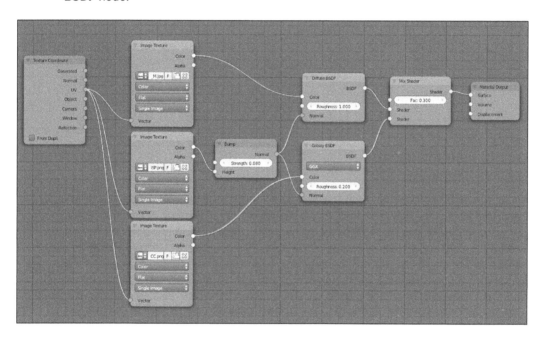

Creating the wooden poles ends

1. In material slot number three, select the **WoodPoles** material from the drop-down menu. Make it single user and rename it WoodPolesEnds.

2. In the **Material** node editor, we need to make every texture single user.

3. For the **Color**, **Bump**, and **Spec** textures, let's load the `WoodEnds.jpg`, `WoodEnds_BUMP.png`, and `WoodEnds_SPEC.png` files, respectively.

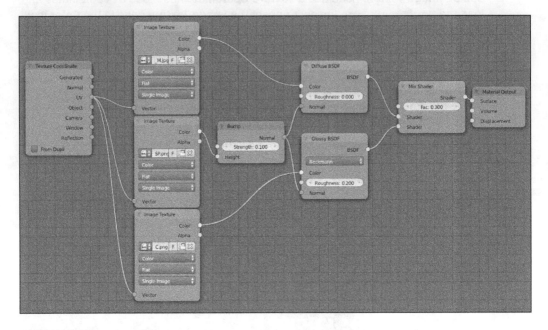

How it works...

Again, the materials we created in this recipe are pretty simple node setups. What is really important here is the way the mesh was unwrapped that allowed us to give the right look to our wooden planks and poles. With the wood poles, we also used two different materials, one for the pole and one for the ends of the poles. We could have reached the same result using maps to distribute different node groups within the same material along the mesh, but sometimes the method we used is now faster and just as effective. We again used a black and white version of the color map as a bump map and this time also as a specular map. We also adjusted the specular intensity using an **RBG Curves** node to darken the image a bit.

There's more...

Using **Image Textures** is not the only way of creating wood. Even though cycles does not have an integrated wood procedural texture yet, it is possible to use the other procedural texture and tweak them a bit to obtain really convincing materials.

See also

In the `AdditionalMaterial.blend` file, there is a procedural wood material completely made using procedural textures. Check it out!

Giving final touches to the image using render passes

Our image is almost ready. We just need a couple of settings for the final render and do some compositing to enhance the final effect.

Getting ready

Before we start, let's add some **DOF** to the scene. Go to the **Camera** settings and set the **DOF** size to 0.0125 and **Blades** to 6.000. We want the area around the tree to be in focus, so set **Distance** accordingly.

Now, let's go to the **Render Layers** menu and in the **Passes** panel, let's activate the **Shadow** and **Environment** passes. Finally, in the **Render** settings, let's set the **Render** samples to 300 and the rest of the settings as shown in the following screenshot. Remember to activate the **Transparent** option in the **Film** panel. Now let's render the image by hitting *F12* or the **Render** button. When the image is ready, move to the **Compositing** node editor and activate the **Use** nodes.

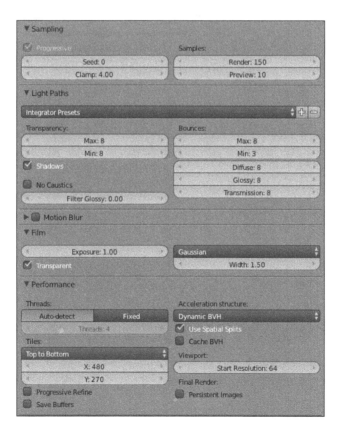

Remember that you can check the **Backdrop** option and use a **Viewer** node (**Add | Output**) to see the compositing result in the background.

How to do it...

Let's see how to give the final touch to our image.

Adding the background and a bloom effect

1. Add a **Mix** node (**Add | Color**) and connect the **Image** output of **Render Layers** to the second **Image** input. Connect the **Environment** output from the **Render Layers** node to the first one. Connect the **Alpha** output from **Render Layers** into the **Fac** input of the **Mix** node. Label the **Mix** node bgPicture.

2. Add a **Hue Saturation Value** node and place it between the **Mix** node and the **Environment** output of the **Render Layers** node. Set the HSV to 0.5, 0.9, 0.75.

3. Add a **Dilate/Erode** node and plug into it the **Alpha** layer from the **Render Layer** node. Set **Mode** to Feather and **Distance** to -7. Add an **Invert** node (**Add | Color**) and place it after the **Dilate/Erode** node. Add a **Mix** node and plug the **Invert** output into the **Fac** value. Label the **Mix** node BloomMASK.

4. Set the image 1 **Color** to black and plug the **Alpha** layer from **Render Layers** into the image 2 input. Add another **Mix** node and set the **Mode** to **Add**. Plug the output of **BloomMASK** into the **Fac** input.

5. Plug the output of the **bgPicture** node into the image 1 input and the **Environment** layer into the image 2 input.

6. Add a frame, label it AddBG, and place all the nodes we just created inside it.

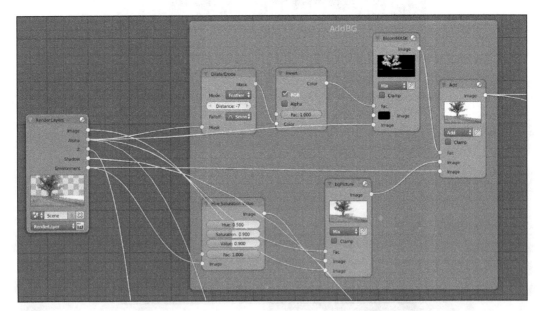

Creating a blur mask for the horizon

1. Add a **Normalize** node (**Add | Vector**) and a **ColorRamp** node. Connect the **Z** layer from the **Render Layers** node to the **Normalize** input and then connect the **Normalize** output to the **ColorRamp** node. Move the black color stop of **ColorRamp** to the right, so that it's almost at the center of the ramp.

2. Add a **Mix** node and connect the color output of **ColorRamp** to the image 2 input. Also, connect the **Alpha** layer to **Fac** input and set the image 1 **Color** to black.

3. Add a **Box Mask** node (**Add | Matte**) and a **Mix** node. Connect the **Mask** output to the **Fac** input and the previous **Mix** output to the image 1 input. Set the image 2 **Color** to black.

4. Set the **Box Mask** position of **X** to 0.500 and that of **Y** to 0.720 and **Width** and **Height** (**Size**) to 1.073 and 0.390. Also set **Rotation** to -1.400.

5. Add a **Blur** node (**Add | Filter**) and place it between the **Box Mask** and **Mix** nodes. Set **Type** to Fast Gaussian and the intensity to **X**: 15 and **Y**: 50.

6. Add a **Frame** node, label it HorizonMask, and place all the nodes we just created inside it.

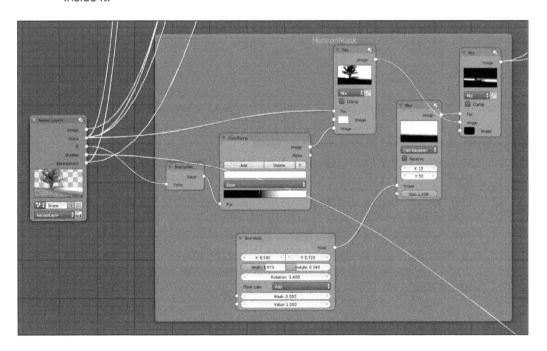

7. Add a **Mix** node and set **Mode** to Mix. Connect the image output of the last **Add** node of the **AddBG** frame to the image 1 input and the image output of the last **Mix** node of the **HorizonMask** frame to the **Fac** input.

8. Copy the **Mix** node and plug the image output of the last **Mix** node to both the image inputs and the image output of the last **Mix** node of **HorizonMask** into the **Fac** value.

9. Add a **Blur** node, set **Type** to `Fast Gaussian` and strength to XY 20, 20. Place it before the image 2 input of the last **Mix** node. Label the **Mix** node `ImageBG_Output`.

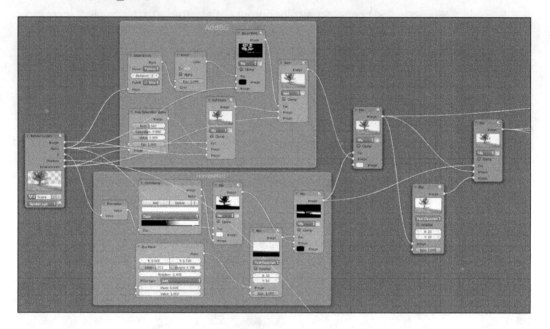

Creating masks for color correction

1. Add an **RGB to BW** node and connect the **Shadow** layer from the **Render Layers** node to it.

2. Add an **Ellipse** mask and a **Blur** node. Connect the mask to the **Blur** node and set the node **Type** to `Fast Gaussian` and intensity to **X**: `723`, **Y**: `200`. Also, set the **Box Mask** position to **X**: `1`, **Y**: `1` and **Size** to **Width**: `0.800`, **Height**: `0.82`.

3. Add a **Mix** node and set **Mode** to **Add**. Connect the **Blur** node output to both the **Fac** and the image 1 input. Connect the **RGB to BW** node output to the image 2 input.

4. Add a frame and label it `LigthenMASK`. Place all the nodes we just created, except the **RGB to BW** one, inside the frame.

5. Copy the frame and the nodes inside it. Change the label to `DarkenMASK`.

6. In the **Ellipse** mask settings, change **Position** to **X**: `-0.150`, **Y**: `0.800` and **Size** to **Width**: `0.800`, **Height**: `0.700`.

7. Change the blur intensity to **X**: `500`, **Y**: `200`.

8. Add an **Invert** node (**Add** | **Color**) and place it after the **RGB to BW** node.

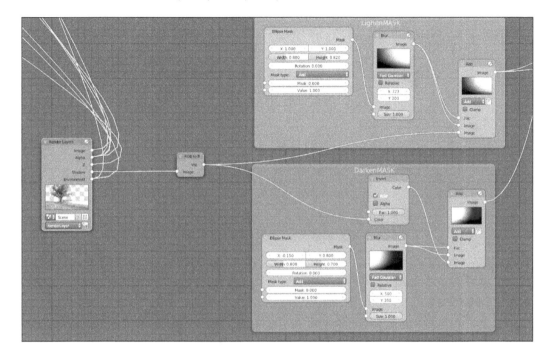

9. Add a **Color Balance** node (**Add** | **Color**) and set **Lift**, **Gamma**, and **Gain** all slightly cooler. Also, make **Gain** a bit darker. (that is, set Lift to RGB: 0.995, 0.975, 1; Gamma to RGB: 1.045, 0.99, 1.12; Gain to RGB: 0.86, 0.87, 0.94).

10. Connect the **ImageBG_Output** node to the **Color Balance** node. Add another **Mix** node and plug the **ImageBG_Output** node into the image 1 input and **Color Balance** into the image 2 input. Finally, plug the last **Add** node of image output **DarkenMASK** into the **Fac** input.

11. Copy the **Mix** node and change its **Mode** to **Add**. Plug the previous **Mix** node into the image 1 input and the last **Add** node image output of **LightenMASK** into the **Fac** input. Set the image 2 **Color** to RGB: 0.42, 0.26, 0.15. Label the **Add** node `MaskCorrection`.

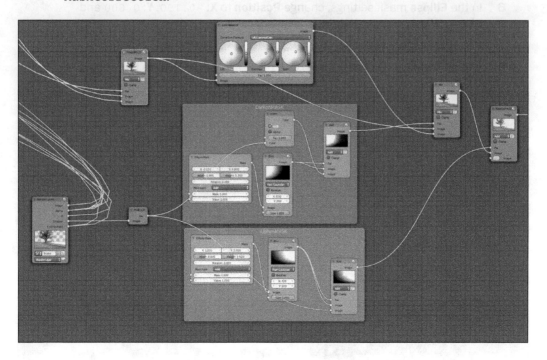

Final touches

1. Add a **Hue Saturation Value** node and place it after the **MaskCorrection** node. Set **Saturation** to `0.900`.

2. Add a **Glare** node (**Add | Filter**) after the **HSV** node and set **Mode** to `Fog Glow`. Set **Threshold** to `0.900` and **Size** to `9.00`.

3. Add a **Mix** node and plug the **Glare** node into the image 1 input and **ImageBG_Output** into the image 2 input. Set **Fac** to `0.400`.

4. Add a **Lens Distorsion** node after the **Mix** node and check the **Fit** option. Set **Distort** to `0.005` and **Dispersion** to `0.007`.

How it works...

Let's analyze what we did step by step.

Adding the background and a bloom effect

Here, we composited the background into the image. By checking the **Transparent** option, the background is rendered as an alpha channel. We also activated the **Environment** layer so that we have the background on a separate level. We used a **Dilate/Erode** node to shrink the **Alpha** mask of the image and create a bloom effect around the edges of the objects in our scene.

Creating a blur mask for the horizon

Here, we created a mask for the horizon and used it to better blend the edge between the sea and the sky. We could also use it to add some atmospheric fog. Using the **Alpha** pass and **Color Ramp**, we tweaked the look of the Z-pass. Then, using **Box Mask**, we excluded the parts we didn't need, obtaining a mask we could use to limit our operations to the horizon. We could then blur it and change its color.

Creating masks for color correction

In this part, we created two complementary masks to correctly color the image in certain areas. The target was to have a warmer color coming from the right, and a cooler one from the left. We used an Ellipse mask to set the **Rough** masks. Since the colors come from the light, we wanted the warmer color to only affect the parts of the objects that are directly hit by the sun. To achieve this effect, we used the **Shadow** pass. Once we had the two masks, we could tweak the colors as we wanted.

Final touches

In this final part, we performed operations for the colors and look of the image. We decreased the saturation and added a bit of a fog glow to enhance the look of the render. We then used a mix node to decrease the effect of the nodes we added until now, mixing the edited image with the original one (just with the background added). In the end, we used a lens distortion to add a slight dispersion effect. It is important to not overdo this, but a really delicate dispersion can add a lot of realism to the render.

There's more...

Compositing offers us an endless amount of possibilities to tweak our image. It is really useful to be able to make changes to the look of our render without actually having to re-render the image. Feel free to experiment with the different passes that Cycles offers us and see what they look like, using the knowledge gained in this recipe. You will be amazed by the possibilities available! In the next three chapters, we will learn more techniques, even about compositing!

See also

- In this tutorial, we can learn an alternative way of producing a Z-pass for use in compositing: `http://cgcookie.com/blender/2013/03/11/creating-mist-blender-cycles-z-depth/`

5
Creating a Cartoonish Scene

In this chapter, we will cover the following recipes in detail:

- ▸ Setting up the environment and lighting
- ▸ Creating skin, teeth, and other body parts
- ▸ Creating the hair material
- ▸ Creating the dress material
- ▸ Compositing the scene

Introduction

Although **Cycles** is a render engine which uses accurate lighting and material system, it can also provide great cartoon looks. We just have to know how to tweak the materials and the lighting. Let's see how in this chapter!

Setting up the environment and lighting

The first thing that we will do is setting up the lighting. We will be using a combination of the sunlight and environment lighting.

Getting ready

Let's open the `chapter05_empty.blend` file. As you can see, this time the interface is slightly different than usual. Due to the nature of the image, a vertical layout should be better for this particular scene. We will start by setting up the lighting and the materials for the environment.

How to do it...

To create the various materials, we will be performing the following steps:

Lighting and render settings

1. Add a **Sun** light and place it behind the camera. The direction has to be similar to the camera's, but the angle to the ground shall be bigger.

2. Set **Color** to RGB 1, 0.98, 0.9 and the **Strength** value to 3.500.

3. Make sure that the Shadows are active and set the **Size** value to 0.050.

4. Go to the **World** tab and set **Color** to **Sky Texture**. Set the sphere lighting so that it comes from the top left, as shown in the following screenshot. In case we want to be really precise with this, we can use the Sun Position plugin that we used in *Chapter 4, Creating an Exterior Scene*.

5. Set the **Strength** value to 1.300.

6. Activate the **Ambient Occlusion** option and set the **Factor** value to 0.25.

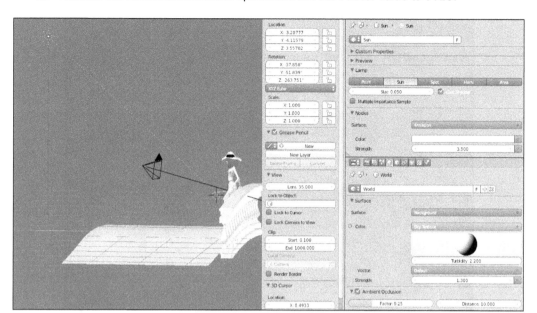

7. Let's go to the **Render** panel now.

8. In the **Sampling** panel, set the **Clamp** value to 4.00. The number of samples for the final render should not be less than **600** samples, while **50** samples will be fine for the preview.

9. In the **Film** panel, activate the **Transparent** option and set the **Exposure** value to 1.30.

10. Set the **Light Paths** panel as shown in the following screenshot:

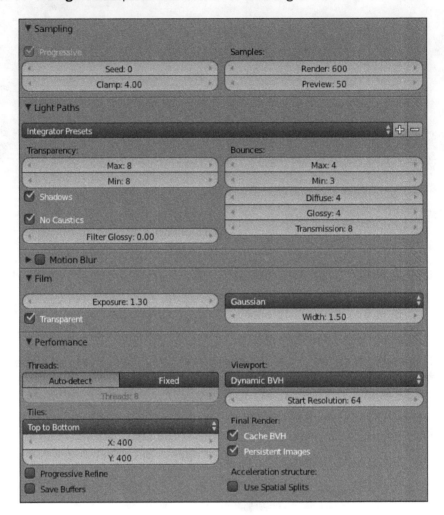

Sea

1. Select the **Sea** mesh and add a new material to it. Name it Sea.

2. In the material node editor, delete the default **Diffuse BSDF** node and add a **Glossy BSDF** node. Set the **Roughness** value to 0.020.

3. Add an **Image Texture** node and a **Texture coordinate** node. Load the SkyRefs.jpg file. For this texture, we will use the **Reflection** coordinates.

4. Add a **Mapping** node and place it between the SkyRefs texture and the **Texture Coordinate** node. Set the **Location** value to XYZ 1.7, 0, 0.

5. Add a **Gamma** node and place it after the SkyRefs texture. Set the **Gamma** value to 1.200.

6. Add a Color **Mix** node and connect the **Gamma** node to its **Color2** socket. Set the **Color1** value to 0.03, 0.42, 0.61. Leave the mode to **Mix** and set the **Fac** value to `0.500`. Connect the **Color** output to the **Color** input socket of **Glossy BSDF**.

7. Add a **Noise Texture** node and set the **Scale** value to `50.000`, **Detail** to `2.000`, and **Distortion** to `1.000`.

8. Duplicate the **Noise Texture** node and change the **Scale** value of the new node to `200.000`. Mix the two **Noise Texture** nodes with a Color **Mix** node. Leave the mode to **Mix** and set the influence of the first **Noise Texture** node (**Scale** is `50.000`) to 70 percent.

9. Add a **Voronoi Texture** node and set the **Scale** value to `40.000`. Leave the mode to **Intensity** and mix it with the previous two textures using a Color **Mix** node in the **Add** mode, **Fac** is `0.500`. Remember to plug the **Voronoi Texture** node into the **Color2** socket.

10. Add a **Wave Texture** node. Set the **Scale** value to `7.000`, the **Distortion** value to `15.000`, **Detail** to `50.000`, and the **Detail Scale** value to `2.000`. Mix it with the previous textures using a Color **Mix** node in the **Mix** mode, with **Wave Texture** influence of 30 percent.

11. Connect the last Color **Mix** node to the **Displacement** socket of the **Material Output** node.

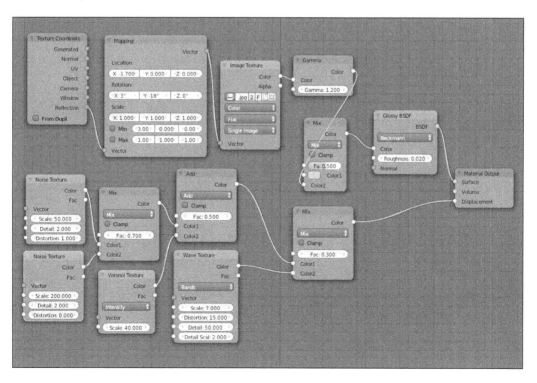

Floor

1. Select the **Floor** mesh and add a new material named **Floor** to it.

2. Add a **Toon BSDF** node and mix it with the default **Diffuse BSDF** node using a **Mix Shader** node.

3. Set the **Toon BSDF** mode to **Glossy**, the **Size** value to 0.225, and the **Smooth** value to 0.100.

4. Add a **Fresnel** node and connect it to the **Fac** value of **Mix Shader**. Set the **IOR** value to 1.900.

5. Add an **Image Texture** node and a **Texture Coordinate** node. Load the ChessTiles_COLOR.png file and use the **UV** coordinates for it. Add a **Bright/Contrast** node and place it after the **Image Texture** node. Set the **Contrast** value to -0.040 and connect the **Color** output to the **Color** input of **Diffuse BSDF**.

6. Add a **Voronoi Texture** node, and set the mode to **Cells** from the drop-down menu. Also, set the **Scale** value to 750.000.

7. After that, add a Color **Mix** node and connect the **Voronoi Texture** node to the **Color1** input. Set the **Color2** value to RGB 0.7, 0.7, 0.7. Leave the mode to **Mix** and set the **Fac** value to 0.350. Finally, connect the **Color** output to the **Color** input of the Glossy **Toon BSDF**.

8. Duplicate the **Image Texture** node and make it single user by clicking on the small number next to the file path. Load the ChessTiles_DISP.png file and connect the **Color** output into the first **Value** socket of a **Multiply** node in the **Multiply** mode. Set the second **Value** to 0.400 and connect the node to the **Displacement** socket of the **Material Output** node.

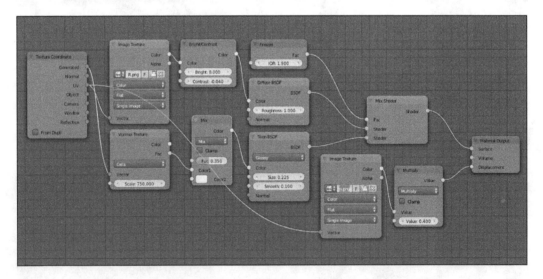

Balustrade

1. Select the **Balustrade** mesh and add a new material named **Balustrade** to it.

2. Add a **Toon BSDF** node and mix it with the default **Diffuse BSDF** node, with an influence of 30 percent for the **Toon BSDF** node.

3. Set the **Roughness** value of **Diffuse BSDF** to 1 and mode of the **Toon BSDF** node to **Glossy**. Also, set the **Size** and **Smooth** value to 0.400.

4. Add an **Image Texture** node and a **Texture Coordinate** node. Load the Balustrade.jpg file and use the **UV** coordinates. Plug the **Color** output of the texture into a **Gamma** node and set the **Gamma** value to 1.200. Finally, connect the **Gamma** node into the **Color** input socket of **Diffuse BSDF**.

5. Add a **Mapping** node and place it between the **Texture Coordinate** and **Image Texture** nodes. Set the **Scale** value to XYZ 15, 15, 15.

6. Duplicate the **Image Texture** node and make the texture single user. Load the Balustrade_SPEC.png file, and connect the **Color** output into the **Color** input of **Toon BSDF** with the **Glossy** mode.

7. Duplicate the **Image Texture** node again, make it single user, and load the Balustrade_DISP.png file. Add a **Bump** node and connect the texture to the **Bump** node's **Height** input socket.

8. Set the **Strength** value of **Bump** to 0.100. Connect the **Normal** output to the **Normal** input of the **Diffuse BSDF** and **Toon BSDF** nodes.

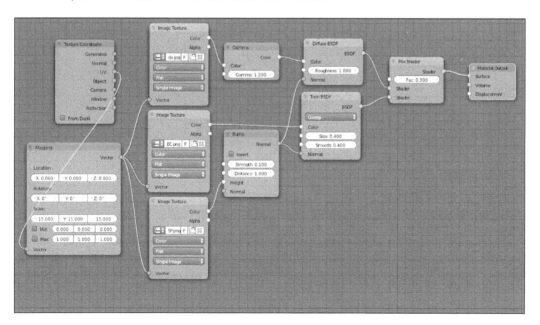

Dust Particles

1. Select the **Dust** mesh and add a new material named Dust.

2. Mix the default **Diffuse BSDF** node with a **Transparent BSDF** node using a **Mix Shader** node. Set the **Color** value of **Diffuse BSDF** to RGB 1, 0.81, 0.53.

3. Add a **Noise Texture** node and set the **Scale** value to 2.000, the **Detail** value to 16.000, and the **Distortion** value to 5.800. Plug the **Fac** output into a **ColorRamp** node and set the color stops as shown in the following screenshot. Finally, plug the **Color** output of **ColorRamp** into the **Fac** input of **Mix Shader**.

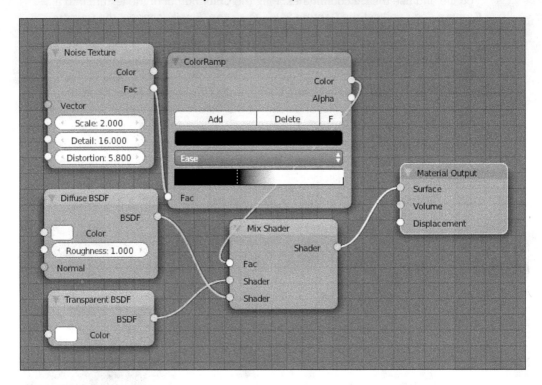

How it works...

In this previous sections, we used some new interesting techniques.

First of all, we can see the **Light Paths** settings for the rendering are quite low. This is because we do not need a strong Global Illumination for the kind of cartoon look we are going for. Also, we deactivated caustics for the same reason. This will require some further tweaks in some of the materials that we will be creating, especially for the transparent ones; but it will allow us to optimize the scene a lot.

Something quite interesting to talk about is how we created the sea material. First of all, we used a simple plane and generated the sea surface using only procedural textures. Moreover, we mapped a texture using the reflections coordinates. This is a great way to fake reflections over a surface. Water is usually almost perfectly transparent and its color is given by the environment such as the sky and the bottom of the sea. In our scene, we do not have much to give a proper color to the sea; but using this technique we could easily fake this. The peculiarity of the reflections coordinates is that the textures change depending on the angle from which we are looking at the mesh, and it would look exactly like a reflective surface. Of course, this is not as accurate as real reflections, but it is perfect for our scene.

Here, we are using the Toon BSDF for the first time. This is particularly good for obtaining a cartoon shading style. We can adjust the **Roughness** value of the specularity changing the **Size** value, while the **Smooth** value sets the overall smoothness of the highlights. There is the possibility to also use this Shader as a diffuse value, but it still gives some problem with the edges between light and shadow as it is under development. Furthermore, we are not aiming for a totally toony style. So, we do not want to overdo the effect.

Finally, for the dust particles, we used a single mesh instanced by a particles system. If we would like to change the size or the position of the dust particles, it would be enough to select the emitter cube and go to the **Particles** menu. There, we can find the settings concerning the size, rotation, and so on.

There's more...

The nice thing about using a procedurally-generated sea is that it is quite easy to animate if needed, unlike a sea that uses image textures. It will be enough to add a **Mapping** node for the textures and animate the rotation or Position values. To insert **keyframes**, it is enough to press the *I* key while the cursor is over the value that we want to keyframe.

Another alternative is to use the ocean modifier. This is a much more accurate way of creating sea animations. But, it is also much more demanding in terms of resources as it will create a lot of polygons. Creating a big water surface with this method can be quite problematic for certain hardware.

Creating skin, teeth, and other body parts

In this recipe, we are going to create some organic toony-style materials such as skin and teeth.

Getting ready

It is now time to set the various materials for the body of the girl. Select the mesh named **Head**, and add a new material to it, naming it `skin`. It is a good idea to solo the mesh to have a faster viewport real-time preview.

How to do it...

To create the materials of this recipe, perform the following steps:

1. Add a **Translucent BSDF** node and mix it with the default **Diffuse BSDF** node using a **Mix Shader** node. Set the **Roughness** value of **Diffuse BSDF** to 1.000. Label the **Mix Shader** node as Dermal.

2. Add a **Layer Weight** node by navigating to **Add menu | Input**, and connect the **Fresnel** output into the **Fac** input of the **Mix** node. Set the **Blend** value to 0.550.

3. Add an **Image Texture** node and a **Texture coordinate** node. In the **Image Texture** node, load the body_unscatter.jpg file and use the **UV** coordinates.

4. Add a Color **Mix** node and plug the texture into the **Color1** socket. Change the mode to **Color** and the **Fac** value to 0.250. Set the **Color2** value to RGB 1, 0.52, 0.38. Finally, plug the **Color** output into the **Color** input of **Diffuse BSDF**.

5. Duplicate the **Image Texture** node and the Color **Mix** node. Make the texture single user and load the body_subder.jpg file. Also, set the Color **Mix** node's **Fac** to 0.500 and the **Color2** value to RGB 1, 0.44, 0.41. Connect the **Color** output into the **Color** input socket of **Translucent BSDF**.

6. Add a **Toon BSDF** node and a **Glossy BSDF** node, and mix them using a **Mix Shader** node. Label the **Mix** node as Specular.

7. In the **Toon BSDF** node, set the type to **Glossy** in the drop-down menu. Then set the **Size** value to 0.300 and the **Smooth** value to **0.250**. Also, set the **Color** value to RGB 0.35, 0.33, 0.3. In the **Glossy BSDF** node, set the **Roughness** value to 0.050 and the **Color** value to RGB 0.6, 0.6, 0.6.

8. Add another **Mix Shader** node and plug the **Dermal** node into the first socket and the **Specular** node into the second socket. Label it Skin.

9. Add an **Attribute** node and type Nails in the **Name** field. Copy one of the **Image Texture** nodes and make the texture single user. Load the body_LIPS.jpg file into it. Mix the two nodes with a Color **Mix** node. Set the mode to **Add** and the **Fac** value to 1.000. Plug the **Color** output of the **Attribute** node into the **Color2** input and the **Color** output of **Image Texture** into the **Color1** input. Label the node as Lips_Nails.

10. Plug the **Lips_Nails** node's **Color** output into the **Fac** input of the **Dermal** and **Skin** nodes.

11. Add a **ColorRamp** node and place it before the **Skin** node's **Fac** input. Set the colors as shown in the following screenshot.

12. Add two Color **Mix** nodes and place them between the **Diffuse BSDF** and **Translucent BSDF** nodes and their **Color** inputs. Set them both to **Mix** and plug the previous **Color** information into the **Color1** socket and the output from the **Lips_Nails** node into the **Fac** input.

13. Set the **Color2** value to RGB 1, 0, 0.

14. Add a **Noise Texture** node and use the generated coordinates for it. Set the **Scale** value to `250.000`.

15. Add a **Bump** node and plug the **Fac** output of the **Noise Texture** node into its **Height** input. Then plug the **Normal** output into the **Normal** input of the **Diffuse BSDF, Toon BSDF, Glossy BSDF**, and **Translucent BSDF** nodes.

16. Set the **Strength** value of the **Bump** node to `0.020`.

17. Apply the skin material to the **Body** and **Legs** meshes.

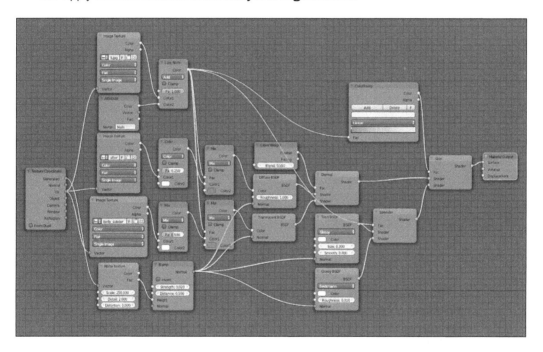

18. In the **Head** mesh, add a new material in the second material slot, and name it `Teeth`.

19. Add a **Translucent BSDF** node and mix it with the default **Diffuse BSDF** node using a **Mix Shader** node. Set the **Fac** value to `0.300`.

20. Set the **Color** value of **Translucent BSDF** to RGB 0.8, 0.62, 0.55 and the **Color** value of **Diffuse BSDF** to RGB 1, 0.92, 0.89.

21. Add a **Glossy BSDF** node and mix it with the previous BSDFs mix using another **Mix Shader** node.

22. Set the **Roughness** value of **Glossy BSDF** to **0.005** and the **Color** value to RGB 0.8, 0.8, 0.8.

23. Add a **Fresnel** node and plug the **Fac** output into the **Fac** input of the last **Mix Shader** node. Set the **IOR** value to `1.800`.

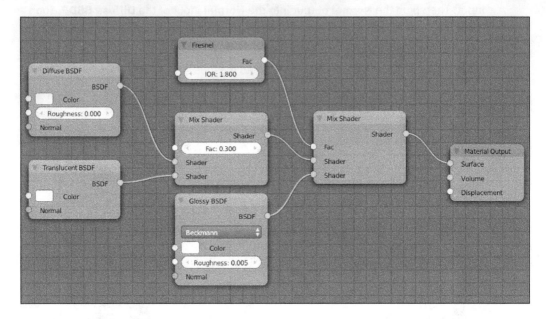

24. Select the **Eye.R** mesh and add a new material into the first material slot. Name it `Eye`.

25. Add a **Translucent BSDF** node and mix it with the default **Diffuse BSDF** node with a **Mix Shader** node. Set the **Diffuse BSDF** node's **Color** to Pure White and the **Roughness** value to `1.000`. Then set the **Color** value of **Translucent BSDF** to RGB 0.8, 0.1, 0.

26. Add a **Layer Weight** node, and plug the **Facing** output into the **Fac** input of **Mix Shader**. Set the **Blend** value to `0.850`.

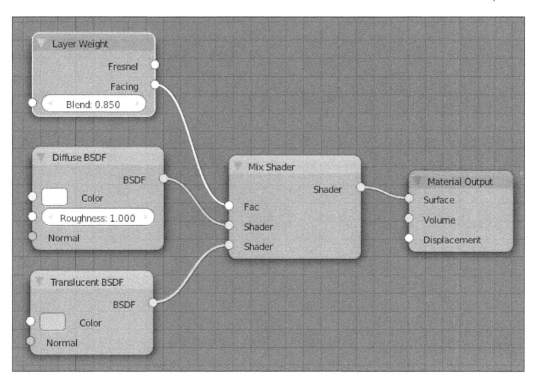

27. Add a new material into the second material slot and name it Iris.

28. Add an **Image Texture** node and a **Texture Coordinate** node. Load the eye.png file and use the **UV** coordinates.

29. Set the **Roughness** value of **Diffuse BSDF** to 1.000.

30. Add a new material in the third material slot and name it Pupil. For this Shader, set the **Diffuse BSDF** node's **Color** to Pure Black.

31. Add a material into the fourth material slot and name it Cornea.

32. Delete the **Diffuse BSDF** node and add a **Glass BSDF** node and a **Glossy BSDF** node. Mix them using a **Mix Shader** node. Add a **Fresnel** node and plug it into the **Fac** value of the **Mix Shader** node. Set the **IOR** value to 1.400.

33. Add a **Transparent BSDF** node and mix it with the previous BSDFs mix using another **Mix Shader** node.

34. Add a **LightPath** node by navigating to **Add menu | Input**, and plug the **Is Shadow ray** socket into the **Fac** value of the **Mix Shader** node. Remember to plug the **Transparent BSDF** node into the second socket of the **Mix Shader** node.

35. Add a **Noise Texture** node and a **Bump** node. Plug the **Fac** output of **Noise Texture** into the **Height** input of the **Bump** node. Set the **Scale** value to 25.000 and the **Detail** value of **Noise Texture** to 0.000. Set the **Strength** value of the **Bump** node to 0.020.

36. Plug the **Normal** output of the **Bump** node into the **Normal** input of the **Glass BSDF** and **Glossy BSDF** nodes.

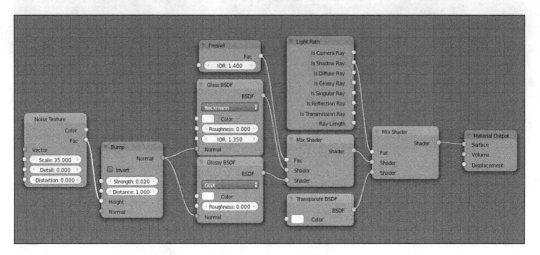

37. Select the **Eye.L** mesh and the **shift select the Eye.R** mesh so that the last one is active and the **Eye.L** mesh is selected. The active mesh will be outlined with a brighter orange line.

38. Press *Ctrl + L* and click on **Materials**.

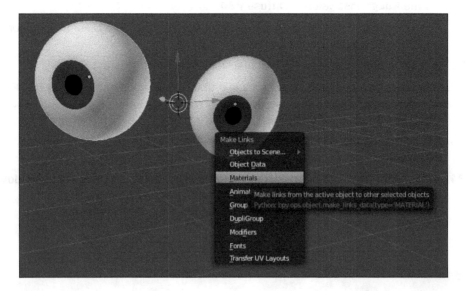

39. For the **Eyelashes.L** and **Eyelashes.R** meshes, use the node setup shown in the following screenshot:

How it works...

When creating computer graphics, we have to always keep in mind that when it is possible to fake something to make it easier and faster, it is a good idea to fake. This is true when creating realistic images and even more so when we are creating cartoon style images. Here, we have the possibility to achieve believable results and different styles without looking for perfect realism. We used this method a lot while creating the Shaders for the body of the girl. We did not aim for realism; on the other hand, we tried to achieve believable and captivating results using any trick and *cheating*, we could. Let's look in detail at what we did for each material.

Skin

Realistic skin uses **SubSurface Scattering** (**SSS**). This is quite a heavy Shader to compute, which is even more problematic in Cycles because at the moment it can only be achieved using CPU. As we said earlier, we are not aiming for realism but believability; so, we can use some tricks. As we have seen in *Chapter 4*, *Creating an Exterior Scene*, SSS is a Shader that lets the light enter an object and be scattered inside it. It takes into account the thickness of the object. This means that the scattering will be more visible where the mesh is thinner and it will become weaker where the is mesh getting thicker.

Let's take a look at our own hand, looking at it with a strong light behind it, preferably the Sun. We will notice that the scattering effect is stronger at the edges of our hand. Simplifying the concept behind SSS a lot, we can apply a translucent effect only at the edges of our mesh. Of course this will be cheating and it will not be a realistic and accurate skin, but it will do the job for the style we are aiming at in a fraction of the time. To achieve the effect, we used a layer weight to balance between Diffuse BDSF and Translucent BSDF. The **Facing** output gives a sharper edge than the **Fresnel** one. To obtain the specularity, we used a combination of a Glossy BSDF and a Toon BSDF.

Finally, we wanted to have a different kind of specularity on the lips and the nails. We used a combination of an image texture and vertex painting to obtain the map needed to mix the BSDFs.

Eye

Here, we used a technique similar to the one we used to create the skin, in order to obtain a fake SSS effect for the sclera. For the cornea, we used a combination of a Glass BSDF and a Glossy BSDF as we wanted the edges to be more reflective and less transparent. This is similar to what we did to create the fake SSS effect, but this time we used a **Fresnel** node in order to obtain a much smoother transition. We also got rid of the shadows using a **Light Path** node. Usually, it is a good idea to do this as shadows do not work so well in spaces so small as the eye. But, in this particular scene, it is really important as we are not using caustics and the shadows from the glass would be fully black.

There's more...

Remember that we can use nodes as the Color Ramp after a **Layer Weight** node or a **Fresnel** node, in order to further tweak the mixing of two BSDFs. We can, for example, make the transition sharper or smoother by moving the color stop. We can also change the colors themselves, so that we will always have a mix of the two BSDFs even at the two extremes. Also, remember that we can mix not only BSDFs, but also virtually whatever we want. Look at the following screenshot for reference:

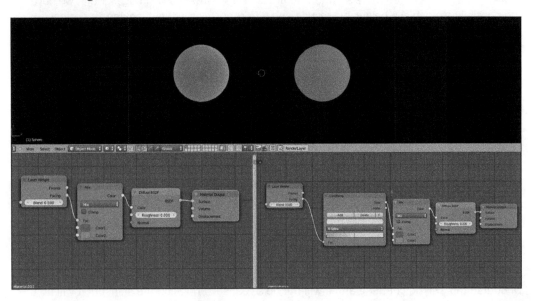

See also

On the Internet, there are a lot of different versions of fake SSS for Cycles. At the following link, you can find a version which used a more complex setup than the one we created. It is really good for studying!

```
http://www.blendswap.com/blends/view/56029http://www.blendswap.com/
blends/view/56029
```

Creating the hair material

It is now time to deal with hair. We are going to create a fairly realistic look for it, which will create a nice contrast with the rest of the materials of the scene.

Getting ready

Before we start, let's have a quick look at how to deal with hair particles in Blender and the options for Cycles. Let's select the **Hair** mesh and move to the **Modifiers** menu. We can see that there are three particles modifiers. As for any other modifier, we can deactivate the usage of the modifier during rendering by clicking on the camera button, or in the viewport by clicking on the eye button. Deactivating the **Viewport Visualization** option is really useful as having hair particles can be quite heavy. Also, doing so can help us make the viewport faster. To modify any other option, we have to go to the **Particles** menu. There, we can see that we have three different particle systems. A really important tab for the rendering is the **Render** tab. Here, we can choose the material we want to use for the hair.

Another really important thing is the **Steps** value. This value determines the number of segments into which every strand is divided. The value we enter is then elevated with a power of two. If this value is too low, our hair will look blocky and lack the organic look. On the other hand, it is important to remember that higher values will require higher rendering times. The **Step** value for the viewport is different and can be found in the **Display** panel. While it can be useful to set it a bit higher when tweaking the hair in order to see what is happening, it is a good idea to keep this value quite low in order to avoid making the viewport really slow and heavy. Finally, in the lower part of the menu, we will find the options regarding Cycles rendering that we explored in *Chapter 3, Creating an Interior Scene*.

How to do it...

To create the hair material perform the following steps:

1. In the **Render** tab, make sure that the **Steps** value is set to 7.

2. In the **Cycles Hair Rendering** tab, let's set the mode to **Accurate**. This option will work for any hair particle system in our scene, so we need to set it only once.

3. Change the **Shape** value to -0.60. In the **Thickness** panel, set the **Root** value to 0.09 and leave the **Tip** value at 0.00. Make sure that the **Close tip** option is active. We need to change these options for every particle system.

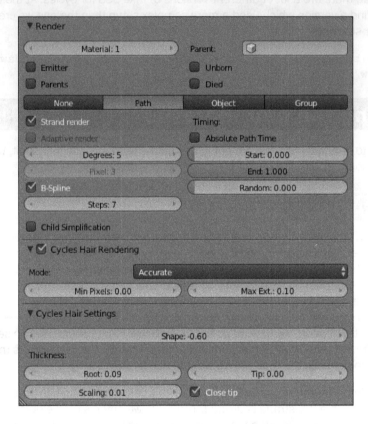

4. Let's move to the material node editor now. Add a **Glossy BSDF** node. Set **Color** to Pure White and the **Roughness** value to 0.005.

5. Duplicate the **Glossy BSDF** node and set the **Roughness** value to 0.09. Also, set the **Color** value to RGB 0.8, 0.65, 0.46. Add the two **Glossy BSDF** nodes using an **Add Shader** node.

6. Mix the output of the **Add Shader** node with the default **Diffuse BSDF** node using a **Mix Shader** node, with 30 percent of influence for the **Add Shader** node. Also, set the **Roughness** value to 1.000 of **Diffuse BSDF**.

7. Add a **Translucent BSDF** node and set the **Color** value to RGB 0.8, 0.57, 0.39. Mix it with the other **Mix Shader** node using another **Mix Shader** node, with 40 percent influence for the **Translucent BSDF** node.

8. Add a **Hair Info** node and a **ColorRamp** node. Connect the **Intercept** output of **Hair Info** into the **ColorRamp** node and set the **ColorRamp** node as shown in the following screenshot. Connect the **ColorRamp** node into the **Color** input of **Diffuse BSDF**.

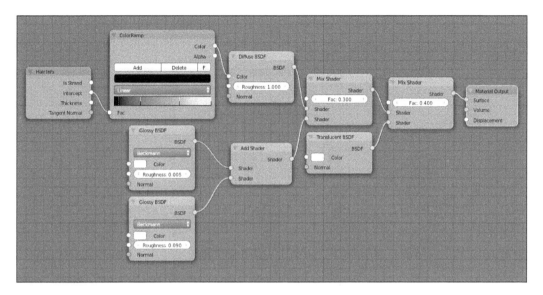

How it works...

The settings for the hair are the same as we saw in *Chapter 3*, *Creating an Interior Scene*. Here, we wanted the hair tip to be closed; so we left the **Close tip** option active. Also, the hair has to be much thinner, hence the value of 0.09 for **Root**.

For the material, using the **Hair Info** node is really important as it allows us to change the color along the length of the strand, using the **Intercept** output together with a **ColorRamp** node. We also used two Glossy BSDF with different **Roughness** values in order to obtain both the soft and sharp reflections over the hair surface. Finally, we have a Translucent BSDF to get the light to be scattered inside the hairs. Sometimes, it could be a good idea to use a black-and-white Color Ramp with the **Intercept** output from the **Hair Info** node in order to have a weaker translucency closer to the root of the hair. As in this scene we are not using caustics, the hair will be generally darker. So, we could leave a solid color for the Translucent BSDF.

We can create some really crazy things using the combination of a **Geometry** node and the **Hair Info** node. With some math, we can combine the **Tangent Normal** output from the **Hair Info** node with the **Parametric** info from the **Geometry** node, and use the result to mix different colors for our use. In the following screenshot, there is an example that shows how to use this method to create strange, colored reflections on the hair. Instead of a Color **Mix** node, we can even use a **ColorRamp** node to mix an even higher number of colors!

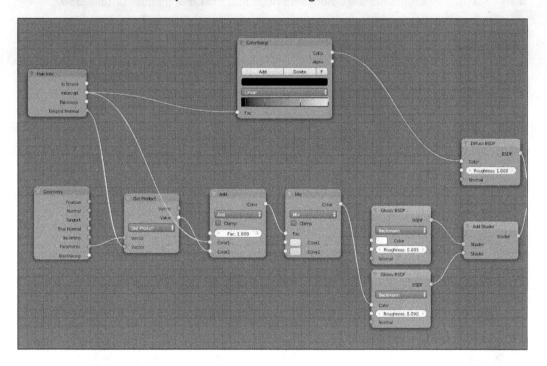

See also

On the **Blender Cookie** website, there is an astonishing tutorial on how to create realistic looking hair. It also covers the particles creation phase. It is not a free tutorial, but it is a great resource to know everything about creating hair in Cycles and Blender: http://cgcookie.com/blender/cgc-courses/styling-and-rendering-long-hair-with-blender-and-cycles/.

Creating the dress material

Let's now create the clothing of the girl in our scene. We will create different kinds of materials such as the fabric for the dress, the leather for the boots, and other kinds of materials for other accessories.

Getting ready

Let's start with the dress. Select the mesh named **Dress**, and add a new material to it. Name it `Dress` and go to the **Material Editor** node.

How to do it...

To create the dress material, we need to perform the following steps:

1. Delete the **Diffuse BSDF** node. Add a **Translucent BSDF** node and a **Velvet BSDF** node. Mix them using a **Mix Shader** node.

2. Set the **Translucent BSDF** node's **Color** to RGB 0.66, 1, 0.45 and the **Velvet BSDF** node's **Color** to a slightly darker green such as RGB 0.58, 1, 0.34. Set the **Velvet BSDF** node's **Sigma** value to `1.000`.

3. Add a **Toon BSDF** node and set it to the **Glossy** mode. Mix it to the previous two BSDFs using a **Mix Shader** node, and set its influence to 7.5 percent.

4. Set the **Color** of the **Toon BSDF** node with the **Glossy** mode to RGB 0.93, 0.96, 0.31; set the **Size** value to `0.200` and the **Smooth** value to `0.500`.

5. Add an **Image Texture** node and a **Texture Coordinate** node. Load the `Dress_BUMP.png` file and use the **UV** Coordinates.

6. Duplicate the **Image Texture** node and make the texture single user. Load the `Fabric.jpg` file. We will use **UV** Coordinates again.

7. Add a **Mapping** node by navigating to **Add menu | Vector**, and place it between the **Texture Coordinate** node and the **Image Texture** node with the `Fabric.jpg` file. In the **Mapping** node, set the **Scale** value to XYZ 18, 18, 18.

8. Add a **RGB to BW** node and place it after the Fabric **Image Texture** node. Mix the two **Image Texture** nodes with a Color **Mix** node, which connects the **Image Texture** node with the `Dress_BUMP.png` file to the **Color1** socket and the **RGB to BW** node (that is after the Fabric **Image Texture** node) to the **Color2** socket.

9. Set the mode to **Multiply** and the **Fac** value to `0.050`.

10. Add a **Bump** node and connect the **Color** output of the **Multiply** node into the **Height** input. Then, connect the **Bump** node's **Normal** output into the **Normal** input of every BSDF.

11. Set the **Strength** value to `0.125`.

12. Add a **ColorRamp** node and place it after the **RGB to BW** node of the Fabric **Image Texture** node. Set the color stops as shown in the following screenshot. Then, connect the **ColorRamp** node to the **Fac** value of the **Mix Shader** node of the **Translucent BSDF** and **Velvet BSDF** nodes.

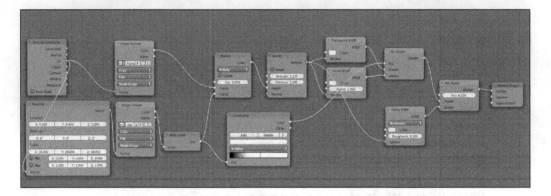

13. Select the **Hat** mesh and add a new material to it. Name it Hat.

14. Delete the default **Diffuse BSDF** node. Add a **Toon BSDF** node and a **Translucent BSDF** node. Set the **Toon BSDF** node's mode to **Diffuse**, the **Size** value to 0.500, and the **Smooth** value to 0.000. Also, set **Color** of both the **Toon BSDF** and **Translucent BSDF** nodes to RGB 0.64, 0.09, 0.

15. Mix the two BSDFs with a **Mix Shader** node and mix this previous node with another **Toon BSDF** node. This time, set the mode to **Glossy**, **Size** to 0.700, and **Smooth** to 0.200. Set the influence of the first mix to 30 percent for the **Translucent BSDF** node and at 20 percent for **Glossy** for the second mix.

16. Add a **Transparent BSDF** node and mix it with the last **Mix Shader** node, connecting the **Transparent BSDF** node to the first **Mix Shader** node socket. Label the node as Pattern.

17. Add an **Image Texture** node, a **Texture Coordinate** node, and a **Mapping** node. Load the Fabric.jpg file and use the **UV** Coordinates for it. Also, set the **Scale** value of the **Mapping** node to XYZ 2.7, 2.7, 2.7.

18. Add an **RGB to BW** node after the **Image Texture** node. Also, add a **Math** node by navigating to **Add menu | Convertor** and set it to **Multiply**. Connect the **RGB to BW** node into the first socket and set the second **Value** to 0.010. Finally, connect the **Math** node output into the **Displacement** input of the **Material Output** node.

19. Add a **ColorRamp** node and connect the **Image Texture** node with the Fabric.jpg file to its input. Set the color stops as shown in the following screenshot and connect the **ColorRamp** node to the Pattern **Mix Shader** node's **Fac** input.

20. In the second material slot, add a new material and name it `HatRibbon`. Delete the default **Diffuse BSDF** node and add a **Velvet BSDF** node. Set the **Color** value to RGB 0.3, 0.56, 0.07 and the **Sigma** value to `1.000`.

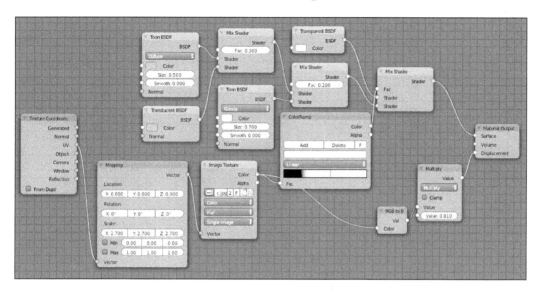

Boots

1. Select the mesh named **Boots**, and add a new material to it. Name it `Boots`.

2. Add a **Velvet BSDF** node and a **Glossy BSDF** node. Mix the **Velvet BSDF** node with the default **Diffuse BSDF** node, with 60 percent of influence for the **Velvet BSDF** node.

3. Change the **Diffuse BSDF** node's **Color** to RGB 0.09, 0.05, 0.02 and the **Roughness** value to `1.000`.

4. Change the **Velvet BSDF** node's **Color** to RGB 0.09, 0.05, 0.02 and the **Sigma** value to `0.800`.

5. Change the **Glossy BSDF** node's **Color** to RGB 0.17, 0.22, 0.26, and set the **Roughness** value to `0.400`.

6. Mix the **Glossy BSDF** node with the previous two BSDFs using a **Mix Shader** node. The influence of **Glossy BSDF** must be five percent.

7. Add a **Noise Texture** node and set the **Scale** value to `500.000`, leaving the other values as default. Add a **Math** node and connect the **Fac** output of the **Noise Texture** node into its first **Value** socket. Set the second **Value** to `0.025` and the mode to **Multiply**.

8. Connect the **Math** node to the **Displacement** socket of **Material Output**.

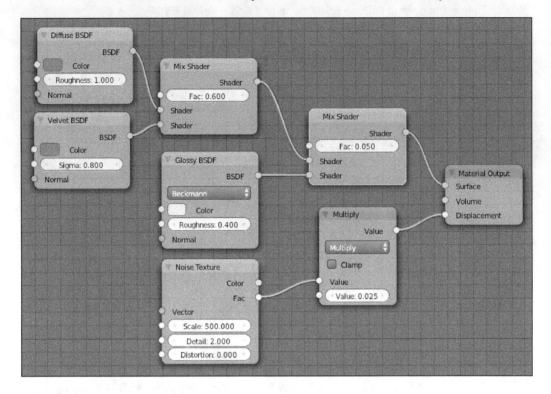

Foular

1. Select the mesh named **Foular** and add a new material to it, calling it Foular.

2. Delete the default **Diffuse BSDF** node. Add a **Translucent BSDF** node and a **Transparent BSDF** node. Set the **Translucent BSDF** node's **Color** to RGB 1, 0.36, 0.21, and set the **Transparent BSDF** node's **Color** to RGB 1, 0.36, 0.21.

3. Mix the two BSDFs using a **Mix Shader** node.

4. Add a **Layer Weight** node by navigating to **Add Menu | Inputs**, and connect the **Facing** output into the **Fac** socket of the **Mix Shader** node.

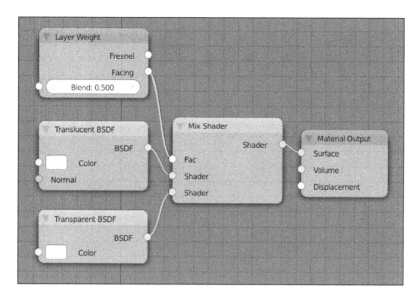

Belt

1. Select the **Belt** mesh and add a material named **LeatherBelt** to the first slot.

2. Here, we will just use the addition of two **Toon BSDF** nodes. One in the **Diffuse** mode with a **Size** value of 0.700 and the other one in the **Glossy** mode with a **Size** value of 0.100.

3. Set **Color** of the **Toon BSDF** node to RGB 0.2, 0.03, 0 for the **Diffuse** mode one and to RGB 0.27, 0.07, 0.01 for the **Glossy** mode one. Leave the **Smooth** value to 0.000 for the **Diffuse** mode one and change the **Glossy** mode one's value to 0.040.

4. Add a material to the second material slot and name it **Metal**.

5. Delete the default **Diffuse BSDF** node and add a **Toon BSDF** node. Set it to the **Glossy** mode and set **Color** to RGB 0.2, 0.2, 0.2. Also, set the **Size** value to `0.150` and the **Smooth** value to `0.030`.

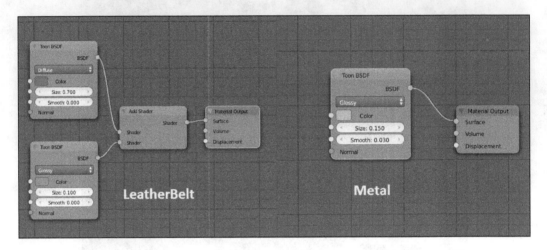

How it works...

In this recipe, we made big use of the Velvet BSDF, which is perfect for creating fabric-like materials. While creating the Hat and the Dress, we also used a pattern texture to drive the transparency or translucency of the material, in order to give the right look to the Shader. With the Hat for example, we wanted to achieve the look of a straw hat. So, we gave quite a large scale to the pattern and made the holes almost completely transparent. To achieve the right amount of transparency, we fine-tuned the texture using a **ColorRamp** node. We can use this technique to get many kinds of pattern over a surface, giving the illusion of the holes without actually having to model them.

The good thing is that this transparency works for shadows as well without any further work on the nodes. Remember that it is always a good idea to use a Diffuse BSDF to check the look of the textures over the surface of an object. It is likely that in future, a proper texture preview node will be implemented in Cycles. But right now, this method works really well. In the Hat and the Boots materials, we used **Displacement** instead of **Bump**, as it tends to give a stronger effect.

While **Bump** only gives the illusion of the bumpiness on a surface without actually changing the geometry, **Displacement** works on the geometry of the object itself. Right now, **Displacement** in Cycles is not finished as a local-surface subdivision function, for improving **Displacement** is still missing. Regardless of this, it already gives really good results in many cases.

To fine-tune the amount of displacement, we can use a **Math** node set to the **Multiply** mode. We plug the texture into the first socket and regulate the intensity with the second. A **Value** of 0.000 will mean no displacement, while 1.000 will make the texture work at 100 percent. We can even push the effect further by giving values higher than one. As in the other recipes, we used the Toon BSDF. This BSDF is really nice because it gives us fine-tuning over the specularity of the objects. While the normal Glossy BSDF only allows us to set the roughness of the reflections, here we can also change the size without actually affecting its roughness. Of course, the Toon BSDF is not suited for realistic results, but here it is perfect for our purpose.

There's more...

There is a technique that we can exploit for using displacement properly. This is not an efficient technique. This means we will not always be able to use it due to the fact that it is really hard on our hardware. Even then, it is a good workaround due to the lack of a dynamic subdivision of the meshes for displacement. To see how it works, let's open a new blend file and set the render engine to Cycles. Add a subdivision surface modifier to the default cube, set it to level four for both the viewport and render, and apply it. Add another subdivision surface and set it to a value such as **4** for the render. It is a good idea not to push the subdivision surface too much in the viewport, as it could be too much to handle for our hardware. Now, add a **Displacement** modifier and add a new texture inside it. As we can see in the following screenshot, the surface of the mesh has been displaced:

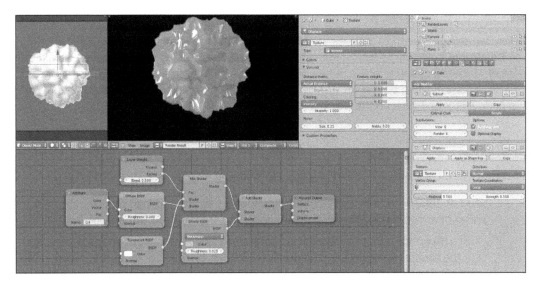

By clicking on the small Show Texture button next to the texture path, we can enter the **Texture** menu and choose what kind of texture we want to use for displacement. We can even use an image texture. Then, from the **Displacement** modifier, we can choose what kind of coordinates we want to use. It is good to repeat that this is not an efficient technique, and we need to have a lot of polygons to properly use this kind of displacement. A dynamic subdivision of the mesh would add more polygons only where needed, keeping the mesh much lighter. Anyway, it is one way to obtain real displacement while we wait for a proper dynamic subdivision for Cycles.

See also

The following thread on Blender Artist shows in detail how to obtain great results with the technique for displacement that we just learned: `http://www.blenderartists.org/forum/showthread.php?273033-Sculpting-with-UVs-and-displacements`.

Compositing the scene

The materials for our scene are ready, but we still need to make the final touches before we can call it ready. To do this, we will do some compositing.

Getting ready

Before we start, we need to activate the **Mist** layer in the **Layer** menu, which is right next to the **Rendering** menu. Here, we need to check the **Mist** option along with the various available passes. Once the option is active, a new **Mist** panel will appear in the **World** tab. Here, we can set the options of **Mist**, but for this scene the default options will be good. Now, let's move to the node editor and click on the **Compositing** button.

How to do it...

To composite the scene, we need to perform the following steps:

1. Add an **Image** node by navigating to **Add menu | Input**, and load the `sky.jpg` file. After that, add a **HueSaturationValue** node and set the **Saturation** value to `0.800`.

2. Add a **Mix** node, plug the **HueSaturationValue** node into the first **Image** socket, and set the second **Image** socket's **Color** to RGB 0.38, 0.59, 0.71. Leave the mode to **Mix** and set **Fac** to `0.500`.

3. Add a **Frame** node and put the three nodes inside it. Label the frame as `BG`.

4. Add a **Box Mask** node and set Position to XY 0.5, 0.9, width to `1.160`, and height to `0.80`. Plug the **Mask** socket into a **Blur** node, set the mode to **Fast Gaussian**, and the **Y** value to `100`.

5. Add a **Mix** node. Plug the **Image** output into the **Fac** value and the **Mist** output from the **Render Layers** node into the first **Image** socket. Set the second **Image** socket's **Color** to Black.

6. Duplicate the **Box Mask** node and the **Blur** nodes. In the **Box Mask** node, change the Y Position to 0.30, and change the **Y** value to 50 in the **Blur** node.

7. Plug the **Blur** node into a new **Mix** node, plug the other **Mix** node into the first **Image** socket, and set the second **Image** socket to Black.

8. Add a **Frame** node and put all these nodes inside, as shown in the following screenshot. Label the frame as HorizonMask.

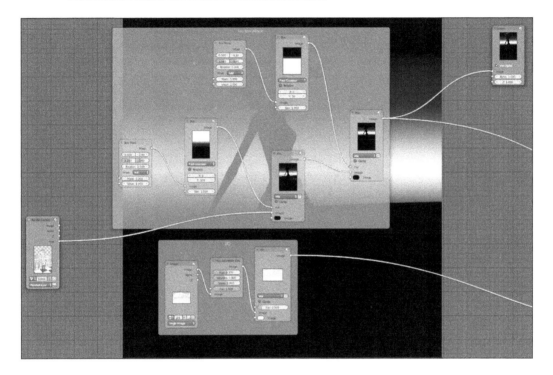

9. Add an **Alpha Over** node. Plug the output of the **BG** frame into the first **Image** socket and plug the **Image** output of the **Render Layer** node into the second **Image** socket.

10. Add a **Mix** node and set the mode to **Add**. Plug the **Alpha Over** node output into the first **Image** Socket and the output of the **HorizonMask** frame into the **Fac** socket. Set the second **Image** Socket to RGB 0.28, 0.37, 0.39.

11. Add another **Mix** node. Plug in both of the **Image** sockets the output of the last **Add** node, and the output of the **HorizonMask** frame into the **Fac** socket. Leave the mode to **Mix**.

12. Add a **Blur** node and place it between the **Add** node and the **Mix** node, so that it goes into the second **Image** socket of the **Mix** node from the **Add** node. This is shown in the following screenshot:

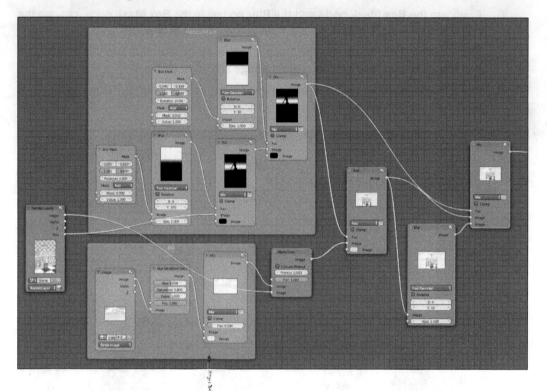

13. Set the **Blur** node's mode to **Fast Gaussian** and the **Y** value to 15.

14. Add a **Crop** node by navigating to **Add menu | Distort**, and place it after the last **Mix** node.

15. Activate both the **Crop Image Size** and **Relative** options. Set **Left** to 0.707, **Right** to 0.293, **Up** to 1.000, and **Down** to 0.000.

16. Add a **Glare** node and place it after the **Crop** node. Set the mode to **Fog Glow** and the **Threshold** value to 0.700. Also, set the **Size** value to 9.

17. Finally, let's plug the **Fog Glow** output into the **Composite** node.

How it works...

In this scene, we used a completely different image for the background and sky than the one we used in the rendering. Having set **Film** to **Transparent**, we can easily composite any kind of image behind our render. In this case, the size of the picture we used was quite different from our render. So, we cropped the image after we composited it, using the **Crop** node.

As in *Chapter 4*, *Creating an Exterior Scene*, we created a mask to be able to tweak the image only in certain areas. This time we used a **Mist** pass. The **Mist** pass is similar to a **Z** pass or **Depth**. The problem is that Cycles produce a really noisy **Z** pass, which is quite difficult to use in most cases. With the **Mist** pass, we obtain almost the same effect, but we have a clean pass which is perfect for use in any situation.

In this case, we used the mask to add some distant fog and blurred the horizon. The concept behind this technique is to use a black and white image as an input for the **Fac** sockets of the **Mix** nodes. The white areas of the map will determine an influence from the second **Image** socket, while the black areas will determine from the first one. This works exactly as the Cycles' **Shader** node system.

With compositing, we can do things such as creating an old picture look for our render. To do something like this, check the node setup in the following screenshot. We need to add it right at the end of our compositing node setup. The image we used is located in the Texture folder and is named OldPaper.jpg.

See also

You can find a really nice tutorial on how to obtain an even more extreme cartoon look using Cycles at the following link: http://www.minimaexpresion.es/?p=1070&lang=en.

6
Creating a Toy Movie Scene

In this chapter, we will cover the following recipes in detail:

- ▶ Setting up the the lighting
- ▶ Creating a realistic plastic material for the characters
- ▶ Creating the environment
- ▶ Achieving a movie look using the compositor

Introduction

In this chapter, we are going to create a particular scene. We are going to populate our scene with toys and create a realistic lighting and environment to make it look like a movie set. Then, we are going to increase the movie look using the compositor. After learning cartoon materials in *Chapter 5, Creating a Cartoonish Scene*, we are coming back to realistic materials.

Setting up the lighting

We will start by setting up the lighting of the scene. This will be created by the light sources that belong to the environment itself and are scattered around the scene, plus some other light sources placed where we need them. However, the main light will be coming from the scenic lights.

Getting ready

Let's get started! Open the `Chapter06_empty.blend` file and select the **Walls** mesh. In the **Shader** list you will find several slots already assigned to various parts of the mesh. We will now create the materials for the slot numbers 2 and 4.

How to do it...

We will start by setting up the lights that belong to the scenery itself.

Setting up scenography lights

Follow the given steps for setting up the scenography lights:

1. Let's add a new material in the second slot and name it `EmitterColumn`.

2. Delete default **Diffuse BSDF** and add an **Emitter BSDF** node in its place. Leave both **Color** and the **Strength** to their default values.

3. Add a new material in the third material slot and name it `EmitterWall`.

4. Delete default **Diffuse BSDF** and add an **Emitter BSDF** node. Leave the **Strength** value to its default value and change the **Color** value to RGB 0, 0.3, 0.8.

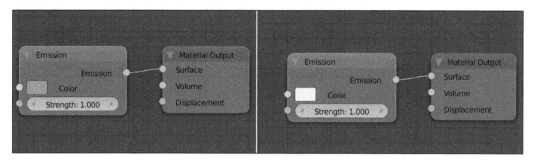

Other lights

Now, we will add three plane emitters to the scene. Let start by adding one plane from the add menu of the 3D viewport.

1. Add a new material to the plane, naming it `Emitter01`. It is enough to use a **Emission BSDF** node with a **Strength** value of `3.000` and default **Color**.

2. Now, let's duplicate the emitter and place the three planes as shown in the following screenshot. To know the exact positions of the planes, you can check the completed blend file of this chapter.

3. Make the material of the two emitters (that are facing the camera) single user by clicking on the small number next to the material name in the material slot. Name the new material `Emitter02`. We want to use this material for the last two emitters we created, which are facing the camera.

4. Change emit **Color** to RGB 0.48, 0.7, 0.8.

5. In the **World** tab, set the **Environment** color to RGB 0.38, 0.48, 0.5 and the **Strength** to `1.400`.

6. Also, turn AO on and set the **Factor** value to `0.50` and **Distance** to `10.000`.

How it works...

The lighting that we created here relies mainly on the real lights placed in our virtual set. This ensures that we have an evenly lighted scene thanks to the lights coming from every direction, and the creation of harsh shadows is avoided. Moreover, having a big scene like this allows us to have a good environment to reflect on our materials, without the usage of a HDRI.

The three point light rig that we placed on the characters ensures a stronger accent on our scene. This is done in order to direct the attention of the viewer towards where we want and to make sure the characters stand out a bit from the environment. We also used different colors for these emitters in order to give a nice contrast on the characters. This helps in making the image more interesting and less flat.

AO is useful in this situation for increasing the overall lighting and reducing the amount of noise without using additional emitters.

The final result is an even lighting over the scene, but the kind of lighting on a movie set varies greatly from scene to scene. Here, it was important to achieve this kind of light.

There's more...

It is always a good idea to look at references when we try to recreate something, even a lighting setup. On the internet, it is easy to find plenty of examples from movies, which can help us to find the right colors for portraying a certain mood for the light. It is important to pay attention to the details, such as the shadows and the highlights. and try to translate what we see in the setup we are building.

▶ At this link, there is a very interesting article about lighting tips by *Ben Simonds*:
`http://bensimonds.com/2010/06/03/lighting-tips-from-the-masters/`.

Lighting is a crucial part of creating stills or videos, both CG and real footage. A good CG artist should at least know about the basic techniques of lighting. There are a lot of manuals available on this topic. For example, this URL talks about lighting from many points of view—in real life and in computer graphics—together with many others interesting topics related to the creation of visually appealing pieces: `http://illuminated-pixels.com/`.

Creating a realistic plastic material for the characters

We will now recreate the material from which the characters are made. It will be a plain plastic material and we will apply some textures on it.

Getting ready

Generally, each character will have three different materials—one for the face, one for the chest, and one for the rest of the body. The plastic of these materials will be very similar, if not the same, but we will be applying the different textures and colors that belong to the different characters.

How to do it...

Let's get started by selecting the **Soldiers** mesh and adding a new material in the first material slot. Name it `Soldiers`.

Creating the material for the soldier's face

Following are the steps for creating the material for the soldier's face:

1. Add a **Glossy BSDF** node and mix it with the default **Diffuse BSDF** node using a **Mix Shader** node.

2. Leave the **Color** value to default and set the **Glossy** node's **Roughness** to `0.003`.

3. Add a **Fresnel** node by navigating to **Add** | **Inputs** and plug it into the **Mix Shader** node's **Fac** value.

4. Set the **Fresnel** node's **IOR** to `2.500`.

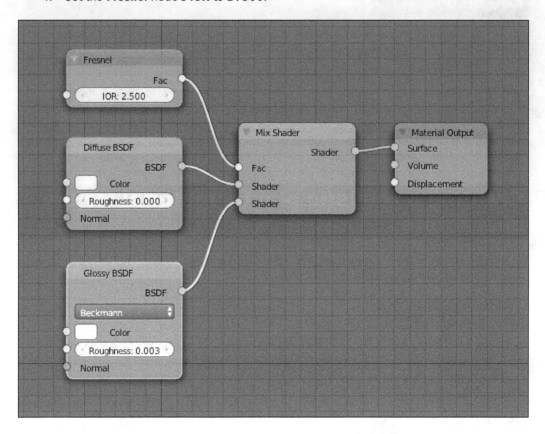

Creating black plastic material

Following are the steps for creating black plastic material:

1. Select the second material slot, and select the **Soldiers** material we just created from the drop-down menu.

2. Make the material single user by pressing the small number next to the name, and rename it to `BlackPlastic`.

3. Change the **IOR** value of the **Fresnel** node to `1.300` and the **Diffuse BSDF** node's **Color** to RGB 0.01, 0.01, 0.01. We do not want this to be fully black.

Creating material for the soldier's chest

Following are the steps for creating material for the soldier's chest:

1. In the third material slot, select the **BlackPlastic** material and make it single user. Rename it to `SoldiersChest`.

2. Add a **Texture Coordinate** node and an **Image Texture** node. Use the **UV** coordinates and load the `SoldiersChest.jpg` file.

3. Plug the **Image Texture** node into the **Diffuse BSDF** node's **Color** input.

4. Set the **Fresnel** node's **IOR** to `1.600`.

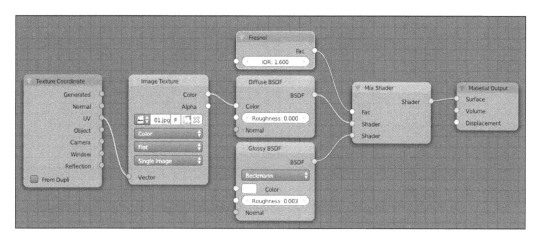

Creating the Officers's plastic material

Following are the steps for creating the Officers's plastic material:

1. Select the **Officers** mesh. In the first material slot, add the **BlackPlastic** material.

2. In the second material slot, add the **BlackPlastic** material again; but this time make it single user and rename it to `Officers`.

3. In the node material editor, change the **Diffuse BSDF** node's **Color** to RGB 0.13, 0.130, 0.13.

4. In the third material slot, add the **SoldiersChest** material and make it single user. Rename it to `OfficersChest`.

5. In the node material editor, make the **Image Texture** node single user and load the `ImpOfficerChest.png` file.

6. Add a color **Mix** node and place it after the **Image Texture** node. Plug the **Alpha** output of the **Image Texture** node into the **Fac** input of the color **Mix** node, and plug the **Image** output into the **Color2** of the color **Mix** node.

7. Set the **Color1** to RGB 0.13, 0.13, 0.13—exactly the same color as the **Officers** material's **Diffuse BSDF** node.

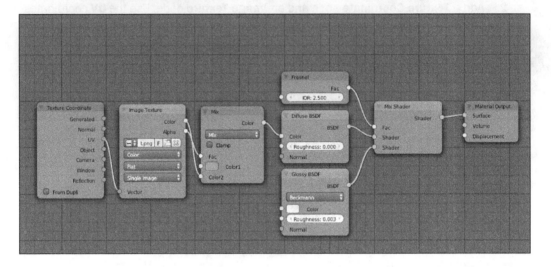

8. In the third material slot, select the **SoldiersChest** material and make it single user. Rename it to **OfficerFace**.

9. In the node material editor, make the image texture single user and load the `OfficerFace01.jpg` file.

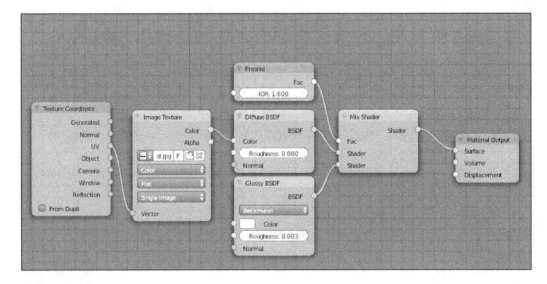

10. In the fourth material slot, select the **BlackPlastic** material.

11. Now select the **Officer** mesh and then press *Shift* and select the **Officers** mesh, so that the latter is the active one. Press *Ctrl + L* and click on **Materials**.

Creating the Darth's plastic material

Following the steps for creating the Darth's plastic material:

1. Select the **Darth** mesh. In the first material slot, select the **BlackPlastic** material.

2. In the second material slot, select the **OfficerChest** material and make it single user. Rename it to `DarthChest`.

3. In the material node editor, make the image texture single user and load the `DarthChest.png` file.

4. Add a **Bright/Contrast** node by navigating to **Add | Color** and place it between the **Color** output of the **Image Texture** node and the **Color2** input of the **MixColor** node.

5. Set the **Contrast** value to `0.020`.

6. In the color **Mix** node, set **Color1** to RGB 0.12, 0.12, 0.12.

7. Delete the **Fresnel** node and put a **Layer Weight** node in its place, connecting the **Facing** output to the **Mix Shader** node's **Fac** input.

8. Set the **Blend** value to `0.100`.

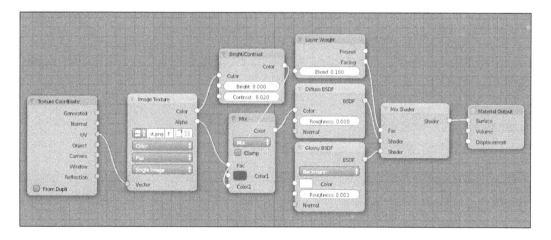

9. In the third material slot, select the **DarthChest** material and make it single user. Rename it to **Darth**.

10. In the material node editor, delete every node contributing to the **Diffuse BSDF** node's **Color** input. The only nodes left will be **Layer Weight**, **Diffuse BSDF** and **Glossy BSDF**, **Mix Shader**, and **Material Output**.

11. Set the **Diffuse BSDF** node's **Color** to RGB 0.12, 0.120, 0.12.

12. Select the **Cloak** mesh and add a new material to it.

13. Add a **Glossy BSDF** and mix it to the default **Diffuse BSDF** using a **Mix Shader** node with 10% influence from the Glossy BSDF.

14. Set the **Diffuse BSDF** node's **Color** to RGB 0.01, 0.01, 0.01 and the **Glossy BSDF** node's **Color** to RGB 0.015, 0.015, 0.015.

How it works...

In this recipe, we created some variations of the same plastic material. As we have seen, with a really simple node setup we can achieve really good results. Moreover, we can achieve some small variation using the **Fresnel** and **Layer Weight** nodes for mixing the BSDFs, which make the materials look more appealing.

It is interesting to see that we were able to apply textures on the materials and mix them with the rest of the surface using the alpha channel of the textures itself. To do this, we need to have PNG images. This is because the JPEG format does not support alpha channel and we would need a separated alpha map to achieve the same result.

There's more...

Going to the modifier's panel for the **Soldiers** or **Officers** meshes, we can see the modifiers of a series of arrays. Thanks to these arrays we can achieve a large number of identical meshes quickly. Moreover, we can switch off the visualization of the modifier in the viewport to improve the scene performance to a great extent. In this way, we will not see all the meshes in the viewport, but they will be visible for the final render.

See also

Check out the material library blend file to find more kinds of plastics!

Creating the environment

We will now create the materials for the environment. Even if the materials are not too complex, we will be able to learn some new interesting techniques.

Getting started

We have to go through several materials. We want to achieve a nice sci-fi look, and we will do this with the help of different textures. Let's start with the floor material.

How to do it...

Let's select the floor mesh and add a new material to it, naming it `Floor`.

Creating the floor

The following are the steps for creating the floor:

1. Add a **Glossy BSDF** node and mix it with the default **Diffuse BSDF** using a **Mix Shader** node.

2. Set the **Diffuse** node's **color** to RGB 0.005, 0.010, 0.020 and the **Roughness** value to `1.000`.

3. Set the **Glossy** node's **Color** to RGB 0.34, 0.34, 0.34 and the **Roughness** value to 0.020.

4. Add an **Image Texture** node and a **Texture Coordinate** node. Load the `FloorDisp.exr` file and use the **UV** coordinates.

5. Add a **Mapping** node by navigating to **Add | Vector**, and place it between the **Texture Coordinate** and **Image Texture** nodes. Set the **Scale** to XYZ 15.000, 15.000, 15.000.

6. Duplicate the **Mapping** and **Image Texture** nodes. Make the **Image Texture** node single user and load the `ScratchesSeamLess.png` file. We will use the **UV** coordinates again.

7. Change the **Scale** value in the **Mapping** node to XYZ 5.000, 5.000, 5.000.

8. Add **RGB** to **BW** by navigating to **Add | Converter** and an **Invert** node by navigating to **Add | Color**. Place them in sequence after the `ScratchesSeamLess` texture.

9. Add a color **Mix** node. Plug the **Image Texture** into the **Color1** socket and plug the output of the **Invert** node from the **ScratchesSeamLess** texture into the **Color2** socket.

10. Leave the mode to **Mix** and set the **Fac** value to `0.200`.

11. Add a **Bump** node and put it after the color **Mix** node. Set the **Strength** to `0.050`. Connect the **Normal** output to the **Normal** input of the **Diffuse** and **Glossy BSDF** nodes.

12. Add a **Noise Texture** node and set the **Scale** to `20.000`, the **Detail** to `2.000`, and the **Distortion** to `0.500`.

13. Connect the **Fac** output to a **Bright/Contrast** node. Set the **Brightness** to `0.100` and the **Contrast** to `0.150`. Also, add an **Invert** node and place it after the **Bright/Contrast** node.

14. Finally, plug the **Color** output from the **Invert** node into the **Fac** input of the **Mix Shader** node.

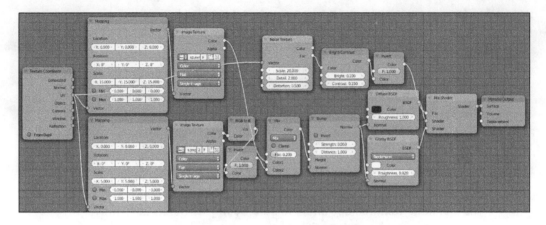

Creating the column wall

Follow the given steps for creating the column wall:

1. Select the **Walls** mesh and add a new material to the first material slot. Name it `ColumnWalls`.

2. Add a **Glossy BSDF** node and mix it with the default **Diffuse BSDF** using a **Mix Shader** node.

3. Set the **Diffuse** node's **Color** to RGB 0.040, 0.050, 0.080 and the **Roughness** to `1.000`.

4. Add a **Texture Coordinate** and an **Image Texture** node. Load the `displacementLow.exr` file and use the **UV** coordinates.

5. Add a **Bump** node and connect the **Image Texture** node's **Color** output to its **Height** socket. Set the **Strength** to `0.100` and connect the **Bump** node's output to the **Diffuse** and **Glossy BSDF** node's **Normal** inputs.

6. Connect the **Image Texture** node's **Color** output also to the **Glossy BSDF** node's **Roughness** and the **Mix Shader** node's **Fac** input.

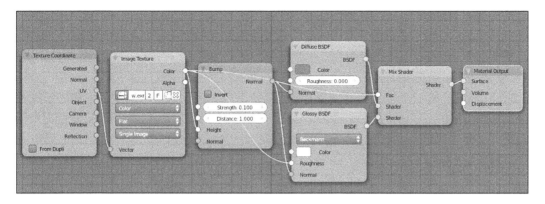

Creating a plain wall

Follow the given steps for creating a plain wall:

1. In the fourth material slot, select the **ColumnWall** material and make it single user. Rename it `PlainWall`.

2. Make the **Image Texture** node's single user and load the `ScratchesSeamLess.png` file.

3. Add a **Mapping** node and place it between the **Texture Coordinate** and **Image Texture** nodes.

4. Set the **Scale** to XYZ 5.000, 5,000, 5,000.

5. Add an **RGB** to **BW** node between the **Image Texture** node and rest of its outgoing connections.

6. Break the connection between the **Image Texture** node and the **Glossy BSDF** node's **Roughness**. Set the **Roughness** to `0.100`.

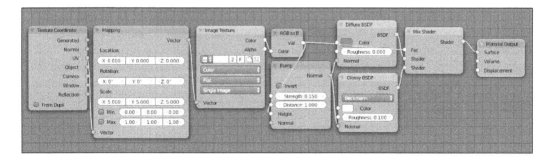

Creating other wall materials

For the last two material slots we will just use two **Diffuse BSDF** nodes with the following **Colors**: RGB 0.020, 0.025, 0.040 and RGB 0.26, 0.03, 0.03. We will call them `WallDark` and `WallRed` respectively.

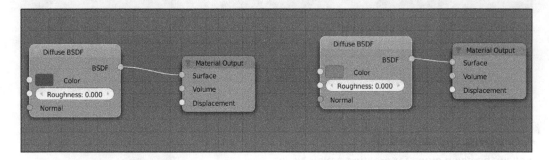

How it works...

The floor material is a simple combination of **Diffuse** and **Glossy BSDF** nodes, but we used several textures to mix them and generate the **Bump** node. The result is an interesting pattern over the floor surface. We also used a **Noise Texture** node to give variation to the glossiness of the surface, which contributed to making the floor look even more natural.

For the wall, we used simple materials that were slightly changed over the different parts to give a more interesting look to the structure. It is interesting to see how we used a texture as an input for different effects in the material, such as bumps, roughness, mix shaders, and fac values. It is always important to keep in mind that in Cycles, and for CG in general, we can use textures for virtually everything.

There's more...

The `displacementLow.exr` file was generated within the Blender by using the bake textures feature. At the moment, Cycles does not support texture baking as it will be implemented later on; but we can still use the **BI** (**Blender Internal**) engine to bake maps such as displacement maps to re-use as we want, even in Cycles. This is a really good way to generate different maps depending on our needs, without having to use any other software!

In the second post of this thread on Blender artists, there is a really good guide on how to bake good displacement maps using BI texture baking!

▸ http://www.blenderartists.org/forum/showthread.php?273033-
  Sculpting-with-UVs-and-displacements

Achieving a movie look using the compositor

It is now time to give the final touch to the image with some compositing, which really improves the look of our renders.

Before we start, we will have a quick look at the render settings so that we can make our final render. Then, we will move on to the compositor. Let's open up the render menu.

Let's open up the render menu and change some of the settings.

Render settings

Follow the given steps to change the render settings:

1. In the **Sampling** panel, set the **Clamp** value to 4.000 and the **Render** value to 150.000.

2. In the **Light Paths** panel in the **Transparency** section, set the **Max** value to 4.000 and **Min** to 1.

3. In the **Bounces** section, set the **Max** value to 16.000 and **Min** to 3.000. Also, set **Diffuse**, **Glossy,** and **Transmission** to 16.000.

4. Make sure that **Shadows** and **Caustics** are active.

5. In the **Film** panel, set the **Exposure** value to 1.400.

6. In the **Performance** panel, activate the **Cache BVH**, **Persistent Image**, and **Use Spatial Splits** options.

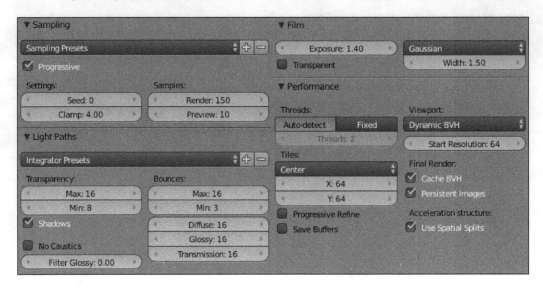

Compositing the image

Follow the given steps for compositing the image:

1. Let's go into the **Render Passes** menu, it is the one next to the render settings. Here, we need to activate the **Emission** pass in the **Diffuse** panel.

2. Now, let's render the image. Once it's finished, we can move on to the compositor.

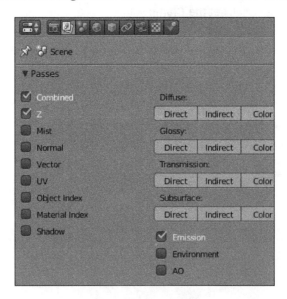

3. Add a **Color Balance** node after the **Render Layer** node's **Image** output. Set **Lift** to RGB 0.965, 1, 1, **Gamma** to RGB 1.1, 1.06, 1.04, and the **Gain** to RGB 0.97, 1.1, 1.1.

4. Add a **Hue Saturation Value** node and put it after the **Color Balance** node. Set the **Saturation** value to 0.9.

5. Add a **Glare** node by navigating to **Add | Effects**, and put it after the **Emit** output of the **Render Layer** node.

6. Leave the mode to **Streaks,** set the **Mix** value to 1, the **Threshold** to 0.9, and **Streaks** to 4.

7. Duplicate the **Glare** node and change the mode to **Fog Glow**. Change **Threshold** to 0.2 and set the **Size** to 9.

8. Combine these two **Glare** nodes using a **MixColor** node. Set the mode to **Add** and the **Fac** value to 1.

9. Mix the output of the color **Mix** node and the **Hue Saturation Value** node from the **Image** output with another color **Mix** node, again in the **Add** mode with a **Fac** value of 1.000.

10. Remember that we can frame the node group to keep the space clean, as shown in the following screenshot:

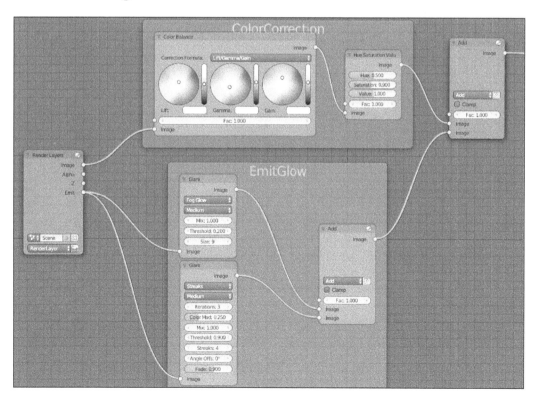

11. Add a **Lens Distortion** node by navigating to **Add | Distort** after the last color **Mix** node, and check the **Fit** option. Set the **Distort** and **Dispersion** values to 0.01.

12. Add an **Ellipse Mask** node by navigating to **Add | Matte** and set **Width** to 0.960 and the **Height** to 0.445.

13. Add a color **Mix** node, plug the **Ellipse Mask** output into the **Color1** socket, and set the **Color2** to black. Set the mode to **Add**.

14. Add a **Blur** node by navigating to **Add | Filter** after the color **Mix** node, set the mode to **Fast Gaussian** and both the X and Y values to 125.000.

15. Frame the **Mask** nodes.

16. Add a color **Mix** node. Plug the output from the **Lens Distortion** node into the **Color1** socket and the output from the **Mask Frame** into the **Color2** socket. Set the mode to **Multiply** and the **Fac** value to 0.600.

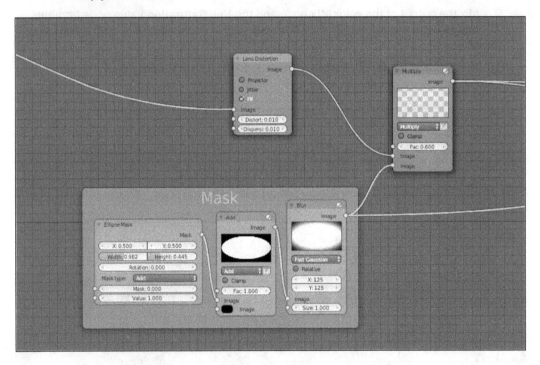

17. Add another **Hue Saturation Value** node and set the **Saturation** to 0.700. Place it after the **Multiply** node.

18. Add a **Lens Distorsion** node after the **HSV** node and activate the **Jitter** option.

19. Add a color **Mix** node and plug the output from the last **Lens Distorsion** node into the **Color1** socket and plug the output from the **Multiply** node into the **Color2** socket. Set the mode to **Mix**.

20. Finally, plug the output from the **Mask** frame into the **Fac** value:

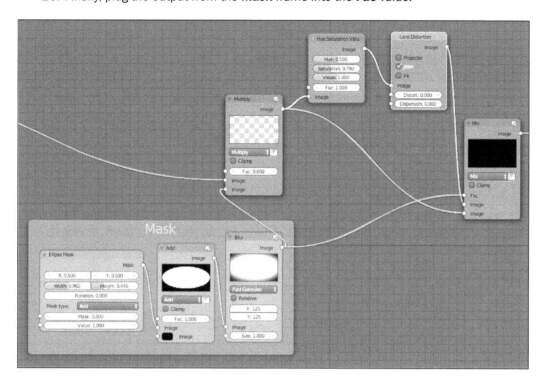

How it works...

The render settings for this scene, as usual for Cycles, are quite simple. We set a pretty low amount of samples for two reasons. First of all, the scene is quite open because apart from the walls, the light is free to travel around. This generates a low amount of noise. The second reason is because images from a movie are always a bit grainy, so a little bit of noise will even help us obtain a better result in this case.

In the compositing phase, we started by color correcting the image. We desaturated it a bit and we gave a colder mood to it by lifting the blues. Then, we created a light glow for the lights in the scene, which is something that often happens when looking at a light source through a camera.

After this, we created a slight vignette using an **Ellipse Mask** node and a bit of lens distortion. The vignette is an effect that movie cameras often generate. It is very important to never overdo these things. A very light effect will help to create the right atmosphere for our image, but one that is too strong will result in cliché.

Finally, we wanted to desaturate our image a bit more along the border. To do this, we used the same mask that we used for the vignette as a map to drive the effect. We also added more noise along the border using the lens distortion's jitter effect.

There's more...

In the render settings, we used a less amount of transparency bounces. This is because in our scene there are no transplant objects and therefore this kind of bounce is not useful in the scene. It is important to always analyze what we needed for a specific situation in order to optimize the render settings in the best possible way.

See also

The Blender foundation created a great live action short movie called *Tears of Steel*, and they released a DVD with a lot of learning material. This is a great resource to learn, among other things, how to achieve a good film look for our scenes:

▸ http://www.blender3d.org/e-shop/product_info_n.php?products_id=143

7

Car Rendering in Cycles

In this chapter we will cover the following recipes in depth:

- ▸ Setting up the lighting
- ▸ Creating the car paint material
- ▸ Creating the material for the tyres and the rims
- ▸ Creating the material for headlights and other details
- ▸ Compositing the scene

Introduction

It is time to learn how to create a really important scenario in computer graphics: rendering a car. A car is made up of several different parts. The most important is of course the car paint, but we will see that there are other important things to make our rendering really stand out.

Setting up the lighting

As we always do, let's start with setting up the lighting. Car rendering can be done in many different lighting conditions, but for our render, we will create a studio lighting.

Getting ready

Open the `Chapter10_empty.blend` file. The lighting, together with the mesh, which we will be using as the ground for the scene, is located in the second layer. Select the **Emit01** mesh and add a new material to it. Name the new material `Emit01`.

How to do it...

1. Delete the default **Diffuse BSDF** node and add **Emit BSDF** in its place.

2. Set the **Intensity** value to `15.000`.

3. Apply the same material to the **Emit02** and **Emit03** meshes.

4. Select the **Emit04** mesh and add a new material in the first material slot, calling it `Emit02`. Also, set the **Strength** value to `15.000`.

5. Add **Holdout BSDF** (**Add | Shaders**) and a **Mix Shader** node.

6. Connect **Holdout** to the first socket and **Emission** to the second one.

7. Add a **Geometry** node (**Add | Input**) and connect the backface output to the **Fac** input of the **Mix Shader** node.

8. Apply the same material to the **Emit05** mesh.

9. For every mesh emitter, deactivate the **Camera** and **Transmission** options in the **Ray Visibility** panel from the **Object** menu.

10. In the **World** menu, set the **Color** to **Environment Texture** and open the file `Studio024.hdr`.

11. Set the **Strength** value to `0.200`.

12. Under the **Settings** panel, activate **Multiple Importance Sample** and set **Map Resolution** to `1024`.

How it works...

The lighting here is quite simple. We tried to give a strong lighting from different angles of the car in order to create some interesting reflection. The HDRI is doing the rest. One thing to notice is how we created the material for the two emitters closer to the wall. Thanks to the **Geometry** node, we can apply two different shaders on each side of the plane so that the light is emitted only towards the car. On the other side, we applied a holdout, which is like a null material or a material that doesn't do anything. In this way, we can make the car stand out from the background, preventing the wall from being overexposed due to the emitting light. We also deactivated the ray's visibility of the **Transmission** node to avoid seeing the emitters through the car glass. This is because even if we turn off the **Camera Ray** visibility, the objects are still visible through glass materials due to the fact that in this case, the rays are treated as transmission rays, and not as a camera.

There's more...

We can achieve the same effect for the one-sided emitters by adding a plane behind the emitter plane. We could make this plane reflective in order to mimic more accurately a real studio light. This method can add some further realism to the lighting, but at a high cost in terms of noise generation. It is worth experimenting with it, but in general, there are very few situations that could noticeably benefit from this method.

See also

On the Internet, you can find a lot of information about this topic. A good tutorial, for example, is this video: `http://www.youtube.com/watch?v=U9iPZ5glrfs`.

Creating the car paint material

Here we are at the core topic of this chapter: the car paint. There are plenty of different types of car paints. In our scene, we will try to reproduce a shiny paint with flakes. Many render engines have an integrated flakes feature, but Cycles still lacks this option. Something like this will probably be added in the future, but for now, we will see how to recreate this effect on our own.

Getting ready

For the creation of the car paint, we will be using a new Cycles feature called **Open Shading Language** (**OSL**). A particular way of creating shaders is by coding them. Such a technique is used for example by Pixar's **RenderMan** engine as well. While creating a material this way is harder due to the fact that knowledge of the Shading language is required, it also opens a wider range of possibilities. In this recipe, we will not be talking about writing a shader, but just how to use it in Cycles. On the Internet, we can already find several OSL shaders. So let's move to layer one and select the **car_body** mesh and add a new material to it. We will call it `CarPaint`. Before we move on, we need to remember that this feature works only with the CPU as of now, so we will not be able to use the GPU to render this scene. Furthermore, we need to activate OSL through the rendering panel. Let's go to the **Render** menu, and in the render panel, right under the device selection menu, we need to activate the **Open Shading Language** option. This is really important because without this, the material that we are going to create for the car paint will not work and will appear to be black in our renders.

How to do it...

1. In the material node editor, duplicate **Diffuse BSDF** and mix the two BSDFs with a **Mix Shader** node using a **Layer Weight** node's **Facing** output with a **Blend** value of 0.950.

2. Set the upper **Diffuse BSDF** node's **Color** to RGB 0.02, 0.035, 0.06, and the lower one to black. Also, set the **Roughness** to 1.000 for both the nodes.

3. Add **Glossy BSDF** and mix it with a **Mix Shader** node using a mix of two **Diffuse BSDF** nodes. Set the **Glossy BSDF** node's distribution mode to **GGX** mode, **Color** to RGB 0.66, 0.9, 1, and the **Roughness** to 0.200. Label the **Mix Shader** node as `BasePaint`.

4. Now we will create the input for the **Fac** value of the **BasePaint** Mix Shader node. Add **Voronoi Texture**, set it to **Cells**, and set the **Scale** to 1000. Plug the **Fac** output into the **Gamma** node's **Color** input.

5. Add a **Layer Weight** node, set the **Blend** value to 0.900, and plug the **Facing** output into a **ColorRamp** node. Set the right color stop to HSV 0, 0, 0.95 and the interpolation mode to **Ease**.

6. Add a color **Mix** node and plug the **ColorRamp** node's **Color** output into the **Fac** socket and the **Gamma** node's **Color** output into the **Color1** socket of the **Color Mix** node. Set **Color2** to black and the mode to **Multiply**. Finally, plug the **Color** output into the **Mix Shader** node's **Fac** input.

7. Add **Anisotropic BSDF** and set the **Roughness** value to 0.010, **Anisotropy** to 0.400, and **Color** to RGB 0.52, 0.24, 1.

8. Add **Glossy BSDF** and set **Color** to RGB 0.52, 0.24, 0.3 and the **Roughness** value to 0.060.

9. Mix the two BSDFs with a **Mix Shader** node, with the **Glossy** node plugged into the first socket and the **Anisotropic** node into the second. As the **Fac** input, we will use a **Layer Weight** node's **Facing** output with a **Blend** value of 0.300. We will label the **Mix Shader** node Coating.

10. Now let's add a **Script** node (**Add | Script**). Load the pyla13.osl file that you will find in the chapter's folder. The node will change to a different interface.

11. Connect the **BasePaint** Mix node to the **Base** socket, and the **Coating Mix** node to the **Layer** socket.

12. Set the **Opacity** value to 0.250, the **Depth** value to 7.000, the **Fresnel** value to 0.800, and **IOR** to 1.390.

13. Finally, connect the **Script** node to the **Surface** socket of the **Material Output** node.

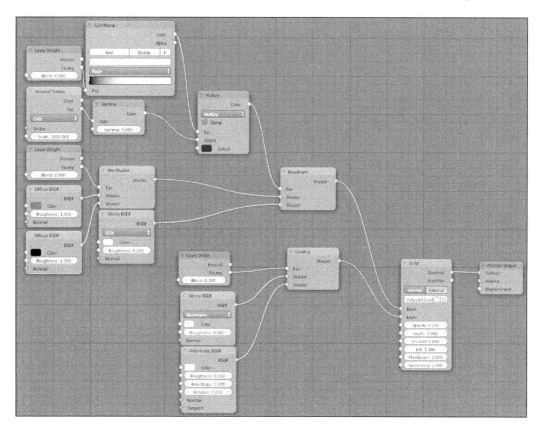

How it works...

The car paint material is made of different parts. First of all, we wanted to create a color variation along the surface of the car, and for this, we mixed the two **Diffuse BSDF** nodes with a **Surface Weight** node. Then we created the flakes using **Voronoi Texture** to generate the map that we then used to mix the **Diffuse** and **Glossy BSDF** nodes. We also used a second **Surface Weight** node to lower the intensity of the flakes on the surface that is less perpendicular to the point of view. We created the coating by mixing an **Anisotropic** and a **Glossy BSDF** node in order to obtain the distorted reflections of the car paint.

To mix the base and the coating, we used an OSL script that allows us to layer materials in a really accurate way. This gives us much more control than just using a **Mix** or an **Add Shader** node, allowing us to achieve a much more realistic result.

There's more...

In order to fully understand the usage and all the options of the pyla OSL script, we can have a look at the documentation on the website of its creator: `http://vadrouillegraphique.blogspot.fr/search/label/OSL`

See also

The script we used in this recipe is just one of the many scripts available on the Internet. You can find more ready OSLs at `http://www.openshading.com/osl/example-shaders/`.

On the same website, the instructions on how to make your first steps towards the creation of your own OSL scripts are also present!

Creating the material for the tyres and the rims

Now that the car paint material is ready, let's move on to other important parts of the car, namely the tyres and the rims.

Getting ready

Select the **Rims** mesh and add a new material to it. Name it `Rims`.

How to do it...

We will start creating the Rims material:

Creating the Rims material

Follow the given steps to create the **Rims** material:

1. In the material node editor, add two **Glossy BSDF** nodes and mix them using an **Add Shader** node.

2. Set the first **Glossy BSDF** node's **Color** to HSV 0, 0, 0.13, and the **Roughness** value to 0.030.

3. Set the second **Glossy BSDF** node's **Color** to HSV 0, 0, 0.4, and the **Roughness** value to 0.200.

4. Add a **Mix Shader** node and plug the output of the **Add Shader** node into the second socket and the default **Diffuse BSDF** node into the first one. Set the **Fac** value to 0.600.

5. Set the **Diffuse BSDF** node's **Color** to HSV 0, 0, 0.05.

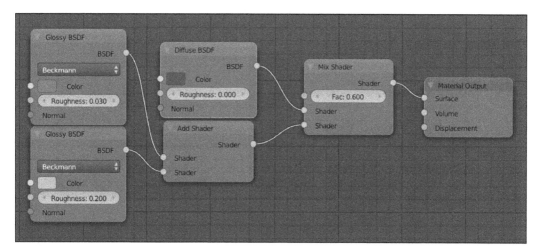

Creating tyres

Follow the given steps for creating tyres:

1. Select the **tyres** mesh and add a new material to it. Name it tyres.

2. Add a **Glossy BSDF** node and mix it with the default **Diffuse BSDF** node using an **Add Shader** node. Set the **Glossy** node's **Color** to HSV 0, 0, 0.07 and the **Roughness** value to 0.200.

3. Set the **Diffuse BSDF** node's **Color** to HSV 0, 0, 0.01.

4. Add an **Image Texture** node and a **Texture Coordinate** node. Load the VPC_FREE_01_tire_sidewall_2.png image and use the **UV** coordinates.

5. Add a **Bump** node and connect the **Image Texture** node to its **Height** input. Set its **Strength** to 0.150 and its **Distance** to 1.000.

6. Connect the **Normal** output to the **Normal** input of the **Glossy** and **Diffuse BSDF** nodes.

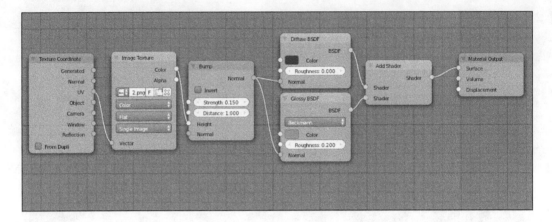

Creating brakes

Follow the given steps for creating brakes:

1. Select the **Brakes** mesh and add a new material in the first material slot. Name it `Brakes`.

2. Mix the default **Diffuse BSDF** node with an **Anisotropic BSDF** node using a **Mix Shader** node, with 90 percent influence for the **Anisotropic** node.

3. Set the **Diffuse** node's **Color** to HSV 0, 0, 0.1 and the **Anisotropic** node's **Color** to HSV 0, 0, 0.65. Also set the **Anisotropic** node's **Roughness** to `0.010` and the **Anisotropy** to `1.000`.

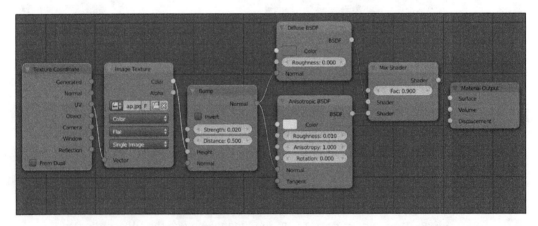

4.	Add an **Image Texture** node with **UV** coordinates and load the `VPC_FREE_01_brakedisk_bumpmap.jpg` image. Use it as a bump map for both the BSDFs with **Intensity** as `0.020` and **Distance** as `0.500`.

5.	Add a new material to the second material slot and name it `BrakesClamps`. This will be a 50 percent mix of a **Diffuse BSDF** (HSV 0, 0, 0.19) node and a **Glossy BSDF** node with **Roughness** `0.200` (HSV 0, 0, 0.55).

How it works...

The materials we created in this recipe are pretty straightforward. In both cases, it is just a combination of **Diffuse** and **Glossy BSDF** nodes. For **Rims**, we used a **Mix Shader** node to mix the BSDFs as we wanted to achieve a result closer to a chrome material, while with the **Add Shader** node for the tyre, we obtained a more rubber-plastic like look.

For the rims, we used two different **Glossy BSDF** nodes in order to give some variation to the reflections, while for the tyres, it was really important to use a height map to obtain the tyre's thread profile.

There's more...

Remember that with the usage of programs like Crazy Bump, we can also generate a normal map to use with our tyres, in order to obtain a more precise effect.

See also

Check out this interesting thread on Blender Artist for some additional material for **Rims** at `http://blenderartists.org/forum/showthread.php?245865-the-rim-wheel-render-for-a-car`.

Creating the material for headlights and other details

We will now create the materials needed for the remaining parts of the car. While we will look at the creation of some of the most interesting materials in great detail, we will only take a brief look at some of the others, as the node setup for them is either similar or identical to other materials handled in previous parts of the book.

Getting ready

Let's start with the headlights. The headlights group is located on layer 11 (the one below the first one) so that it will be easier to work on them. Let's select the **HeadlightGlass** mesh and add a new material to it. Name it `HeadLightGlass`.

How to do it...

1. For the **HeadLightGlass**, we will just use a **Glass BSDF** node with transparent shadows (to see how to create transparent shadows, see *Chapter 2, Creating Different Glass Materials in Cycles*), **Roughness** to `0.000`, and **IOR** to `1.450`.

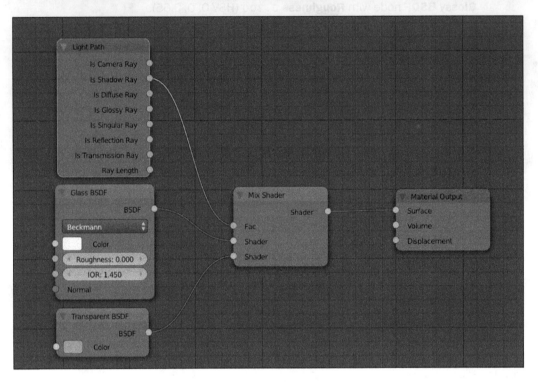

2. Hide the **HeadLightsShadow** by pressing *H* while the mesh is selected.

3. Select the **HeadLights** mesh. Add a new material in the first material slot and name it `HeadLightsChrome`.

4. Add an **Anisotropic** node and a **Glossy BSDF** node and mix them using an **Add Shader** node.

5. Set the **Anisotropic BSDF** node's **Roughness** to `0.010` and the **Color** to HSV 0, 0, 0.7.

6. Set the **Glossy BSDF** node's **Roughness** to `0.200` and the **Color** to HSV 0, 0, 0.65.

7. Mix the **Add Shader** node with the default **Diffuse BSDF** node using a **Mix Shader** node with 70 percent influence for the **Add Shader** node.

8. Set the **Diffuse** node's **Roughness** to 1.000 and the **Color** to HSV 0, 0, 0.5.

9. Add a **Noise Texture** node and a **Texture Coordinate** node. Use the **Generated** coordinates and set noise **Scale** to 200.000.

10. Add a **Bump** node and connect the **Noise Texture** node's **Fac** output to the **Height** input. Set the **Strength** value to 0.250 and **Distance** to 0.500.

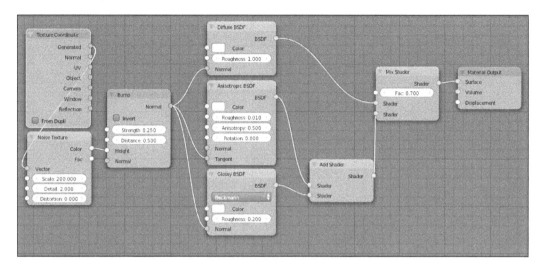

11. Connect the **Normal** output to the **Normal** input of every BSDF in the material node tree.

12. Both the materials that go in the second and third slots will be a simple emission BSDF for the actual lights. The first one should have **Strength** of 15.000 and the second one **Strength** of 6.000. Set both of their colors to HSV 0.55, 0.25, 1. Name the two materials HeadLightsEmit01 and HeadLightsEmit02 respectively.

Creating the tail lights

Follow the given steps for creating the tail lights:

1. Select the **TailLightsGlass** mesh and add a new material to it. Name it TailLightsGlass.

2. Delete the default **Diffuse BSDF** node and add a **Glass BSDF** node. Set the **IOR** value to 1.550.

3. Add a **Texture Coordinate** node and an **Image Texture** node. Load the VPC_FREE_01_taillights_glass2.png file and use the **UV** coordinates.

4. Add a color **Mix** node and plug the **Image Texture** node into the **Fac** socket. Set **Color1** to RGB 1, 0, 0 and **Color2** to white. Plug the color **Mix** node's **Color** output into the **Glass BSDF** node's **Color** socket.

5. Duplicate the **Image Texture** node and make the texture accessible for a single user. Load the VPC_FREE_01_chrome_lights_bump.png image and set **Scale** to 10.000 using a **Mapping** node, using the **UV** coordinates for its vector input.

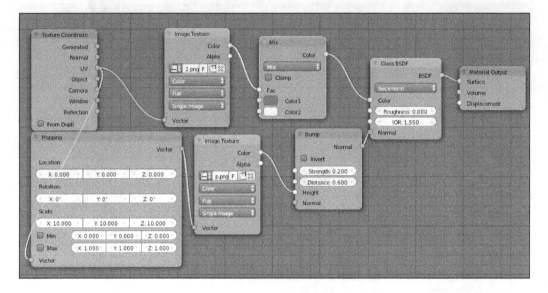

6. Add a **Bump** node and connect the last texture to its **Height** socket. Set **Strength** to 0.200 and **Distance** to 0.600. Connect the **Normal** output to the **Normal** input of the **Glass BSDF** node.

7. Select the **TailLights** mesh. For the first material slot, apply the **LightsChrome** material.

8. In the second and third material slots, we will be using two simple **Emission** nodes, both with **Strength** of 15.000, and the first with **Color** of HSV 0.55, 0.24, 1, and the second with **Color** of HSV 1, 1, 1. Name them TailLightsEmit01 and TailLightsEmit02 respectively.

Creating other parts

For the remaining materials, just recreate the node trees shown in the screenshots:

▸ The following screenshot shows the creation of **Chrome finitures**:

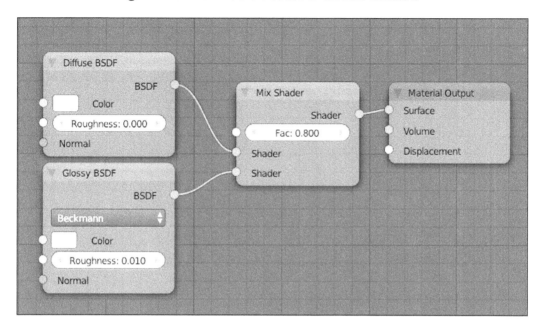

▸ The following screenshot shows the creation of **Chassis**:

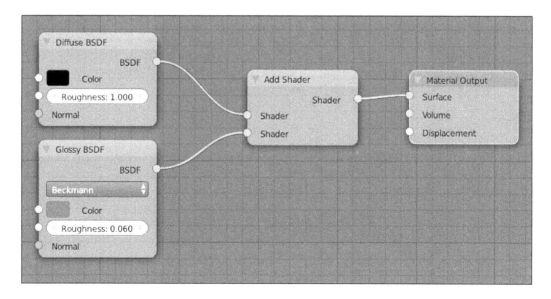

▶ The following screenshot shows the creation of **GroundPlane**:

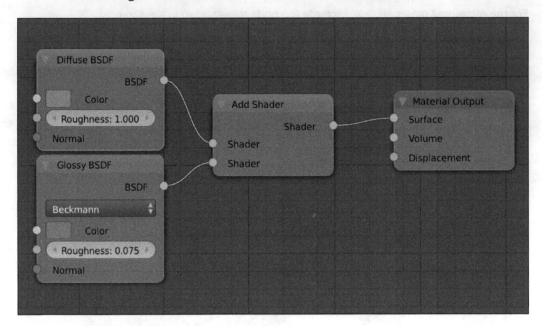

How it works...

The materials created in this recipe are quite simple. For the lights, we wanted to create a chrome material with a bit of a bump. We added a **Diffuse BSDF** node in it so that it would not show up as completely dark, due to the generally dark environment. We used a combination of an **Anisotropic** and **Glossy BSDF** node to obtain the right reflections.

Finally, we wanted to make the emitters strong enough to penetrate through the glass. A slight blue color helps to make the scene feel more high tech, and in the next recipe, we will see how to increase this effect even more thanks to compositing.

There's more...

The tail light glass used a black and white map to drive the different colors over the surface using a single **Glass BSDF** node. This technique can be a great time-saver as you don't have to create different materials over the surface.

See also

The following is a really good guide for creating and rendering a car in Blender and Cycles:

> ▶ http://www.instantshift.com/2013/02/22/modeling-and-rendering-a-car-in-blender-and-photoshop/

On the following Blender Artists thread, there is a large amount of general information about the creation of a car in Blender. The information is quite sparse, but there are a lot of great things to pick up on:

> ▶ http://blenderartists.org/forum/showthread.php?261547-Modelling-Jam-01-Iconic-Movie-Car-Join-in

Compositing the scene

Our scene is almost ready, but we will give it a final touch in compositing to make it really stand out.

Getting ready

Let's change the mode of the node editor to **Compositing** and check the **Use Nodes** option in the lower part of the screen.

How to do it...

1. Add a **Glare** node (**Add | Filters**) and connect the **Image** output from the **Render Layer** node to it. Leave the mode to **Streaks** and set the quality to **High**. Change the **Iterations** to 5.000 and the **Color Modulation** to 0.500. Also change the **Mix** value to 1.000 and the **Threshold** value to 3.100. Finally, set the **Streaks** value to 2.000 and the **Fade** value to 0.970.

2. Duplicate the **Glare** node and change the mode to **Fog Glow**. Change the **Threshold** value to 1.000 and the **Size** to 9.000.

3. Mix the two filters using a color **Mix** node in the **Add** mode with a **Fac** value of 1.000.

4. Add a **Color Balance** node and connect the **Image** output of the **Render Layer** node to it. Set the following values for **Lift**, **Gamma**, and **Gain** respectively: HSV 0, 0, 0.98, HSV 0.55, 0.12, 0.89, and HSV 0.4, 0.06, 1.35.

5. Mix the output of the combination of the two glare nodes with the **Color Balance** node using another **Mix** node in the **Add** mode, with the color-corrected **Image** into the first **Image** socket and the **Filters** into the second one.

6. Add a **Lens Distortion** node (**Add | Lens Distortion**) after the last **Mix** node in the **Add** mode and check the **Fit** option. Set the **Distortion** value to 0.015 and the **Dispersion** to 0.010. Connect the node to the **Composite** node.

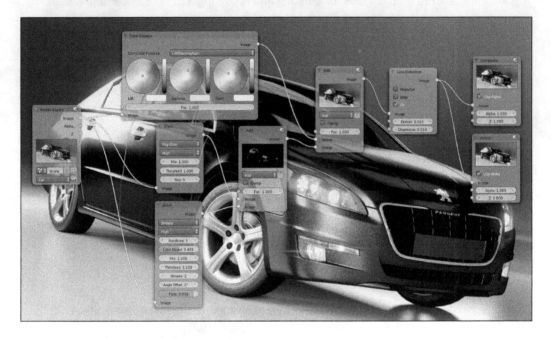

How it works...

First, we added a bit of color-correction using the **Color Balance** node in order to make the image more appealing. We increased the contrast and over-exposed the highlights a bit. We also added a touch of blue to make the environment feel more cold and futuristic.

We then used the **Glare** and **Fog Glow** filters to give the right look to the lights. Thanks to the glare, we added a kind of high-tech effect to the headlights, while with the **Fog Glow** filter, we created a halo.

Finally, we added a touch of lens distortion and chromatic aberration to add an extra bit of realism to the scene.

There's more...

Filters such as **Glare** and **Fog Glow** have a value called **mix**. When this value is set to 0, the effect is applied directly over the original image, while setting it to 1 will make only the effect visible.

Using the mix with the value 1 allows us to composite the effect over the original image in a second moment, giving us a much finer control over the final look of the image. This also allows us to make further changes to the image before compositing the effects onto it, so that these are not affected by any other filter or correction we may want to apply to the image. For example, if we would like to darken the image, our **Glare** and **Glow** filters would lose much of their intensity. Setting the mix to 1 and compositing them after the color correction allows us to darken the image as we want and then put the filters in with their intensity still intact.

See also

Check out the following links for tutorials on compositing a car rendering:

- ▸ http://www.youtube.com/watch?v=dVl_HvTUCZo
- ▸ http://www.youtube.com/watch?v=ZmzzfVYN39Y

Check the following link where you can find an entire course about Blender compositing: http://cgcookie.com/blender/2012/09/12/compositing-in-blender-production-complete-and-pre-orders-ending/.

8
Creating a Car Animation

In this chapter, we will cover the following recipes in depth:

- ▸ Setting up the lighting
- ▸ Creating a car paint material
- ▸ Creating the materials for the exterior environment
- ▸ Setting up the scene for the animation
- ▸ Compositing the scene

Introduction

In this chapter, we will be creating our first animation in Cycles. This will involve using some new options in Cycles that are made especially for animations. Among other things, we will also learn about new materials and techniques. Here is the final animation that we'll have created at the end of this chapter:

Setting up the lighting

Let's start with the lights as we always do. For this time in this scene, we will deal with both an exterior and an interior environment.

Getting ready

We will be using a combination of the sun and environment lighting for the general lighting, plus some emitter and a portal for the interior. To start, open the `Chapter07.blend` file.

How to do it...

1. Add sun light, and set the rotation to XYZ 2.85, -37, -22. This can be set from the properties panel of the viewport, which can be activated by pressing *N*. **Rotation** is in the **Transform** panel.

2. In the **Lamp** menu, set **Shadow Size** to 0.05 and **Strength** to 5. Set **color** to white. Also make sure that the **Cast Shadow** option is active.

3. Select the **InteriorLights** mesh, and add an **Emission** material to them with a **Strength** of 7 and the RGB color value as 0.520, 0.760, 0.800. Call the material `InteriorLights`.

4. Select the **Portal** mesh, and add a material to it. Name it `Portal`. Delete the default Diffuse BSDF, add **Emission BSDF** and set **Strength** to 6.

5. In the object menu of the **Portal** mesh, we need to deactivate the camera, transmission, and shadow-ray visibility.

6. Select the **SunDisk** mesh, add a new material to it, and name it `Sun`. Make it **Emitter** with **Strength** of 2.

7. Now let's move to the World node editor. Add Sky Texture and an RGB curve. Plug **Sky Texture** in the RGB curve, and set them as shown in the screenshot.

8. Plug the RGB curve inside the **color1** socket of a **Color Mix** node, and set the mode to **Color** and the **Fac** value to 0.5. Finally, plug the **Color Mix** node into a **Background** node.

9. Now add a **Texture coordinate** node and an **Environment Texture** node. Load the vp_sky_v3_047_GOODsmall.jpg file, and use the **Generated** coordinates for it.

10. Set its rotation to XYZ 0, 180, 0 with a mapping node

11. Plug the **Environment Texture** inside another **Background** node. We can either duplicate the other (by pressing *Ctrl + D* when the node is selected) one or add a new one (**Add** menu | **Shader**).

12. Add an **Add Shader** node, and use it to mix the two **Background** nodes. Finally, set Sky Background **Strength** to 0.4 and Environment Texture Background **Strength** to 2.

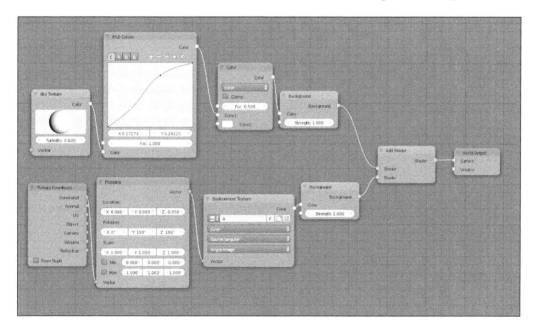

How it works...

The lighting that we created in this scene is probably the most complete one that we have created so far. First of all, we have both the interior and exterior lighting.

The exterior is quite similar to the one that we created in *Chapter 4, Creating an Exterior Scene*. It is a mix of a sky texture and an environment texture plus a sun lamp. In this case, we did not use the sun-position plugin to set everything up, but we rotated the sky, the sun and the textures by hand to achieve the effect that we wanted. It is not as accurate as using the plugin, but we can fine-tune the lighting enough to obtain the effect that we are looking for.

For the exterior, we also used the SunDisk mesh. This emitter will contribute a lot when we will composite the scene at the end of the chapter. The contribution of this mesh, in terms of pure lighting, is close to zero, but we will see how to turn this into a real sun in the final two recipes of this chapter.

Finally, the interior lighting is also quite straightforward. It comprises of a portal light and a series of mesh lights that work as real lights in the room. The portal as not only the camera and the shadow ray visibility are turned off, but also the transmission one, in order to avoid seeing it through the car glass.

There's more...

The interior lights are created using an array modifier. This kind of modifier allows us to create a large number of meshes from a single mesh. We can also add some variation to the position and rotation of the generated meshes through the settings of the modifier. This method is really good, as it saves a lot of time while creating a big number of similar meshes.

See also

- There is a great new array modifier under development called **advanced array modifier**. It will allow a much greater control and fine-tuning over the creation of arrays. Sadly, it is still not available to be officially used, but there are a couple of demonstrations of its use at:

  ```
  http://www.blendernation.com/2012/01/05/advanced-array-
  modifier/
  ```

- There is also the possibility of trying it out using some special build from **graphicall**, like this one:

  ```
  http://www.graphicall.org/537
  ```

For those who do not know what graphicall is, it is a portal where all experimental Blender builds are uploaded for everyone to try. Be aware that these are not official versions reliable for production; but if someone would like to try out a new feature which is still not included in the official version, this is the right place to go!

Creating a car paint material

It is now time to create the material for our car. We already saw in detail how to create a car paint material in *Chapter 7, Car Rendering in Cycles*, but nothing forbids us to learn about another kind of car paint material!

Getting ready

Let's get started, and select the car mesh. As we can see, there are several material slots already assigned to the mesh. The materials that we will be using for the car mesh that really interest us are just a couple, that is the ones related to car painting, which we will explore in detail.

How to do it...

We will start by creating the white part of the car paint material. Let's add a new material in the first slot, and name it `CarPaintWhite`.

To create a car paint, carry out the following steps:

1. Mix the default **Diffuse BSDF** node with an **Anisotropic BSDF** node using a **Mix Shader** node with the **Fac** value of 0.5.

2. Using the **LayerWeight** node's **Facing** output with a **Blend** value of 0.1 as input for the **Fac** value of a **MixColor** node, create a mix of two colors (**Color1**: RGB: 0.090, 0.090, 0.090 and **Color2**: RGB: 0.700, 0.940, 1.000) in the **MixColor** node. Then plug the **Color** output into the **Color** input of **Diffuse BSDF**. Also set the **Diffuse BSDF Roughness** to 1.

3. Add a **Fresnel** node, and set **IOR** to 1.3. Plug it into the **Anisotropic BSDF's Roughness** input. Set the color to RGB 0.600, 0.600, 1.000 and **Anisotropy** to 0.5.

4. Mix the two BSDFs with a Glossy BSDF using another **Mix Shader** node. As with the **Fac** input, we will use the **Layer Weight** node's **Facing** output with a **Blend** value of 0.3. The Glossy BSDF should go into the second **Shader** socket.

5. Set the **Glossy BSDF** color to RGB 0.590, 0.900. 1.000 and the **Roughness** to 0. Also set **Mode** to **Sharp**.

6. Frame all the nodes that have been created so far, and name the frame `PAINT`:

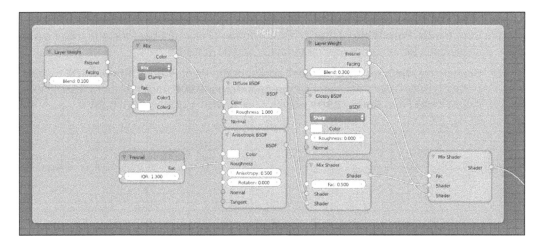

7. Mix **Diffuse BSDF** and a **Glossy BSDF** with a **Mix Shader** node, with 70 percent of influence for Glossy BSDF.

8. Set Diffuse Color to HSV 0.000, 0.000, 0.360, the Glossy BSDF mode to **Sharp** and the **roughness** to 8.000. Also set the Glossy Color to pure white.

9. Add a **Bump** node, and plug it to both the Diffuse and Glossy BSDFs' normal sockets. Set **Strength** to 0.020 and **Distance** to 0.600. Also activate the **Invert** option.

10. Frame these nodes, and name the frame SCRATCHES. Add a **Mix Shader** node, and plug into the first **Shader** socket the output of the **PAINT** frame, and in the second one the **Scratches** frame.

11. We will now create the input for this **Mix Shader** node's **Fac** value and for the bump node. Add an **Attribute** node, and put Col in the namespace. Plug it into the **RGB Curves** node, and set it as shown in the screenshot.

12. Mix the output of the **RGB Curves** node with **Noise Texture** using a **Color Mix** node set to **Multiply** with a **Fac** value of 1.000. Set **Noise Texture Scale** to 150.000, **Details** to 5.000, and **Distortion** to 1.000.

13. Add an **Image Texture** node, and load the MetalScratches0040_1_M.jpg file, using the **Generated** coordinates set the **Scale** to XYZ 5.000, 5.000, 5.000 using a **Mapping** node. In the **Image Texture** node, set the **Projection** method to **Box** and set the Blend to 0.500.

14. Add an RGB value **to** the **BW** convertor after the **Image Texture** node, and finally mix it with the previous node using another **Mix Color** node. We will plug the image texture into the **Color2** socket, while the previous **Multiply** node into the **Fac** value. Finally, we need to set the **Color1** socket to HSV 0, 0, 0.5. Leave the mixing method to **Mix**.

15. Frame all these nodes, and name the frame **MASK**.

16. Now we need to plug the output of this **Mix** node into the **Height** socket of the **Bump** node and into the **Fac** value of the **Mix Shader** node that is mixing the other two frames.

17. Copy the **CarPaintWhite** material into the material slot number four, and make it a single user. Rename the new material to CarPaintRed.

18. Change the **MixColor** node's **Color2** socket of the Paint Frame **Diffuse BSDF** to RGB 0.230, 0.000, 0.000. Also change the **Anisotropic BSDF** node's color to RGB 1.000, 0.250, 0.000 and **Glossy BSDF** node's color to RGB 1.000, 0.600, 0.260.

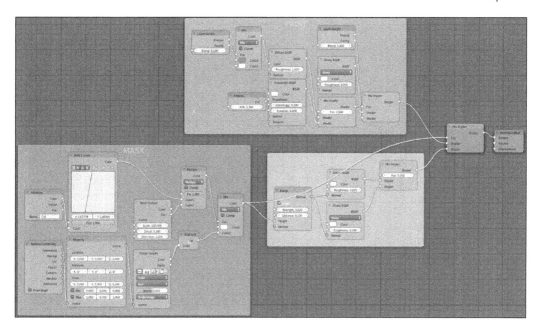

Now we'll create other parts of the car. The following materials are really basic. Their setup is explained with the screenshot:

▸ **Slot 2**: CarBlackDetails

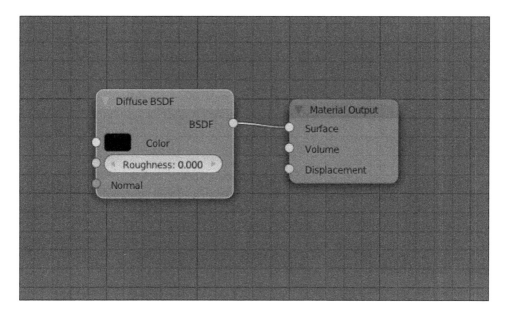

▶ **Slot 3**: Car Glass

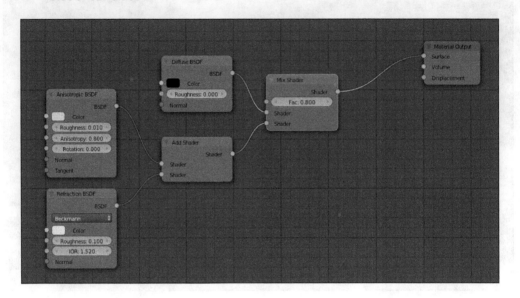

▶ **Slot 5**: CarLightsGlass

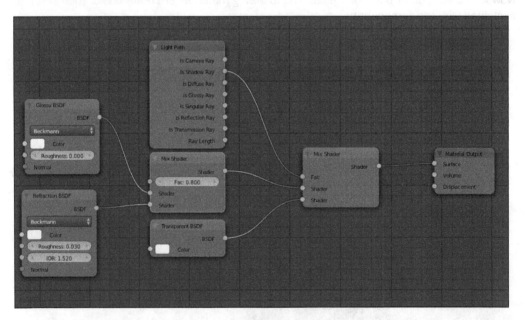

▸ **Slot 6**: CarTailLights

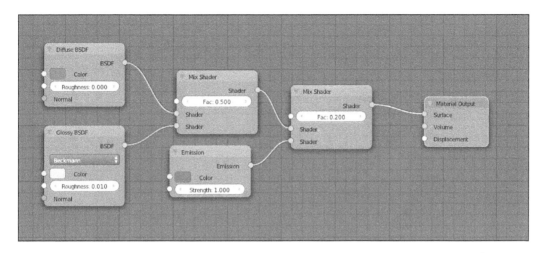

▸ **Slot 7**: CarLightsReflections

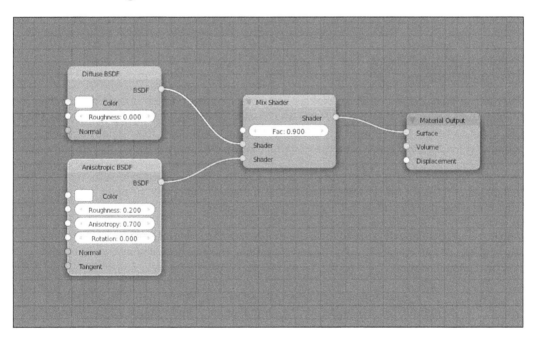

► **Slot 8**: CarLights

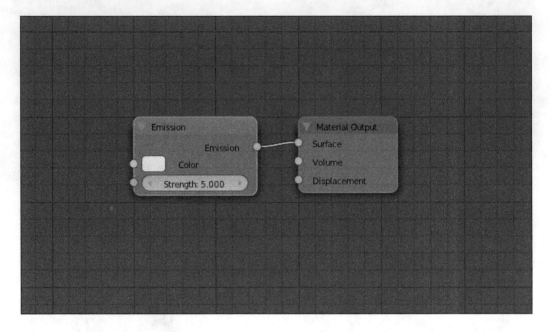

How it works...

The new car paint material that we created is simpler compared to the one we made for *Chapter 7, Car Rendering in Cycles*. Here, we do not have flakes, and we did not use the PYLA OSL script as we did then to layer the different material levels (for further details about the script refer to *Chapter 7*). However, the material that we created is effective for our purpose.

We used a combination of anisotropy and glossiness to achieve the right look for the reflections and a base made with Diffuse BSDF. In this version of the car paint, we also used the vertex paint to create a ruined part of the chassis.

Finally, we used a **Fresnel** node to drive the roughness of the anisotropic BSDF. As we are learning, the possibilities offered by Cycles in terms of the creation of shaders are limited only by our imagination!

The rest of the materials created for the car are really basic. We will see later on in the chapter how to prepare the car model for the animation in order to obtain all the information needed to do a proper composition with it.

There's more...

For the creation of the car paint, we used the vertex paint as a mask to separate the two different shaders. Moreover, we used the same mask as a source for the bump map, so that we could have zones where the paint has been removed with scratches and so on.

See also

▸ Check out the other car paint shaders in the additional materials file that is provided with the book!

Creating the materials for the exterior environment

Let's now take care of the exterior parts of our scene!

Getting Started

We have different interesting techniques to use here. We will see how to create a great-looking rocky cliff, a desert, and some sci-fi structures! Let's get started.

How to do it...

The main piece of the exterior is the cliff rock with the desert on it. Let's select the mesh called **Land** and add a new material to it. We will call it `Cliff_Desert`.

To create the desert environment, we'll carry out the following steps:

1. In the material node editor, let's add two **Image Texture** and a **Texture Coordinates** node. Load `SoilSand02.jpg` and `SoilSand01.jpg` using the **UV** coordinates for them. Mix them using a **MixColor** node with **Fac** of `0.5` and **Mix** mode.

2. Add another **Image Texture** node, and load the `SoilCracked.jpg` file. Also for this texture, let's use the **UV** coordinates, and let's set the **scale** to XYZ 25, 25, 25 using a **Mapping** node.

3. Mix the last image textures with the mix of the previous two using another **Mix Color** node with **Fac** `0.5` and **Mix** mode.

4. Add a **Voronoi Texture** node, change the mode to **cells**, and **Scale** to `600`. Multiply the voronoi texture to the previous textures with a **Mix** node with **Fac** of `0.6`.

5. Add another **Mix Color** node, plug the textures into the **Color1** socket, and set **Color2** to RGB 0.660, 0.160, 0.020. Set the mode to color and **Fac** to 0.600.

6. Finally add an **HSV** node, and set **Saturation** to 0.8; then plug it into the **Diffuse BSDF** node.

7. Frame all the nodes that we created, and name the frame **Desert**.

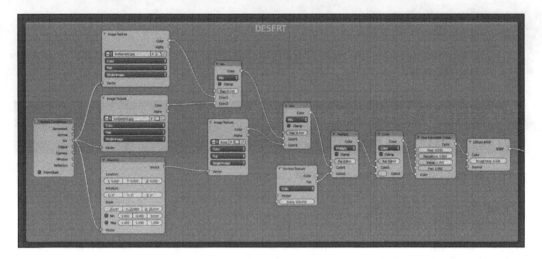

Let's create the cliffs:

1. Add two **Image Textures** nodes, and load the AridRocks.jpg and Cliff.jpg files. Use the **UV** coordinates for the AridRocks.jpg image while adding an **Attribute** node, and use the **CliffUVs** for the Cliff.jpg image.

2. Mix them using a **Mix Color** node with **Fac** as 1.000 and the **Add** mode. Put the Cliff.jpg texture into the **Color2** socket.

3. Add another **Mix Color** node, and set it to the **Multiply** mode. Plug the sum of the two textures into the **Color1** socket ,and set the **Color2** to RGB 0.1, 0.08, 0.075 and the **Fac** to 0.8.

4. Plug the result of these textures into the **Diffuse BSDF** color socket and also into an **RGB to B** node and a **Gamma** node (with **Gamma** 1.6), and plug them into a **Glossy BSDF Color** input. Set the **Roughness** to 0.4.

5. Add the two BSDFs using an **Add Shader** node.

6. Add two new **Image texture** nodes and load the RocksArid_height.tiff and RocksArid_normal.tiff files again using the **UV** coordinates.

7. Also add a **Noise Texture** node and set **Scale** to 300.000, **Detail** to 2.000, **Distortion** to 0.500, and Add it to the RocksArid_height texture using a Mix Color node with **Fac** 1.000. For the **Noise Texture** we want to use the **Generated** coordinates.

8. Plug this last node into the **Height** socket of a **Bump** node. Also add a **NormalMap** node and plug `RocksArid_Normals` into it. Set **Strength** to `0.5` and plug it into the **Normal** socket of the **Bump** node.

9. Set Bump **Strength** to `0.6` and **Distance** to `1` and plug it into the **Normal** input of **Diffuse** and **Glossy BSDFs**.

10. Frame all the nodes that we created and label the frame as `Cliff`.

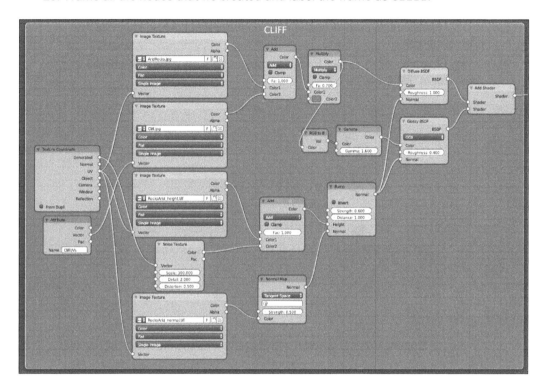

11. Let's mix the two frames using a **Mix Shader** node. We will plug the **Desert** frame into the first socket and the **Cliff** frame into the second one.

12. As **Fac** input let's use an **Attribute** node. Into **Name** let's write `Col` and plug into the **Fac** socket the **Color** output.

Let's create the metal structure:

1. Select the **MetalStructure** mesh and add a new material into the first Material Slot. Name it `PanelMetal`.

2. Mix default **Diffuse BSDF** with **Anisotropic BSDF** using an **Add Shader** node. Set Diffuse BSDF **Roughness** to `1`, Anisotropic BSDF **roughness** to `0.2`, **anisotropy** to `0.5`.

3. Add two **Image Texture** nodes and load the `SciFiPanel.jpg` and `SciFiPanel_normal.tiff` files. We will use the UV coordinates and set the scale to XYZ 5, 5, 5 using a mapping node.

4. Add a **Bump** and **Normal Map** node. Plug the **Normal** map output into the **Bump**'s normal input. Plug the normal map image texture into the **Normal Map** node and the `SciFiPanel` image texture into the **Height** socket of the **Bump** node.

5. Set Bump **Strength** to `0.1` and **Distance** to `0.5`. Also set **Normal Map strength** to `0.1`. Plug **Bump**'s normal output into the **Diffuse** and **Anisotropic BSDF's** normal inputs.

6. Finally plug the `SciFiPanel` **Image texture** color output into the **Diffuse** and **Anisotropic BSDF** node's color inputs.

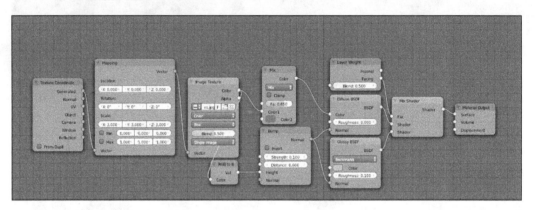

Let's create the cupola:

1. Select the **Cupola** Mesh and add a new material into the first material socket. Name it `Cupola`.

2. Mix the default **Diffuse BSDF** with a **Glossy BSDF** using a **Mix Shader** node. Plug a **Layer Weight** node's **Facing** output into the **Fac** value and set **Blend** to `0.5`. Also set Glossy Color to HSV 0, 0, 0.14 and **Roughness** to `0.1`.

3. Add an **Image Texture** node and load the `MetalScratches.jpg` file. Use the **Generated** coordinates and set **Scale** to XYZ 3, 3, 3 using a **Mapping** node. In the **Image Texture** node, set the **Projection** method to **Box** and the **Blend** to `0.5`.

4. Plug the **MetalScratches** texture into the **Color1** socket of a **Color Mix** node in the **Mix** mode, with **Fac** value of `0.65`. Set **Color2** to HSV 0, 0, 0.05. Finally plug the **Mix** node output into the Diffuse BSDF color input.

5. Add an **RGB to BW** convertor after the **Image Texture** node and plug it into a **Bump** node. Set **Strength** to `0.1` and **Distance** to `0.6`. Plug the **Bump** node into the **Normal** sockets of the **Diffuse** and the **Glossy BSDF** nodes.

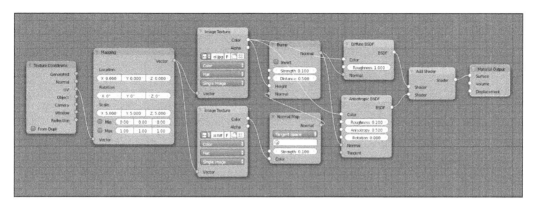

6. Add a new material into the second material slot and name it **CupolaMetal**.

7. Mix default **Diffuse BSDF** with **Anisotropic BSDF** using a **Mix Shader** node, with a **fac** value of 0.5. Set Anisotropic **roughness** to 0.2, **anisotropy** to 0.9 and **rotation** to 0. Also set **Color** to pure white.

8. Add an **Attribute** node and write Col into the namespace. Plug the **Color** output into the **Color2** socket of a **Mix Color** node, in the **Multiply** mode and a **Fac** value of 0.5. Set **Color1** to HSV 0, 0, 0.035. Finally plug it into the **Color** socket of **Diffuse BSDF**. Let **Color** be set by default:

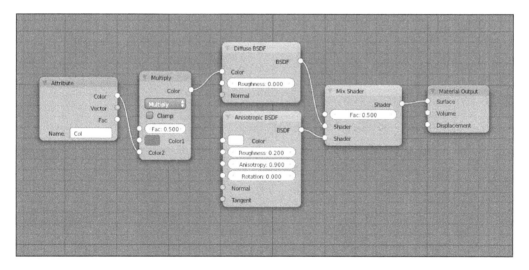

Let's create the sea:

1. Select the **Sea** mesh and add a new material to it. Name it Sea.

2. Mix **Refraction** and **Glossy BSDF** using a **Mix Shader** node, with 80 percent influence from **Glossy BSDF**. Set the **Refraction** color to white and **Roughness** 0.02 and **IOR** to 1.333. Set the **Glossy** color to white and **Roughness** to 0.02.

3. Add an **Image Texture** node and load the `disp_00000.jpg` file that you will find in the `Ocean` folder contained in the main textures folder. Click on the drop-down menu where it says **Single Image** and select **Image Sequence**. Set **Frames** to 400, **Start Frame** to 0, and **Offset** to 0. Check the **Autorefresh** option. This process will allow us to use a sequence of images based on the frame that we will be rendering, instead of a single image.

4. For **Texture**, we will use the **UV** coordinates, and we will set the scale to XYZ 30, 30, 30 using a **Mapping** node.

5. Plug **Image Texture** into the **Bump** node's **Height** socket and set **Strength** to 3 and **Distance** to 1. Finally plug the **Bump** node into the **Refraction** and **Glossy BSDF's** normal inputs:

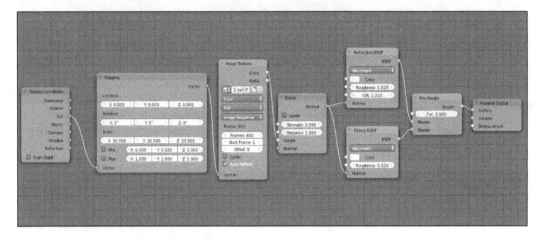

Let's create the bridge structure:

▸ **First Material slot: Cement.**

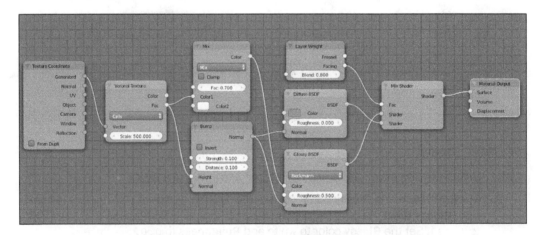

▸ **Second Material slot**: **SteelCable.**

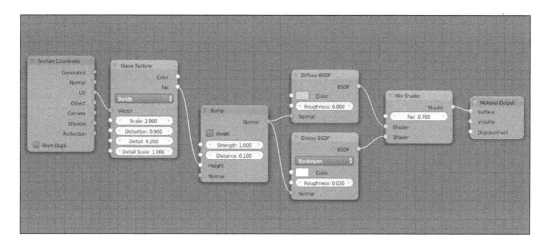

Let's create the road:

The image texture file to be used is `Road.jpg`:

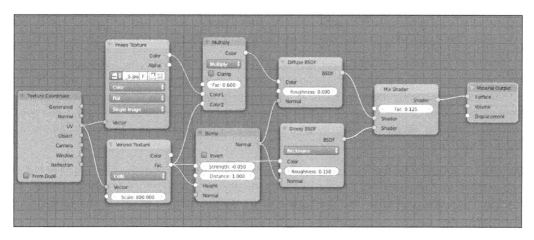

Let's create the floor:

The image texture file to be used is `MetalScratches.jpg`:

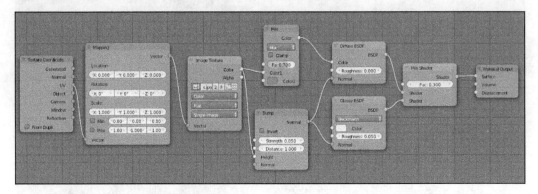

How it works...

In this recipe, we learned some new, interesting things. The most complex material that we created is the one for the land mesh. Using the vertex paint as a mask, we mixed two really big node groups and smoothly combined them together. As we did in *Chapter 4, Creating an Exterior Scene*, we are using a displace modifier to obtain the proper displacement as this function is still missing in Cycles. We will see how to optimize this for our animation in the next recipe.

Another really interesting material is the one for the sea. For the first time, we used an animated texture in our shader. This is a really useful function that will allow us to use different textures during the animation. As we obviously want the sea to move throughout the time of the animation, an image sequence is the best technique to obtain this effect. To have animated textures, we can also use video sequences, but in general, image sequences will allow us more control.

We need to set the total number of frames and the number with which the first image of the sequence is named, which in our case is `00000`. Finally we can offset the beginning of the image sequence through the timeline in case we want the texture to not be animated from the beginning.

There's more...

> ▶ The image sequence that we used for the sea is obtained from the ocean modifier included in Blender. This modifier simulates the movement of the sea displacing the surface of a mesh. This is great because it allows us to have a big amount of detail, but it is also quite demanding in terms of hardware. Anyway, thanks to the same modifier, we can also bake the sea movement as bump and normal map sequences, which we can later use on a simple plane. Using the last option will result in a much lighter scene, and will be less demanding in terms of hardware and lower render times.

See also

▶ Have a look at this tutorial to understand the usage of the ocean modifier better:

`http://www.youtube.com/watch?v=2V0Q0kDkm9Y`

Setting up the scene for the animation

In this recipe, we will optimize our scene as best as we can in order to decrease the total render time.

Getting ready

It is better to underline something from the beginning. As we said earlier in this book, rendering can be a quite long story. Rendering an animation is a much longer story. No matter how much we are going to optimize the scene, our rendering is quite heavy, and we have to render 375 frames. With that said, let's get started!

How to do it...

Optimizing the scene means we need to get rid of what is not strictly necessary in a certain moment. It will happen during our animation; something that is really close to the camera and needs a lot of detail in a certain moment will be far away and almost invisible later on. And when the thing is not so close to the camera, it is useless to have the maximum detail possible. We will start by optimizing the heaviest mesh, the **Land mesh**.

Let's optimize the Land mesh:

1. Select the Land mesh and go to the modifier menu.

2. The first modifier of the list is a subdivision surface one. Right now **Render Subdivision** is set to 5. Let's go to frame number 114 on our timeline and with the mouse cursor placed over the Render Subdivision number, let's press *I* on the keyboard. The number will become yellow. You can also add a key frame by pressing the right button on the value and clicking on **Add Keyframe.**

3. Go to frame 113 (the number will become green) and set the subdivision number to 4. With the cursor over it, press *I* again.

4. Now go to frame 199. The number of subdivisions should again be 5, but they should be green in color. Press *I* while the cursor is over the number, and it will become yellow again.

5. Go to the next frame (200), set the number to 4, and add another key frame by pressing *I*:

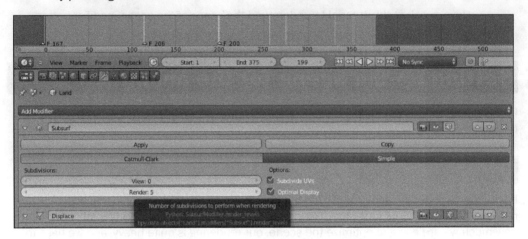

6. Let's go to the sampling panel. While the timeline is set to frame 1, add a key frame to the **Seed** value. Then go to the last frame (375) and set the **Seed** value to a value higher then 375; 400 will be good. Add another key frame.

7. Now let's move to frame 199, set **Render Samples** to 400, and add a key frame. Then move to the next frame (200), set **Samples** to 800, and add another keyframe.

8. Set the **Clamp** value to 8.

9. In the **Light Paths** panel, check the **No Caustics** option and set the remaining settings as shown in the following screenshot.

10. Check the **Motion Blur** option and in the panel, set **Shutter** to 0.3.

11. In the **Film** panel, check the **Transparent** option.

12. In the **Output** panel, set **Format** to **OpenEXR** and check the **RGBA** and **Float(Half)** options:

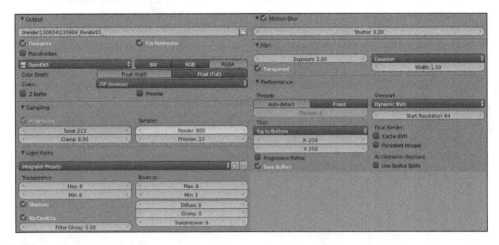

Let's render the layers and indexes:

1. The last thing that we want to take care of are render passes. Let's go in the **Render Layers** menu and in the **Passes** panel, let's activate the following passes: **Mist, Object Index, Material Index, Emission**, and **Environment**.

2. Now select the **SunDisk** mesh and in the **Object** menu, go to the **Relations** panel. Set **Pass Index** to 2.

3. Select the **Car** mesh and set **Pass Index** from the object menu to 1. Also go to the the material menu and select the **CarTailLights** material. In the **Settings** panel, set the **Pass Index** to 1.

4. Now we are finally ready to render the animation!

How it works...

The first thing that we did was to optimize the amount of geometry used for the Land mesh. The displacement requires quite a lot of polygons in order to have a good result, but we really see the cliff only in the second shot of the animation. This is why we set the number of subdivisions to 5 only in that fragment. The rest of the animation will be much quicker to render, and we will not see the loss of detail on the cliff.

Another important thing that we did was to animate the seed. The seed is a random value for the noise of the render. No matter how many samples we compute, there will always be a small amount of noise in some area. When the seed is constant the noise does not change its pattern during the animation, and this is not a pleasant effect at all. So, we want the seed to have a different value at each frame in order to resemble the real noise.

We also changed how many samples we want for different parts of the animation, as for the open air shots we need far less in order to get a clean image as compared to the indoor shot.

The pass indexes that we set will allow us to use masks for the objects and materials for which we set the index during compositing in order to create effects that are otherwise impossible to obtain.

 Another really useful thing is the **OpenEXR** format that we are using to render. This format will allow us to have a single file for each image that we render with all the data that we need for compositing contained in it. When we import the file in Blender later on, we will be able to use all the passes that we activated, without having a lot of different images for each frame. This is of great help!

There's more...

In order to change the active camera in the scene, we used markers. We can add innumerable markers on our timeline and bind the cameras to each one of them. At the frame where the marker is placed, the active camera will change to the one that is assigned. This is a really useful method to have multiple cameras in our scene and render the sequence in one time.

See also

▶ This quick tutorial will show us how to bind camera to markers in order to change the active camera during animation:

    http://www.youtube.com/watch?v=gQSvjyV78OE

Compositing the scene

It is now time to composite the scene after rendering it.

Getting ready

After the rendering is completed, we will open up a new Blender scene and go to the node editor. Let's delete the default render layer and add an image input node (**Add** menu | **Image**). Here we will load the **exr** image sequence that we just rendered. We need to change the mode to image sequence and set the number of frames, exactly as we did for the sea-animated texture. You will see that we now have all the sockets with the render passes that we activated before. Let's dive into the compositing process!

How to do it...

We will start by compositing the image over the sky background:

1. From the **Image** output, add the following in sequence: a **Glare** node (**Add** menu | **Filters**), a **Mix Color** node, and an **Alpha Over** node (**Add** menu | **colors**).

2. Set **Fog Glow** with **Mix** to 1, **Threshold** to 0.55 and **Size** to 9 and plug it in the second socket of the **Mix** node. Plug the original **Image** output into the first socket of the **Mix** node and set it to the **Add** mode, **Fac** 0.2.

3. Finally plug it into the second socket of the **Alpha Over** node.

4. After the **Environment** output, add a **Color Balance** node and set it as shown in the picture. Then plug it into the **Alpha Over**'s first socket.

5. After the same **Color Balance** node, add another **Glare** node in the **Fog Glow** mode with **Mix** 1, **Threshold** 0 and **Size** 8. After this, add a **Blur** node (**Add** menu | **Filters**) in the **Fast Gaussian** mode and set it to XY 2, 2.

6. Add a **Color Mix** node and plug the output of the **Blur** node into the second socket while setting the first one to black. Then plug the original **Alpha** output into the **Fac** socket.

7. After this, add another **Color Balance** node and set it as shown in the picture.

8. Finally add another **Mix color** node in the **Add** mode and plug the output of the **Color Balance** node into the second socket and the output of the **Alpha Over** node into the first one. Set **Fac** to 0.75.

9. Frame all the nodes that we created and label the frame **Background**.

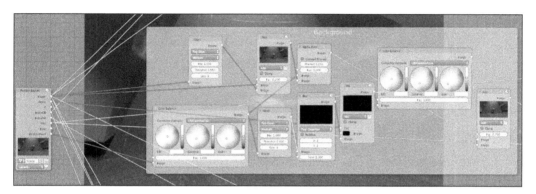

Let's create the glare:

1. Add an **ID Mask** node (**Add** menu | **convertor**) and connect the **IndexOb** output to it. Set **Index** to 1.

2. Add a **Color Mix** node and connect the **ID Mask** node to the **Fac** value, set the first socket to black, and connect the original **Image** output into the second socket.

3. Add a **Glare** node and set it to the **Streaks** mode. Set **Iterations** to 4, **Color Modulation** to 0.5, **Mix** 1, **Threshold** to 0.3, **Streaks** to 4, **Angle** to 14 and **Fade** to 0.96. Set a key frame for **Threshold** at frame 199 and set another key frame at frame 200 with a value of 2.3.

4. Add another **Mix** color node and connect the original **Image** output into the second socket and original **Alpha** into the **Fac** value of the **Mix** node. Set the first socket to black and leave the mode to **Mix**.

5. Duplicate the **Glare** node and put the new one after this **Mix** color node. Leave all the settings as they are except for **Threshold** that we want to set to 1.400.

6. Mix the two **Glare** nodes with a **Mix** color node in the **Add** mode with the first **Glare** node connected to the first socket and the last one to the second socket. Set **Fac** to `0.100`.

7. Frame all these nodes and label the frame **Glare**:

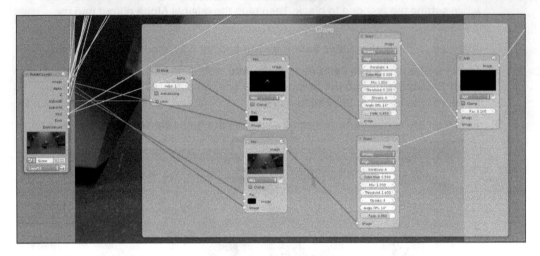

Let's add the taillights:

1. We need to create the same initial mask using the the **ID Mask** and Color **Mix** nodes as we did for the glare; only this time we will use the **IndexMaterial** output.

2. After this, we need to create a node setup, as shown in the following screenshot:

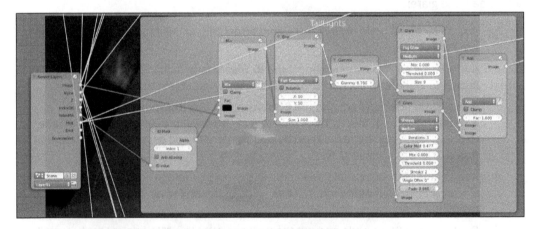

3. We will create two masks again using the **ID Mask** and **Mix** nodes. We will use the **IndexObject** output again, but this time we need to set **Index** of the node to 2.

4. For one of the masks before the **Mix Color** node, we will add a **Dilate/Erode** (**Add** menu | **Filters**) node and set the mode to **Step** and **Distance** to -6.

5. Now that these two masks are created, let's create a node setup, as shown in the following screenshot:

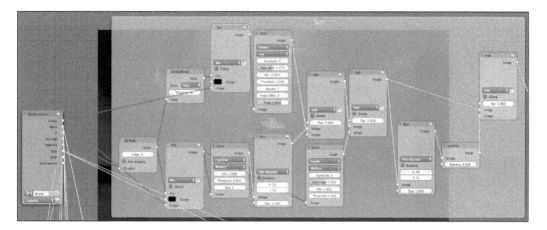

6. Before we move on to the last frame of our composition, let's start assembling everything together.

7. With a **Mix Color** node in the **Add** mode, mix the **Background** frame (first socket) and the **Glare** frame (second socket). Set **Fac** to `0.500`.

8. Connect this **Add** node to the first socket of another **Add** node and connect the **TailLights** frame to the second socket. Set **Fac** to `0.000` and set a key frame with this value at frame 256 (by pressing *I* while the cursor is hovering over the value that you want to set a key frame for). Set another key frame at frames 257 and 350 with a value of `1.500`. Finally set the last key frame at frame 351 with a value of `0.000`.

9. Plug this last **Add** node to the first socket of another **Mix Color** node in **Add** mode and plug the **Sun** frame into the second socket of the **Add** node. Set **Fac** to `1.000`.

Let's create the distant fog frame:

1. Connect the **Original Mist** output (the one coming directly from the **exr** image input sequence node) to a **ColorRamp** node and set it as shown in the screenshot.

2. Add a **Bokeh Blur** node (**Add** menu | **Filters**) and a **Bokeh Image** node (**Add** menu | **Inputs**). Set **Bokeh Image Flaps** to 5 and connect it to the the **Bokeh** input of the **Bokeh Blur** node. Set **Max Blur** to `16.000`, **Size** to `0.300` and **Bounding** to `1.000`.

3. Now connect the **Add** node that is mixing all the previous frames with the **Sun** frame to the **Bokeh Blur** image socket and to the first socket of a new **Mix** color node. Then we will connect the **Bokeh Blur** image output into the second **Mix** socket and the **ColorRamp** node into the **Fac** socket.

4. Add another **Color Mix** node and set the mode to **Screen**. Add the **Original Mist** output into the **Fac** socket and the output of the last **Mix** node into the first socket. Finally set the second socket to RGB 0.290, 0.270, 0.215.

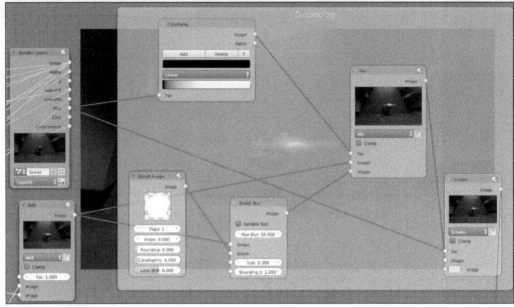

SHAPE

5. As a final thing, we will add a **Lens Distortion** node (**Add** menu | **Distort**) right after the **DistantFog** frame. Check the **Fit** option and set **Distort** to 0.01 and **Dispersion** to 0.008.

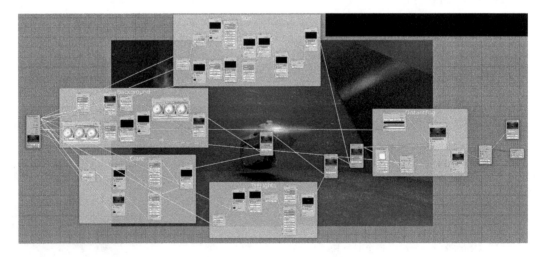

How it works...

This was quite a big compositing session! Thanks to the passes that we activated, we were able to work a lot on the image, and exactly where we wanted. Let's see what we did, a bit more in depth.

First of all, we composited the background (the sky) on all the geometry that we rendered. Using the Fog Glow node, we were able to create a bit of light wrapping from the background, so that they blend seamlessly with the foreground. We also made a little bit of color correction on both of them.

Then we created two glare effects: one for the car alone and the other one for the whole scene. To create the mask for the car, we used an ID Mask node. Thanks to this node, we can isolate the objects or the materials for which we set the index prior to the rendering process. It is important to remember that these masks are not of really good quality as they are quite aliased. Anyway, they are good enough for our purposes. In the Blender compositor, as in any other part of the software, we can add key frames for everything. As the light situation in the outside and the inside scenes is quite different, we animated the threshold, so that we could obtain the amount of glare we wanted.

For the taillights and the sun, we followed a quite similar process. We created a mask to work on the part of the image that we wanted, and then we applied the right effects for it. We animated the fac of the mix node for the taillights again so that they would shine only while the car is braking.

In the last frame, we used the Mist output to create a distant fog effect and a bit of blur. For the blur, we used a bokeh blur that allows us to simulate the bokeh effect that is given by the shape of the blades of the camera lens.

There's more...

While working with such big node groups, it is important to work in the environment that is most comfortable for us. We can change the look of the compositor from the user preferences by going to the **Theme** tab in the node editor menu. For example, we can change the curving of the wires by making them straight or by changing the color of the active wires, so that they will be more visible in the intricate net of nodes.

The usage of groups is also worth remembering in order to keep our workspace clear and clean.

See Also

> ▸ This link will show you a good tutorial about the usage of the Bokeh and Vector blur in the Blender compositor:
>
>   http://www.youtube.com/watch?v=xEnQJ6v4Xt4

9
Creating an Iceberg Scene

We will cover the following recipes in this chapter:

- ▸ Creating the ice and snow materials
- ▸ Creating the sea material in Cycles
- ▸ Compositing the scene

Introduction

In this chapter we will see how to create snow and ice material, and how to mix them together according to the position of the mesh. These two materials will be quite complex and will make use of many of the techniques we have learned until now. From now on we will focus more on the creation of the materials, as the lighting will be the same as the one we already created several times.

Creating the ice and snow materials

In this recipe we are going to create all the material for an iceberg. Our target is to have snow on the flat surfaces and ice on the slopes, where it is too steep for the snow to stay. Let's get started!

Getting ready

We will create the ice and the snow using a single material, and mix them using a new technique. Select the iceberg mesh and add a new material to it.

How to do it...

We will now see the steps required to create the ice as well as the snow material.

Creating ice

The following are the steps to create ice:

1. Add **Glossy BSDF** and **Glass BSDF** and mix them using a **Mix Shader** node. Let's put **Glossy** in the first socket and **Glass** in the second one.

2. As input for the color of both the BSDFs, we will use a color **Mix** node with **Color1** as white and **Color2** as RGB 0.600, 1.00, 0.760.

3. As input for the **Fac** value of the color **Mix** node, we will use a **Voronoi Texture** node with the **Generated** coordinates, **Intensity** mode, and **Scale** 100. Invert the color output using an **Invert** node and plug it into the **Fac** value of the color **Mix** node.

4. As the input for **Roughness** of the **Glossy BSDF**, we will use the **Layer Weight** node's **Facing** output with a **Blend** value of 0.800. Then we will plug this into a **ColorRamp** node and set the color stops as shown in the following screenshot. The first color stop is HSV 0.000, 0.000, 0.090 and the second one is HSV 0.000, 0.000, 0.530. Remember to plug the **ColorRamp** node into the **Glossy BSDF** roughness socket.

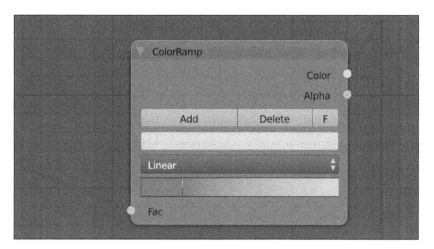

5. Finally, set **Glass BSDF** node's **IOR** to 1.310 and **Roughness** to 0.080.

6. Now we will create the **Fac** input for the **Shader Mix** node of the two BSDFs. Now we will add **Noise Texture** to the **Generated** coordinates with a **Scale** of 130, **Detail** of 1, and **Distortion** of 0.500. Plug this into a **ColorRamp** node and set the color stops as shown in the the following screenshot.

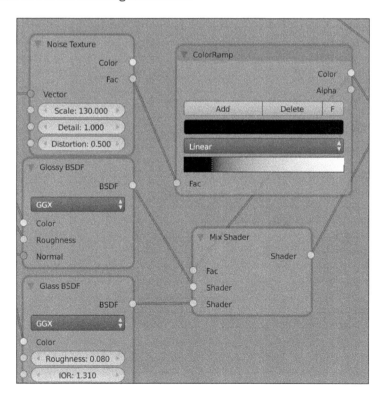

7. Let's now add a **Subsurface Scattering** node. Set the mode to **Compatible**, the **Scale** to 10.000 and the **Radius** to 0.070, 0.070, 0.10.

8. As a color input, let's add another color **Mix** node with **Color1** as RGB 0.780, 0.960, 1.000 and **Color2** as RGB 0.320, 0.450, 0.480.

9. The **Fac** input for the color **Mix** node will be the same as for the color **Mix** node of the Glass and Glossy BSDFs. Now mix the **SSS** node with the mix of the other two BSDFs, using an **Add Shader** node.

10. Now, we will create the normals for the shader. Add three **Image Texture** nodes. In the first one, let's load the `IceScratches.jpg` file. We will use the **Generated** coordinates with a **Scale** of XYZ 20.000, 20.000, 20.000. Set the projection mode to **Box** and the **Blend** to 0.500.

11. In the second **Image Texture** node, load the `ice_snow_DISP.png` file, using the **UV** coordinates.

12. Finally, load the `ice_snow_NRM.png` file in the third **Image Texture** node, using again the **UV** textures.

13. Now let's mix the `IceScratches.jpg` with the `ice_snow_DISP.png` textures, using a color **Mix** node with the **Displacement Texture** into the **Color1** socket and the scratches texture into the **Color2** socket. Set the **Fac** value to 0.100.

14. Plug the mix of the textures into the **Height** socket of a **Bump** node and then plug the `ice_snow_NRM.png` texture into the **Color** socket of a **Normal Map** node. Finally, plug this one into the **Normal** socket of the **Bump** node.

15. Set the **Normal Map** node's **Strength** to 0.050, the **Bump** node's **Strength** to 0.500 and the **Distance** to 1.000.

16. Plug the **Bump** node into all of the BSDFs we added so far.

17. Frame every node we created and label the frame `ICE`.

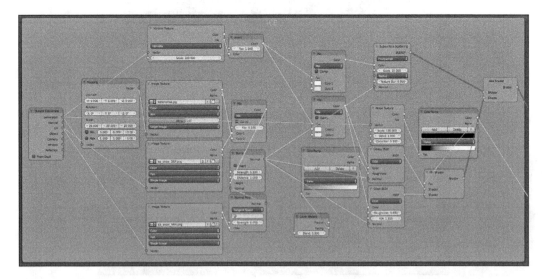

Creating snow

1. The nodes we will add now will still be within the same material, but outside the **ICE** group we just created. Add a **Glossy** and a **Subsurface Scatter BSDF** nodes. Mix them using a **Mix Shader** node with 20 percent of influence from the **Glossy BSDF** node.

2. Set both the colors to white. Also, set the SSS **Scale** to 3.00 and the **Radius** to 0.400, 0.400, 0.450. Set the Glossy mode to **GGX** and the **Roughness** to 0.600.

3. Add a **Noise Textures** node and set **Scale** to 2000.000, **Detail** to 2.000 and **Distortion** to 0.000. We will use **Generated** coordinates for this texture.

4. Connect the **Fac** output of the **Noise Texture** node to the **Height** socket of the **Bump** node and set the **Strength** to 0.200 and the **Distance** to 1.000. Connect the **Normal** output of the **Noise Texture** node to the **Normal** input of the **Subsurface Scatter BSDF** and **Glossy BSDF** nodes.

5. Now let's mix the **Mix Shader** node of the **Subsurface Scatter BSDF** and **Glossy BSDF** nodes with an **Emission** shader using another **Mix Shader** node.

6. Add new **Noise Textures**, this time with **Scale** as 2500.000, **Detail** as 2.000, and **Distortion** as 0.000.

7. Connect the **Fac** output of the **Noise Texture** node to the **Color** input of the **Gamma** node, with a **Gamma** value of 8.000, and then add the **Color** output of the **Gamma** node to the **Fac** input of the **ColorRamp** node. We will set up the color stops as seen in the next screenshot.

8. Connect the **ColorRamp** node's **Color** socket to the **Fac** socket of the previous **Mix Shader** node. Remember to use the **Color** output of the **ColorRamp** node.

9. Frame all these nodes and label the frame SNOW.

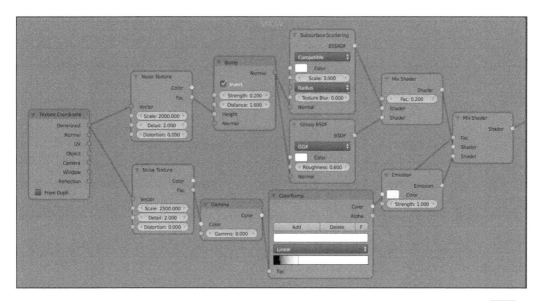

Mixing ice and snow

1. Add a **Geometry** (**Add | Input**) and a **Normal** node (**Add | Vectors**). Connect the **Normal** output from the **Geometry** node to the **Normal** input of the **Normal** node.

2. Now connect the **Dot** output of the **Normal** node to the first socket of a **Multiply** node and set the mode to **Multiply** and the second value to 2.000.

3. Add a **Mix shader** node and connect the **ICE** frame into the first **Shader** socket and the **SNOW** frame into the second one. Finally, connect the output of the **Multiply** node into the **Fac** value of the **Mix Shader** node.

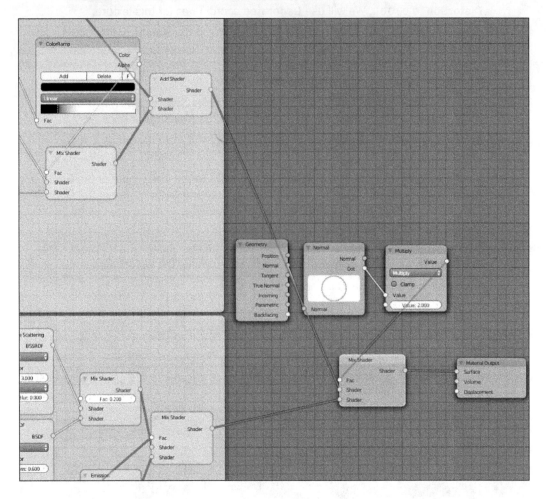

How it works...

Let's see the most interesting points of this material in detail. For the ice material, we used a **Voronoi Texture** node to create a pattern for the surface color. Then we mixed the **Glass** and **Glossy BSDF** nodes using a **Noise Texture** node to simulate both, the more and less transparent areas: for example, the ice may be less transparent due to some part of it being covered with snow, difference in purity of the water, or the thickness of the ice. Then we mixed the two BSDFs with a **Subsurface Scatter** node to simulate the dispersion of the lighting inside the ice. Note that we used the **ColorRamp** node quite often in order to fine tune the various mixing and inputs.

The snow material is quite similar for the main concept, but is missing the refractive part of the ice. Here we did something else. We used a **Noise Texture** node with some tweaking (**Gamma** and **ColorRamp**) to make it really contrasted to mix an emission shader to the rest of the material. This will create a small emission dot over the snow surface that we will use in compositing to create the flakes.

It is really interesting how we mixed the two materials. We wanted the snow to be placed only on the flat surfaces of the iceberg, while we wanted the slopes to be just ice. To obtain this effect, we extracted the normal information about the mesh and used it to understand which part of the mesh is facing upward. We must imagine the normals to be working like the sunlight falling on the surface of the earth. Half of the sphere is in darkness, and half is hit by the light. We can decide from which direction the light hits the surface. Now imagine the same principle applied to the shape of our mesh. In this way we can create a white mask on the areas that are hit by the normal sphere direction. With the **Normal** node, we can orient this effect wherever we want. The default position of the sphere is exactly what we needed: the parts of the mesh that are faced upward are made white, while the rest of the mesh is black. Turning the sphere around will make the direction of the ramp that has been created, change accordingly.

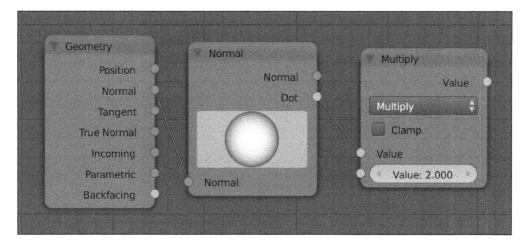

The sphere, maybe, is not the best way to set these kind of things as it lacks a bit of precision (as for the setting of the sky), but this will probably change in the future with something that allows more precise settings. Finally we used a **Multiply** node to multiply the value coming from the **Normal** node and increased the contrast of the mask.

There's more...

The normal method we just saw in this recipe is not the only way of mixing materials. Just some time ago, two new plugins have been developed. The first one allows us to obtain the same results we got in this recipe by creating a weight map or a vertex paint based on the slope of the mesh, while the second creates the same based on the altitude. This opens up many possibilities not only in terms of material creation, but also for the distribution of particle systems! The plugins can be downloaded from the following links, where we can find some instructions about them:

```
http://blenderthings.blogspot.nl/2013/09/height-to-vertex-weights-
blender-addon.html
```

See also

In the following link, *Andrew Price* teaches us how to create a different kind of ice material; for example, material that is more suitable for ice cubes. Surely worth a watch!

> ▸   `http://www.blenderguru.com/videos/how-to-create-realistic-ice/`

Creating the sea material in Cycles

Although we've already created some sea material, this one is going to be something new. While the other sea materials were just a mix of reflective and refractive shaders, now we are going to try to mimic a real mass of water, where the color and the roughness of the refraction changes with the change of the depth. To obtain such an effect in computer graphics the most useful thing would be volumetrics. This, for now, is not yet implemented in Cycles, so we will have to fake it. Anyway, as we've already learned, cheating is quite normal while creating 3D graphic scenes, and the result will be great anyway! Let's get started.

Getting ready

Select the sea mesh and add a new material to it. Name it `sea`.

How to do it...

To create the sea material, follow the ensuing steps:

1. Let's add a **Refraction BSDF** node and a **Glossy BSDF** node and mix them together using a **Mix Shader** node, with **Refraction** to the first socket and the **Glossy** to the second one. As input for the **Fac** socket, we will use a **Fresnel** node with **IOR** 1.120.

2. Let's set the **Refraction** node's **IOR** to 1.333 and the **Glossy** node's **Roughness** to 0.005. Also set the **Glossy** color to white.

3. Now we are going to create the input for the **Refraction BSDF** roughness. Add a **Camera Data** node (**Add** | **Input**) and a **Multiply** node. Connect the camera data **View Distance** output to the first **Value** socket of the **Multiply** node. Set this to the **Multiply** mode and set the second **Value** to 0.001.

4. Finally, connect the **Multiply** node to the **Roughness** socket of the **Refraction BSDF** node.

5. Now it's time to create the sea bump. Add a **Noise Texture** node to a **Wave Texture** node using a **Mix** color node in the **Add** mode. Set the **Wave Texture** node's **Scale** to 30.000, **Distortion** to 14.000, **Detail** to 4.000, and **Detail Scale** to 2.000. Then, set the **Noise Texture** node's **Scale** to 400.000, **Detail** to 2.000, and **Distortion** to 0.000. Finally, set the **Mix** color node's **Fac** value to 1.000.

6. Add a **Voronoi Texture** node in the **Intensity** mode and multiply it to the sum of the two previous textures. Set the **Fac** value of the **Mix** node to 0.400. Also, set the **Voronoi Texture** node's **Scale** to 400.000.

7. Connect the previous **Mix** node to the **Height** socket of a **Bump** node. Set **Strength** to 0.250 and **Distance** to 1.000. Finally, connect the **Normal** output to all the **Normal** inputs of the BSDFs.

8. Now we want to create some fake water-like caustics. Add another **Voronoi Texture** node and set **Scale** to 200.000 and the mode to **Intensity**. Connect the **Fac** output from the **Voronoi Texture** node to an **Invert** node.

9. Then add a **ColorRamp** node after the **Invert** node and set the interpolation mode to **Constant**. Set the color stops as shown in the following screenshot. After the **ColorRamp** node, add a **Math** node and set it to **Multiply**. Set the second socket's value to 5.000.

10. Connect the **Math** node to a **Transparent BSDF** node. Mix the **Transparent BSDF** node with the mix of the other two BSDFs using a **Mix Shader** node. Make sure the **Transparent BSDF** node is connected to the lower socket.

11. Finally, add a **LightPath** node and connect the **Is Shadow Ray** to the **Fac** value of the **Mix Shader** node.

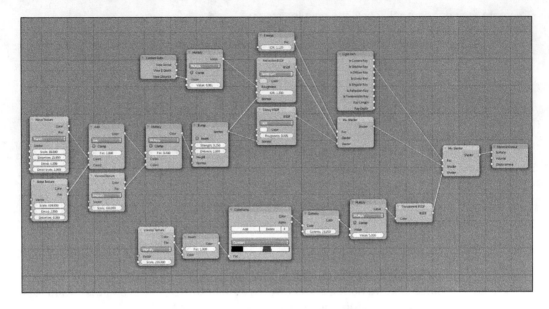

How it works...

Let's understand the most important things about this sea material. Surely, even if it is quite simple, the most interesting thing is how we achieved a variable roughness for the **Refraction BSDF** node. The **Camera Data** node, as the name says, gives us information about the camera. We need information about the distance of the shading point from the camera. We can use **View Z Depth** of **View Distance**. The difference between the two is that, the first one gives a constant distance from the plane, which is perpendicular to the view vector of the camera. The second one returns the distance exactly from where the camera rays are shot, which is the camera itself.

It is important to note that while we are in real-time preview mode, the distance is calculated from the point from where we are looking at the scene, even if this point is not the camera. Of course, while rendering, this point can only be the active camera of our scene.

As we said at the beginning of the recipe, this method is not accurate, and for our purpose, can work only for a still image. Anyway, the effect that we can get is enough for our purpose. Using **View Distance**, we can create some sort of a depth spherical map around the camera.

This means that the roughness will increase not only with the depth, but also with the distance from the camera over the water surface. This last thing is not exactly what we want, but from our camera's point of view, it will not be a big problem.

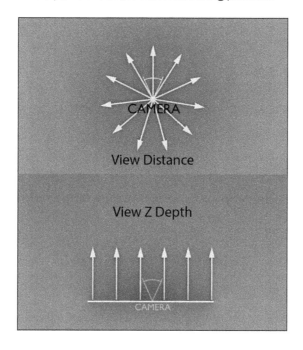

After this we created a bump using a combination of procedural textures and some fake caustics, using the method we learned in *Chapter 2, Creating Different Glass Materials in Cycles*, with the addition of a **Voronoi Texture** node to generate the initial pattern.

There's more...

As said at the beginning of the recipe, the correct way to achieve the variable roughness in the water would be through volumetric, which at the moment, is still not supported in Cycles. Anyway, as I am writing these words, there are already experimental builds on Graphicall that contain a very early version of the volumetric shading. For those who would like to play a bit with them, I advise you to download the builds released by *Tungers* under the name *GSoC 2013— DingTo* (Google *summer of code*). For example, this one: `http://graphicall.org/1049`.

See also

This thread on Blender artists (also in the following pages) has the first experiments with the volumetric in Cycles. There are some interesting node setups, tips, and tricks to pick up!

> ▸ `http://blenderartists.org/forum/showthread.php?216113-Brecht-s-easter-egg-surprise-Modernizing-shading-and-rendering/page650`.

Compositing the scene

It is time to make some quick compositing to our scene to give the final touch. Apart from the background and some other minor things, it will be important to make the snowflakes sparkle, as they ideally should. Let's see how!

Getting ready

Before we render the scene, we need to activate the **Emission** passes from the **Render Layers** panel.

How to do it...

Let's go to the node compositor and get started. We will start by compositing our image over the background.

1. Connect the **Alpha** output from the **Render Layer** node to a **Dilate/Erode** node (**Add | Filters**). Set the mode to **Feather** and **Distance** to -7.

2. After this, add a **Blur** node; set it to **Fast Gaussian** and set the **Strength** to X: 5, Y: 5. Connect the **Blur** node to an **Invert** node.

3. Add a **Mix** node, and connect the **Alpha** output from the **Render Layer** node into the **Fac** value and the output from the **Invert** node into the lower **Image** socket. Set the upper **Image** socket to black. Label the **Mix** node **HorizonMask**.

4. Copy the **Dilate/Erode** node and the **Invert** nodes. Again, connect the **Alpha** output from the **Render Layer** node to the **Dilate/Erode** node and set the **Distance** to -30 and then connect this to the **Invert** node. Plug its output into the **Fac** socket of a new **Mix** node and plug the **Environment** output from the **Render Layer** node into the lower **Image** socket. Set the first **Image** socket to RGB 0.58, 0.62, 1. Label the **Mix** node Sky.

5. Add an **Alpha Over** node (**Add | Color**) and plug the **Image** output from the **Render Layer** node into the lower socket and the **Environment** output into the upper one.

6. Add another **Mix** node and set it to the **Add** mode. Connect the **HorizonMask** Mix node into the **Fac** socket, the output of the **Alpha Over** node into the upper **Image** socket and the **Sky** Mix node into the lower one.

7. Frame all the nodes we have created so far and name the frame Background.

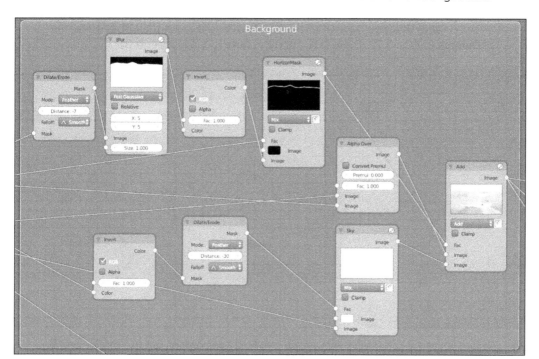

8. Add a **Glare** node after the **Background** frame and set the mode to **Fog Glow** and the quality to **High**. Also set **Mix** to 1.000, the **Threshold** to 0.400 and the **Size** to 9.000.

9. Mix this with the output of the **Background** node using a **Mix** node; set to the **Add** mode. Make sure the **Glare** node goes into the lower **Image** socket and set **Fac** to 0.600.

10. Add a **ColorRamp** node after the **Emission** output of the **Render Layer** node and set the color stops as shown in the following screenshot. After this, add another **Glare** node in the **Streaks** mode. Set the quality to **High**, **Iterations** to 4.000, **Color Modulation** to 0.550, **Mix** to 1.000, **Threshold** to 0.200, **Streaks** to 7.000, **Angle Offset** to 0.000, and **Fade** to 0.940.

11. Connect this to the lower **Image** socket of a **Mix** node in the **Add** mode, and connect to the upper **Image** socket to the previous **Add** node. Set **Fac** to 2.500.

12. Add a **Color Balance** node after the last **Add** node and set the **Lift** to white, the **Gamma** to RGB 0.77, 0.84, 0.84, and the **Gain** to 1.11, 1.04. 0.96.

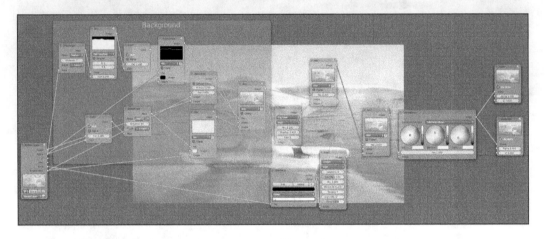

How it works...

The compositing we created here is quite simple. First, we composited the render over the background, creating a mask over the edge of the geometry to mix the background and the render in a better way. To achieve this effect we used a **Dilate/Erode** node for increasing the size of the **Alpha** output a bit, then blurred it and finally cut out the **Alpha** channel again to obtain only a small mask at the edge of the render.

After this we created the snowflakes using the **Emission** output. We increased the contrast as much as we could using a **ColorRamp** node and then applied a **Glare** filter. In order to make the flakes more visible, we used a value higher than 1 for the **Add** node **Fac** value.

There's more...

We can increase the size of the horizon mask by decreasing the value of the **Dilate/Erode** node, blur it more, or decrease its intensity by putting a **ColorRamp** node right before the **Add** node and make the white color stop a shade of gray.

See also

In Blender, it is also possible to create masks manually, which can then be used in compositing, or in many other ways. This link has a tutorial that will show how a mask can be created and used in compositing, plus a lot of other useful things to learn!

▶ http://www.youtube.com/watch?v=RBTwXdcLL-M.

10
Creating Food Materials in Cycles

We will cover the following recipes in this chapter:

- ▶ Creating grapes in Cycles
- ▶ Creating parmigiano cheese
- ▶ Creating bread
- ▶ Learning the Branched Path Tracing render

Introduction

In this final chapter, we are going to learn how to create some tasty food. Achieving believable organic materials is quite challenging, and we are going to use most of the techniques we learned so far.

Creating grapes in Cycles

We will start out by creating the material for the grapes. For this purpose, we will be using an **OSL** (**Open Shading Language**) that we also used in *Chapter 7, Car Rendering in Cycles*, to realistically layer different shaders. The plugin is the **PYLA** and you can find it in Chapter 7 files.

Getting ready

Let's select the grape mesh and add a new material to it. Name it Grapes. Then let's move to the material node editor.

How to do it...

1. Let's add a **SubsurfaceScatter BSDF** node. Set the mode to **Compatible**, **Color** to RGB 0.66, 0.68, 0.12, and the **Scale** value to 0.6. Also, set the **Radius** value to 0.6, 0.7, 0.3.

2. Add a **Diffuse BSDF** node and a **Glossy BSDF** node, mix them using a **Mix Shader** node, and make sure the **Glossy BSDF** node is plugged into the lower socket. Set Glossy **Color** to RGB -.24, 0.3, 0.98 and the **Roughness** value to 0.04. Also, set the mode to **GGX** and the Diffuse node's **Roughness** value to 1.

3. Add a **Noise Texture** node and set the **Scale** value to 5, **Detail** to 2, and **Distortion** to 0.4. Plug this into a **ColorRamp** node and set the color stops, as shown in the following screenshot. Finally, plug the color ramp into the **Fac** socket of a **Color Mix** node and set **Color1** to RGB 0.43, 0.5, 0.275 and **Color2** to RGB 0.65, 0.65, 0.65. Plug the **Color** output into the **Color** input of the **Diffuse BSDF** node.

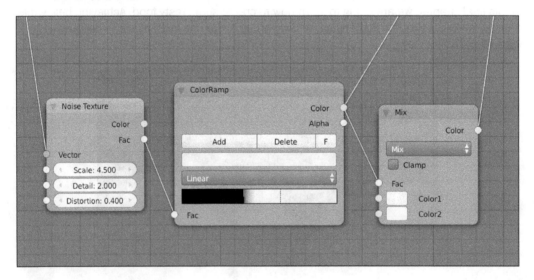

4. Also, plug the **ColorRamp** output from the **Noise Texture** node into the **Fac** socket of the **Mix Shader** node.

5. Add a **script** node (**Add | Script**) and load the PYLA.py file. Plug the **SSS BSDF** node into the **Base** socket and the mix of the other two BSDFs into the **Layer** socket.

6. Set the **Opacity** value to 1, the **Depth** value to 2.5, **Fresnel** to 0.4, **IOR** to 1.333, **Mask Layer** to 0.9, and **SecondaryLayer** to 1.

7. Add another **Noise Texture** node and set the **Scale** value to 6.6, the **Detail** value to 2, and the **Distortion** value to 0. Again, we will use **UV** coordinates. Plug the texture into a **ColorRamp** node and set the color stops, as shown in the following screenshot.

8. Add another **PYLA script** node, plug the previous **PYLA** node output into the **Base** socket, and the **Color Ramp** node from the previous **Noise Texture** node into the **Opacity** socket.

9. Add a **Diffuse BSDF** node, set the **Roughness** value to 1, and **Color** to RGB 0.25, 0.18, 0.08. Plug it into the **Layer** socket of the **PYLA** node.

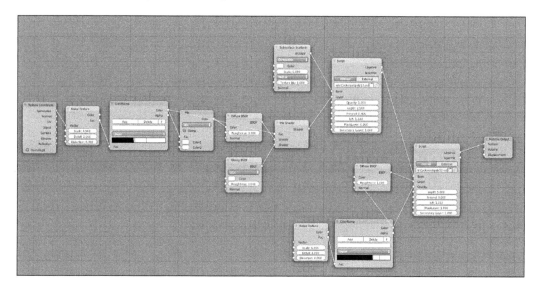

How it works...

Once again, the usage of the PYLA plugin was really useful for us to get the right look for our material. A real grape is made of different levels—the inside and the skin.

We recreated the inside using a **Subsurface scattering BSDF** node, and then used the **PYLA OSL** node to realistically layer the other BSDF that we used to recreate the skin. Using a **Noise Texture** node, we gave some color variation to the skin.

Finally, we used another Diffuse BSDF to add some burnt and dirty part over the grape skin.

 For a normal **Mix Shader** node, we could use **Texture** as the mixing factor of the two layers. This of course can be done for each of the sockets of the **PYLA OSL** node.

There's more...

Since the coordinates we used for the textures in this material are **UV**, the pattern among the different berries of the grape will be the same. There is an easy way to give some further variation. We can create a second **UV** layer for the grapes and just click on **unwrap**. This will create a new **UV** set that will be different for each one of the berries. Now in the material, we can use an **Attribute** node to use the new **UV** layer with some of the textures and give variation among the grapes. Notice that the scale of the new **UV** layer is much smaller compared to the first layer, so we will have to adjust the scale of the textures accordingly. In the following screenshot, there is an example of how we could set up the material using this method.

See also

▸   In the following link, there is a nice topic about the creation of the material for a red grape using handmade textures, which is really interesting: `http://blenderartists.org/forum/showthread.php?283157-Grapes-SOLVED`.

Creating parmigiano cheese

Now, let's see how to create the material for the parmigiano cheese. This time, we will not be using the **PYLA** script, but again, there will be **SSS** in the **shader** node setup, as this shader is really useful for the creation of organic materials such as food.

Getting ready

Select the parmigiano mesh and add a new material to it. Name it `Parmigiano`.

How to do it...

1. Add a **Subsurface Scatter BSSRDF** node and set the mode to **Cubic**. Set the **Scale** value to `1.2`, the **Radius** value to 0.12, 0.12, 0.1, and the **Sharpness** value to `0.4`.

2. Duplicate the **SSS BSDF** node and mix it with the previous one using an **Add Shader** node.

3. Add a **Glossy BSDF** node, set the mode to **GGX**, and the **Roughness** value to 0.3. Add it to the sum of the two **SSS BSSRDF** nodes using another **Add Shader** node.

4. Add an **Image Texture** node using **UV** coordinates and load Parmigiano_cavity. tga. Add a **ColorRamp** node after the texture and set the color stops as shown in the following screenshot. Also, set the interpolation mode to **ease**.

5. After the **ColorRamp** node, add a **Mix Color** node, set the mode to **Multiply**, and the **Fac** value to 0.2. Set **Color1** to RGB 0.5, 0.39, 0.295 and plug the output of the **Color Ramp** node into the **Color 2** socket.

6. Plug the **Mix Color** output into the two **SSS BSDF** nodes' color input sockets.

7. Duplicate the **Mix Color** node and again plug into the **Color2** socket the output from the **ColorRamp** node. Set **Color1** to RGB 0.12, 0.11, 0.1 and the **Fac** value to 0.8. Plug the output into the **Color** input socket of **Glossy BSDF** nodes.

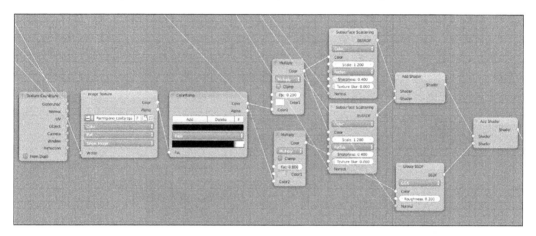

8. Add a **Noise Texture** node, set the **Scale** value to 150, **Detail** to 3, and **Distortion** to 1. For this texture, we will use **Generated** coordinates.

9. Add a **ColorRamp** node after the **Noise Texture** node and set the color stops as shown in the following screenshot.

10. Add an **Image Texture** node with **UV** coordinates and load ParmigianoDISP.tga.

11. Add a **Color Mix** node, set the mode to **Multiply**, and the **Fac** value to 1. Plug into the **Color1** socket the ParmigianoDISP.tga image texture, and in the **Color2** socket, the output of the **ColorRamp** node coming from the **Noise Texture** node.

12. Add another **Color Mix** node in the **Multiply** mode and set the **Fac** value to 1 after the previous one; plug the latter into the **Color1** socket while plugging the **ColorRamp** node from the Parmigiano_cavity.tga image texture into the **Color2** socket.

13. Add a **Bump** node and plug the last **Multiply** node into the **Height** socket. Set the **Strength** value to 0.4 and the **Distance** value to 1.

14. Add another **Image Texture** node with **UV** coordinates and load the `ParmigianoDISP_normal.tga` file. Plug it into a **Normal Map** node and then plug this into the **Normal Input** socket of the **Bump** node. Set the **Normal Map Strength** value to `0.4`.

15. Finally, plug the **Bump** node output into the input of each one of the BSDFs we have added so far.

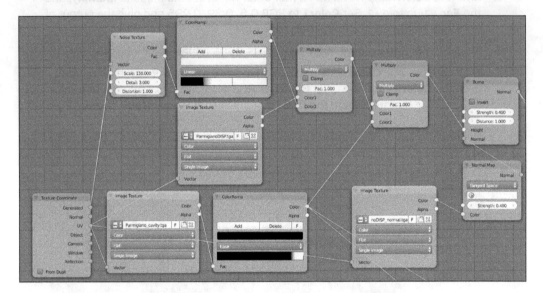

16. Frame all the nodes we added so far and label the frame **Inside**.

17. Add a **Subsurface Scatter BSDF** node, set **Color** to RGB 0.35, 0.3, 0.19, the **Scale** value to `0.6`, and the **Radius** value to 0.12, 0.12, 0.1. Also, set the mode to **Compatible**.

18. Add a **Glossy BSDF** node, set **Color** to RGB 0.18, 0.16, 0.08, and the **Roughness** value to `0.05`. Also, set the mode to **GGX**.

19. Mix the two BSDFs using an add shader and then plug the output into the lower socket of a **Mix Shader** node while plugging the output of the frame labeled **Inside** into the upper socket.

20. Add an **Attribute** node and write `Col` into the namespace. Plug the **Color** output into a **ColorRamp** node and set the color stops as shown in the following screenshot.

21. Finally, plug the **ColorRamp** output into the **Fac** input of the **Mix Shader** node.

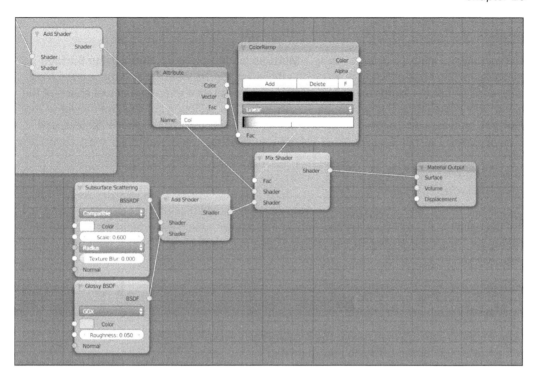

How it works...

Let's see in detail the most important parts of this shader. To create the base material, we used the addition of two **Subsurface Scatter** nodes with the same settings. This is because sometimes, **SSS** can get a bit dark in certain areas, and this technique helps us to avoid this effect. A material like the parmigiano cheese can scatter a lot of light inside, so we don't need dark areas. To obtain the reflections, we used a simple Glossy BSDF.

The texture setup we used is quite a complex one. To obtain the color input of the various BSDFs, we used a color multiplied by a cavity map. This helps us to stress the cavities of the surface and maintain the detail. One of the problems of the **SSS** shader, in general, is that it can make the surface quite flat. Multiplying the color with a cavity map will help us to enhance the detail of the surface even with an SSS BSDF.

Then we created the bump using a combination of **Bump**, **Normal**, and **Generated Noise Texture**, and again the **Cavity** map. The **Bump** texture is also really important to try to maintain the details that we could lose because of the SSS BSSRDF.

Finally, we created a simple shader for the crust of the parmigiano cheese and mixed it with the previous shader using **Vertex Paint** as the mask.

There's more...

The parmigiano mesh is sculpted using a **Multires** modifier. Like the **Subdivision Surface** modifier, we can set a different amount of subdivision for the viewport and the render. A big difference is that the **Multires** modifier also stores information about the actual shape of the mesh. This makes it ideal for sculpting. At the end of the sculpting process, we can leave the **Multires** modifier using a lower rendering subdivision level to keep the scene lighters, and add the remaining details using maps baked from **Multires**.

See also

Cycles still do not have a map baking system, but we can do this kind of operation with the BI engine. In the following link, there is a nice tutorial, which will explain the process of baking textures in BI, which can then also be used in Cycles: http://www.youtube.com/watch?v=U7PQGgz1RII.

Creating bread

Now, we will create the material for the bread. This is an Italian kind of bread named schiacciata or focaccia. Let's see how to do it!

Getting ready

Select the **bread01** mesh and add a new material to it. Name it bread.

How to do it...

1. Add a **Subsurface Scatter BSSRDF** node and set the mode to **Cubic**, the **Scale** value to 0.6, the **Radius** value to 0.11, 0.12, 0.1, and the **Sharpness** value to 0.5.

2. Add a **Diffuse BSDF** node and mix it with the **SSS BSSRDF** node using an **Add Shader** node. Set the **Roughness** value to 1.

3. Add an **Image Texture** node and load the SchiacciataCOLOR_COLOR.tga file. We will use **UV** coordinates.

4. Add **RGB Curves** after the **Image Texture** node and set the **Combined curve** node as shown in the following screenshot. Also, add a **Hue Saturation Value** node, set the **Saturation** value to 1.1, and **Value** to 0.9. Finally, plug the **HSV** node output into the **Color** socket of the **SSS** and **Diffuse** nodes.

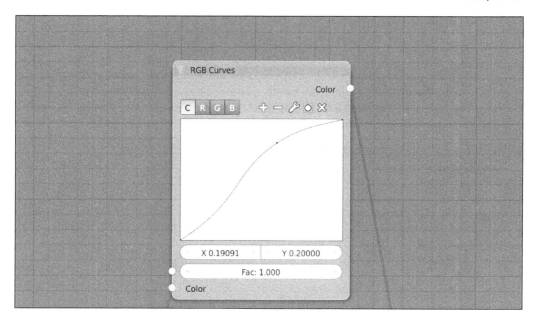

5. Add a **Glossy BSDF** node and mix it with the sum of the previous two shaders using a **Mix Shader** node, plugging the **Glossy BSDF** node into the lower socket. Set the Glossy mode to **GGX** and the **Roughness** value to 0.5.

6. Add another **Image Texture** node, again with **UV** coordinates, and load the SchiacciataCOLOR_SPEC.tga file. Plug it into a **Color Ramp** node and set the color stops as shown in the following screenshot. Plug the **Color Ramp** node into the **Fac** input of the **Mix Shader** node.

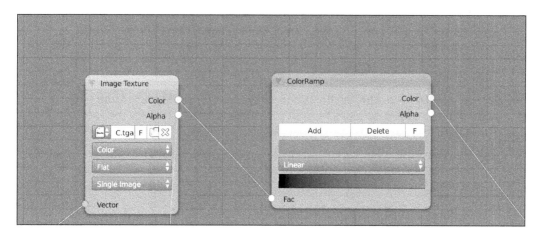

7. Add again an **Image Texture** node and load the `SchiacciataCOLOR_DISP.tga` file. Again, we will be using **UV** coordinates. Plug the **Color** output into the **Color1** socket of a **Mix Color** node. Set the mode to **Multiply** and the **Fac** value to 1.

8. Add a **Noise Texture** node and set the **Scale** value to `180`, the **Detail** value to `2`, and the **Distortion** value to `1.4`. For this texture, we need to use **Generated** coordinates. Add a **Color Ramp** node after it and set the color stops as shown in the following screenshot:

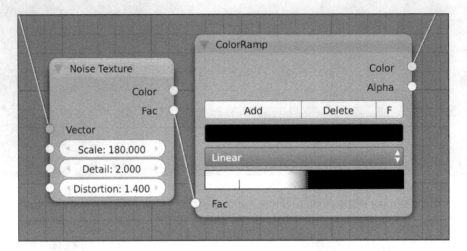

9. Plug the **Color Ramp** node into the **Color2** socket of the **Mix Color** node.

10. Add a **Bump** node and plug the **Color Mix** node into the **Height** socket. Set the **Strength** value to `0.5` and the **Distance** value to `1`.

11. Add another **Image Texture** node with **UV** coordinates and load the `SchiacciataCOLOR_NRM.tga` file. Plug the output into a **Normal Map** node and set the **Strength** value to `0.5`. Plug the **Normal Map** node into the normal input of the **Bump** node. Finally, plug the **Bump** output into each one of the BSDF normal inputs.

12. Add a **Math** node after the **Color** node that is mixing the **Noise Texture** node and the `SchiacciataCOLOR_DISP.tga` image texture. Set the mode to **Multiply** and plug into the **Material Output Displacement** socket.

13. Add a **Hue Saturation Value** node after the `SchiacciataCOLOR_COLOR.tga` image texture and set the **Saturation** value to `0.5` and **Value** to `0.5`. Plug it into the **Color** input of **Glossy BSDF**.

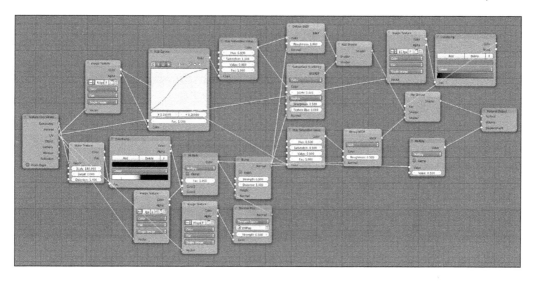

How it works...

Again, the most important part of the creation of the bread material is the use of **Subsurface Scattering**. This time we mixed it with a **Diffuse BSDF** node as the bread is scattering less light than the cheese.

Also, here we paid much attention to the creation of the bump, as maintaining the details is really important in **SSS**. This time we also plugged the **Bump** map into the **Displacement** socket of the material output. Again, it is important to remember that real displacement is still not working in Cycles, but this helps the bump anyway.

To tune the intensity of the displacement, we used a **Math** node in the **Multiply** mode.

There's more...

At the moment, the **Subsurface Scatter** node is still under development, and this means that it could change in the future. However, it is already important to get the main ideas behind it. The color of **SSS BSSRDF** represents the color of the surface of the object, while the scale defines the general distance of the light being scattered inside the object. A smaller scale will mean that the light will be able to travel inside the object much less than with a high scale.

The radius defines the amount of scattered light for each channel. This is useful to define the internal color of an object, and how much we want the light to travel inside for each color channel. Higher values will make the object scatter a higher amount of light.

The mode defines the algorithm used to define how much and where the light is being scattered. The developers say that the model closest to reality in most cases is the gaussian one.

In this mode, we also have a sharpness option. Increasing this value will help to maintain the details on the surface, but overdoing it could result in a loss of the scattering effect.

See also

In the following link, *Andrew Price* will show us how to create a different kind of bread. The most interesting part is where he explains how he created the textures for the bread: `http://www.youtube.com/watch?v=rrP1-ZJz3GA`.

Learning the Branched Path Tracing render

For this final recipe, we will have a look at the **Branched Path Tracing** rendering mode. This rendering mode will allow us to have a much higher level of control on each aspect of the render so that we will be able to optimize much more. Of course, more control means more things to know. So let's learn how to set up the render!

Getting ready

Go to the **Render** menu and click on the **Sampling** tab. From the drop-down menu, select the **Branched Path Tracing** mode. Let's get started!

How to do it...

1. Check the **Square Samples** option.
2. Set the **Clamp** value to 10.
3. Set **AA Samples for rendering** to 5.
4. Set **Samples for Diffuse** to 4, **Glossy** to 5, **Transmission** to 3, **AO** to 1, **Mesh Light** to 3, and **Subsurface** to 5.
5. Set the **Light Paths** settings as shown in the following screenshot:

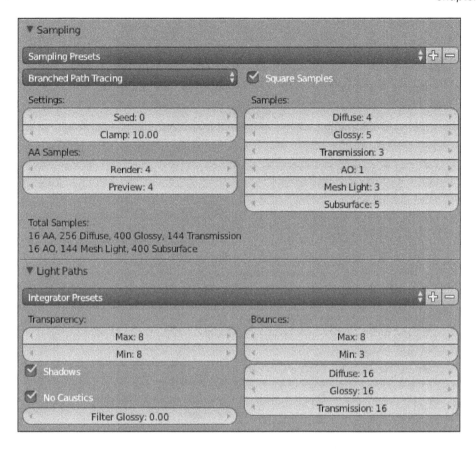

How it works...

As we just saw, the settings for the sampling in this rendering mode are more than the normal **Path Tracing** mode. This allows us to set the number of samples for each different part of the rendering in order to give more samples only where it is really needed.

The idea is that the samples will equal to the AA samples multiplied by each one of the other sampling settings (Diffuse, Glossy, and so on). So, if for example, we have four AA samples and four Diffuse samples, we will have a final number of samples for the Diffuse of 16. However, we checked the **Square Samples** option, so we actually have 16 AA samples and 16 Diffuse samples for a total amount of 256 samples.

The most important things here are the Glossy and the Subsurface, and as we can see, each of them get five (25) samples.

Then we have a mesh light, but its contribution to the lighting is really low, so we can have a lower samples number for this. Also, the AO contribution for the scene is not so important, so we could set the number of samples to 1.

In the lower part of the **Sampling** tab, we can see the total number of samples for each one of the different settings to help us have a better overview.

The options for the **Branched Path Tracing** rendering mode are not in the **Render** menu only. We can set the individual samples for each lamp in the scene (from the **Lamp** menu) or for the world (in the **World** menu).

There's more...

Another important aspect of the **Branched Path Tracing** mode is that the rendering algorithm is actually different from the normal **Path Tracing** mode. This means that not only can we calculate individual number of samples, but also the way the noise will be removed is different. Don't worry, the look of the rendering will be the same. But things such as **Cubic Subsurface Scattering** will be handled much better in the **Branched Path Tracing** mode rather than in the normal one.

Another thing to notice is that right now, this mode is available only for CPU, but for our scene, it does not make any difference, as we already had to use CPU because of **Subsurface Scattering** and the Open Shading Language.

See also

▸ The following tutorial will explain in detail the usage of the **Branched Path Tracing** mode. It is always better to have more than one source for our studies: `http://cgcookie.com/blender/cgc-courses/cycles-non-progressive-integrator/`.

Index

Thank you for buying
Blender Cycles: Lighting and Rendering Cookbook

About Packt Publishing

Packt, pronounced 'packed', published its first book "*Mastering phpMyAdmin for Effective MySQL Management*" in April 2004 and subsequently continued to specialize in publishing highly focused books on specific technologies and solutions.

Our books and publications share the experiences of your fellow IT professionals in adapting and customizing today's systems, applications, and frameworks. Our solution based books give you the knowledge and power to customize the software and technologies you're using to get the job done. Packt books are more specific and less general than the IT books you have seen in the past. Our unique business model allows us to bring you more focused information, giving you more of what you need to know, and less of what you don't.

Packt is a modern, yet unique publishing company, which focuses on producing quality, cutting-edge books for communities of developers, administrators, and newbies alike. For more information, please visit our website: www.packtpub.com.

About Packt Open Source

In 2010, Packt launched two new brands, Packt Open Source and Packt Enterprise, in order to continue its focus on specialization. This book is part of the Packt Open Source brand, home to books published on software built around Open Source licences, and offering information to anybody from advanced developers to budding web designers. The Open Source brand also runs Packt's Open Source Royalty Scheme, by which Packt gives a royalty to each Open Source project about whose software a book is sold.

Writing for Packt

We welcome all inquiries from people who are interested in authoring. Book proposals should be sent to author@packtpub.com. If your book idea is still at an early stage and you would like to discuss it first before writing a formal book proposal, contact us; one of our commissioning editors will get in touch with you.

We're not just looking for published authors; if you have strong technical skills but no writing experience, our experienced editors can help you develop a writing career, or simply get some additional reward for your expertise.

Blender 2.6 Cycles: Materials and Textures Cookbook

ISBN: 978-1-78216-130-1   Paperback: 280 pages

Over 40 recipes to help you create stunning materials and textures using the Cycles rendering engine with Blender

1. Create naturalistic materials and textures such as rock, snow, ice, and fire using Cycles

2. Learn Cycle's node-based material system

3. Get to grips with the powerful Cycles rendering engine

Blender Game Engine Beginner's Guide

ISBN: 978-1-84951-702-7   Paperback: 206 pages

The non programmer's guide to creating 3D video games

1. Use Blender to create a complete 3D video game

2. Ideal entry level to game development without the need for coding

3. No programming or scripting required

Please check **www.PacktPub.com** for information on our titles

Blender 2.5 Character Animation Cookbook

ISBN: 978-1-84951-320-3   Paperback: 308 pages

50 great recipes for giving soul to your characters by building high-quality rigs and understanding the principles of movement

1.   Learn how to create efficient and easy-to-use character rigs

2.   Understand and make your characters, so that your audience believes they're alive

3.   See common approaches when animating your characters in real-world situations

4.   Learn the techniques needed to achieve various setups, from IK-FK blending to corrective shape keys and eyes controllers

Blender 2.5 HOTSHOT

ISBN: 978-1-84951-310-4   Paperback: 332 pages

Challenging and fun projects that will push your Blender skills to the limit

1.   Exciting projects covering many areas: modeling, shading, lighting, compositing, animation, and the game engine

2.   Strong emphasis on techniques and methodology for the best approach to each project

3.   Utilization of many of the tools available in Blender 3D for developing moderately complex projects

Please check **www.PacktPub.com** for information on our titles